CONTENTS

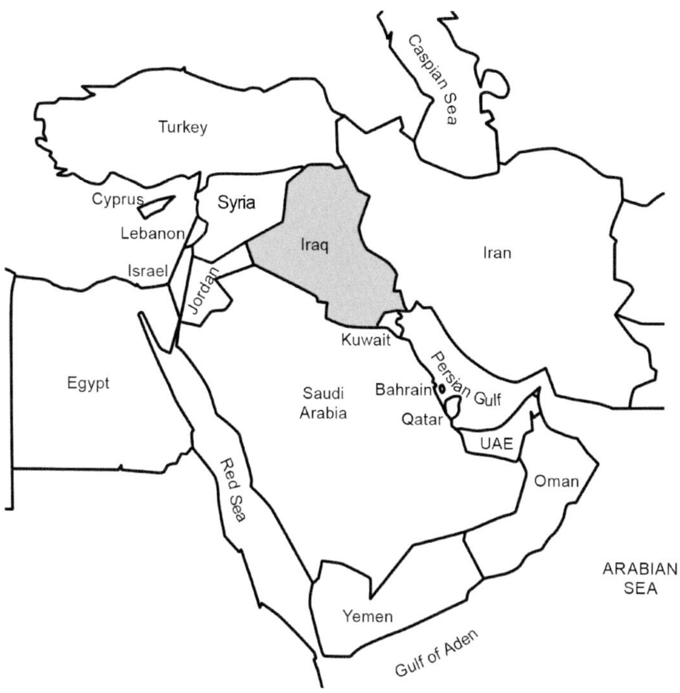

Helion & Company Limited
Unit 8 Amherst Business Centre, Budbrooke Road, Warwick CV34 5WE, England
Tel. 01926 499 619
Fax 0121 711 4075
Email: info@helion.co.uk Website: www.helion.co.uk Twitter: @helionbooks Visit our blog http://blog.helion.co.uk/

Published by Helion & Company 2019
Designed and typeset by Farr out Publications, Wokingham, Berkshire
Cover designed by Paul Hewitt, Battlefield Design (www.battlefield-design.co.uk)
Printed by Henry Ling Ltd, Dorchester, Dorset

Cover: The second group of Iraqi Mirage-pilots with their French instructors at Mont-de-Marsan AB in 1981, in front of the Mirage F.1BQ serial number 4001. (Dassault/Aimé Marion via Hugues de Guillebon)

ISBN 978-1-912390-31-1

British Library Cataloguing-in-Publication Data.
A catalogue record for this book is available from the British Library.

Note: In order to simplify the use of this book, all names, locations and geographic designations are as provided in The Times World Atlas, or other traditionally accepted major sources of reference, as of the time of described events. Similarly, Arabic names are romanised and transcripted rather than transliterated. For example: the definite article al- before words starting with 'sun letters' is given as pronounced instead of simply as al- (which is the usual practice for non-Arabic speakers in most English-language literature and media). For the reasons of space, ranges – which are usually measured in feet and nautical miles in international aeronautics – are cited in metric measurements only.

ABBREVIATIONS

AAA anti-aircraft artillery
AAM air-to-air missile
AB air base
ADAR *autodirector anti-radar* (seeker head of the AS.37 Baz-AR anti-radar missile)
ADOC Air Defence Operations Centre (C3 or operational HQ of the IrAF)
AEW airborne early warning
AMD-BA Avions Marcel Dassault – Bréguet Aviation
An Antonov (the design bureau led by Oleg Antonov)
AOI (The) Arab Organisation for Industrialisation
ARM anti-radar missile
ASCC Air Standardisation Coordinating Committee
ATMS automated tactical management system
AWACS airborne early warning and control system
AWACW Airborne Warning and Control Wing (USAF)
BAC British Airspace Corporation (later BAe Warton)
BAe British Aerospace
BAI battlefield interdiction
BVR beyond visual range
C3 command, control and communication
CAP combat air patrol
CAS close air support
CEV *Centre d'essais en vol* (Flight Test Centre, France)
Chaff reflective jamming device made up of thin, lightweight metallic strips, cut to one-half length of the target's radar wavelength
CO commanding officer
COIN counter-insurgency
COMINT communications intelligence
CTL considered total loss
DGA *Délégation Générale pour l'Armement* (General Delegation for Armament, former DMA re- named in 1977)
DIA *Direction des Affaires Internationales* (Direction of International Affairs, part of the DMA, France)
DIA Defence Intelligence Agency (USA)
DMA *Délégation Ministérielle pour l'Armement* (Ministerial Delegation for Armament, France, 1965-1977)
DMI Directorate of Military Industries
ECM electronic countermeasures
ECCM electronic counter-countermeasures
ELF European Liaison Force (USAF)
ELINT electronic intelligence
FCS fire-control system
Flare pyrotechnic device released from an aircraft causing an infra-red homing missile or target tracker to follow it rather than the aircraft
FMC fully mission capable
GMID General Military Intelligence Directorate (Iraq)
GP general-purpose (bomb)
HAWK Homing-All-The-Way-Killer (US-made SAM)
HE high-explosive
HPIR High Power Illuminator (Doppler) Radar (X-band tracking radar guiding MIM-23 HAWK SAMs)
IADS integrated air defence system
IAP international airport
IFR in-flight refuelling
I-HAWK Improved Homing-All-The-Way Killer (US-made SAM)
Il Ilyushin (the design bureau led by Sergey Vladimirovich Ilyushin, also known as OKB-39)
IIAF Imperial Iranian Air Force
INA Iraq News Agency
IrAAC Iraq Army Aviation Corps
IrAF Iraq Air Force (official designation since 1958)
IRGC Islamic Revolutionary Guards Corps
IRIAA Islamic Republic of Iran Army Aviation
IRIAF Islamic Republic of Iran Air Force
IRIN Islamic Republic of Iran Navy
IRNA Iranian News Agency
KGB *Komitet gosudarstvennoy bezopasnosti* (Committee for State Security, USSR)
KSA Kingdom of Saudi Arabia
Lock-on continuous and automatic tracking of a target by the radar and the FCS
MANPAD man-portable air-defence system (shoulder-fired anti-aircraft missile)
MIC Military Industrialization Commission (latter DMI, Iraq)
MICA *Missile d'Interception et de Combat Aérien* (interception and air combat missile)
MiG Mikoyan i Gurevich (the design bureau led by Artyom Ivanovich Mikoyan and Mikhail Iosifovich Gurevich, also known as OKB-155 or MMZ 'Zenit')
NATO North Atlantic Treaty Organisation
nav/attack navigational and attack (avionics suite)
OCU Operational Conversion Unit
ONI Office of Naval Intelligence (US Navy)
OPEC Organization of Petroleum-Exporting Countries
OTU Operational Training Unit
RAF Royal Air Force (of the United Kingdom)
Raphael TH *Radar de hHotographie Aérienne Electronique á transmission hertzienne* (airborne-photography radar with electronic transmission)
RHAW radar homing and warning (system)
RIO radar intercept officer (back-seater in the F-14A Tomcat)
RPL *Réservoir Pendulaire Largable*
RSAF Royal Saudi Air Force
RWR radar warning receiver
SAM surface-to-air missile
SAMP *Societe des Ateliers Mécaniques de Pont-sur-Sambre* (Company of the Mechanical Workshops of Pont-sur-Sambre)
SAR search and rescue
SEPECAT *Société Européene de Production de l'avion Ecole de Combat et d'Appui Tactique* (European Company for Production of Training, Combat, and Tactical Support Aircraft; joint venture of Breguet and BAC)
SIGINT signals intelligence
Su Sukhoi (the design bureau led by Pavel Ossipovich Sukhoi, also known as OKB-51)
TWT travelling wave tube
UAE United Arab Emirates
ULCC ultra-large crude carrier ('supertanker' with a hull length of more than 400 metres)
USAF United States Air Force

USN	US Navy
USSR	Union of Soviet Socialist Republics (also 'Soviet Union')
VLCC	very large crude carrier ('supertanker' with a hull length of more than 330 metres)
VVS	Voyenno-Vozdushnye Sily (Soviet Air Force)

FOREWORD AND ACKNOWLEDGMENTS

For much of the 1980s, hardly a month passed without the newspapers reporting an attack on one of the 'supertankers' underway in the Persian Gulf. However, none of the reports in question ever hit the headlines: hidden somewhere between the page three and five, nearly all included little more than few lines, usually citing the name and the nationality of the ship in question, Baghdad's announcement of a successful attack on a 'very large naval target', and that this was happening within the context of the ongoing Iran-Iraq War. There was no recognisable pattern behind such attacks: they took place randomly and at, apparently, very different locations within the Persian Gulf; the ships attacked not only waved the flag of very different nations, but were also underway to very different destinations – and frequently carrying cargos owned by Iraqi allies.

In those days there was no internet, and the Falklands War was still much more often discussed – in the specialised press, at various conferences, and even in 'squadron ready rooms' of the different air forces around the World – than the 'hard to cover' Iran-Iraq War, about which there was next to no reliable information. Indeed, although colloquially known as the 'Gulf War', it appeared that the latter conflict included no naval warfare component at all. Thus, it took quite some time before the specialised press began revealing at least some details. One of these was the quite surprising fact that France had leased five Dassault Super Etendard fighter-bombers armed with Aerospatiale AM.39 Exocet anti-ship missiles to Iraq, a country with next to no coast.

After earning themselves quite some reputation during the Falklands War, Super Etendards were announced as a major escalation in what soon became known as the 'Tanker War'. The latter was considered as a 'bi-product' of, the often entirely irrational, Iran-Iraq War, that had been raging since September 1980. However, before long, related reporting stopped: on the contrary, reports began surfacing about Iraq operating Dassault Mirage F.1 fighters armed with Exocets instead. Although the frequency of related reports continued increasing, most of these were still ignored by the public. This situation experienced a dramatic change only in May 1987, when – reportedly – an 'Iraqi Mirage' hit the US Navy's frigate USS *Stark* (FFG-37) with two Exocets, killing 37 seamen. During the following months, the media went head over heels into reporting from the Persian Gulf: accusations and counter-accusations were flying, Iraqis first stopped then re-started their attacks on the international shipping, the Iranians followed in fashion, then the Kuwaiti tankers were put under US flag, and the US Navy, the Royal Navy of the United Kingdom and the French Navy entered the Persian Gulf in force to escort them. Over the following year, warships from around a dozen navies reached the area, more attacks by Iraqi Mirages were reported, while exchanges of fire between the US and Iranian forces culminated in Operation *Praying Mantis*, in April 1988, and then the downing of the IranAir airliner by the US Navy's cruiser USS *Vincennes* (CG-49), in July 1988. It was only some time after this particular tragedy that the Iran-Iraq War finally came to an end.

This is only a brief summary for how the authors of this volume recall the *origins* of the story about 'Iraqi Mirages': a giant mess of superficial, usually non-related reports, further 'spiced' by countless rumours, even more so since the comparatively recent emergence of social media. It was more than a decade later that the first authoritative accounts about the Tanker War began emerging: however, while detailing most of the effects, they barely 'scratched the surface' of the topic of 'Iraqi Mirages'. It took another – and this time a far bigger, more dramatic and longer-lasting – tragedy, the US-led invasion of Iraq in 2003, and the flight of millions of Iraqis to nearby countries, for any kind of authoritative details on this topic to become available at all.

More recent publications have created an entirely different image: indeed, one whereupon Mirage F.1s were de-facto representing 'everything' there is to say about the Iraq Air Force (IrAF) of the 1980s, perhaps even of the 1990s; of these single-handedly defeating the Iranian air force, and then destroying the Iranian economy and thus forcing Tehran into accepting the UN-sponsored cease-fire that ended the war with Iraq. In the social media, this is often 'celebrated' as a sort of a clear-cut victory for Iraq in that conflict. The conclusion is at hand that one is likely to get a rather 'black-or-white' picture about the operational history of the Iraqi Mirages – and the situation is not made any better by reports about multiple falsifications of related Iraqi military documentation, all of which was either destroyed or looted after the US invasion of 2003.

It is thus that even nowadays researching this topic actually remains extremely problematic. An additional issue is that while the Iraqis are – invariably – generous and hospitable people, ready to go out of their way to cooperate, they are also deeply suspicious and morbidly sensitive. They have a strong propensity for ignoring uncomfortable facts. Working with them thus requires much more than an 'extremely delicate balance': on one side, it is easy to forfeit their trust and confidence; on the other, some of them are ready to go as far as to intentionally provide diametrically opposite information to two different researchers at the same time. It is for such reasons that – except for whatever Iraqi documentation became available over time – our work on this project was strongly reliant upon a number of, apparently, 'unrelated' sources. Foremost amongst these was an entire series of extensive de-briefs with Brigadier General Ahmad Sadik (IrAF, ret.); further contacts that strongly influenced this project were the Iranian researcher Farzin Nadimi, engineer Günther Jakowitsch from Austria, and Sirous Ebrahimi, a pilot of the Iranian Merchant Navy.

The reasons are unlikely to appear obvious at first glance. However, and although never managing to show, share or transfer more than only a small friction of their extensive documentation and knowledge, all of these sources have provided consistent information over the years – and then information that, with few minor exceptions, proved highly reliable when cross-examined. This is little surprising considering their backgrounds.

Ahmad Sadik used to serve with the little known IrAF Intelligence Directorate in the early 1980s, before being assigned the position of a liaison officer to the French military advisory mission in Iraq. By 1990-1991, he was appointed to one of top positions for the al-Hussein project and then, in the mid-1990s, he served as a liaison officer between the Iraqi government and the UN weapons inspectors in the country.[1] While his very existence alone is hotly disputed by some, supposedly authoritative Iraqi sources – and this despite the fact that Sadik was also interviewed by numerous other Western journalists over time – in this place it is sufficient to say that in 2003 Ahmad felt forced to flee to Syria: like nearly all the other former officers of the IrAF, he found himself facing death threats from the notorious Islamic Revolutionary Guards Corps (IRGC) of Iran.[2]

It was in Syria that co-author Cooper met and de-briefed Sadik on four different occasions, the two became close friends and confidantes, and began cooperating with regards to research. Sadik has provided English transcriptions of not only 200-page-long curriculum vitas of two highly-decorated Iraqi Mirage-pilots (see Bibliography). Tragically, long before our cooperation could have been further expanded, Sadik was arrested by the notorious Air Force Intelligence (of Syria), on charges of being a 'threat for national security', and incarcerated. The last we have heard from him, back in 2016, is that one of his guards 'informed' him he is going to remain imprisoned, 'for another ten years'.

Farzin Nadimi used to work as editor of one of the top Iranian military aviation journals, before embarking on running a major project for his PhD thesis about the effects of the Iraqi aerial offensive upon the Iranian oil-exporting industry. He was the first 'outsider' granted permission to work with the archives of – amongst others – the National Iranian Oil Company. Combined, Sadik's insider knowledge and documentation, and Nadimi's findings have formed the backbone not only for an entire series of articles published in France during the late 2000s, but for this project, too.

Günther Jakowitsch used to run several major construction projects in Iraq of the 1980s – all related to water-supply and irrigation – and never stood in any kind of relation to the local military. However, in 2004, he was contacted by one of his close friends from Iraq: indeed, a member of the family of the former chief Iraqi negotiator (or 'commercial agent') for some of the most important arms deals between Baghdad and Paris that were ever signed.[3] The request he received on that occasion was to shape much of his subsequent life, and exercise a strong influence upon our research over the last 10 years.

The story Jakowitsch has to tell is likely, at first, to remind the reader of plots for diverse techno-thrillers, or an online scam – if it wasn't as well-supported by extensive documentation as it is. In late February 1982, on the night of his return from France, the Iraqi middleman that played the crucial role in negotiating the contract for the Project Baz-3 was literally 'disappeared', and that on the orders of top commanders of the IrAF. The reason for his 'disappearance' may have been the content of the contracts he had negotiated. Specifically, because the President of Iraq from 1979 until 2003, Saddam Hussein Abd al-Majid at-Tikriti (colloquially 'Saddam') mistrusted the French preparedness to share their best available high-technologies with Iraq, he appears to have demanded his counterparts in Paris grant him a payment of US$10 million for each French-made combat aircraft that would be shot down in the war with Iran – to his personal account in a bank in Switzerland. Rumours always spread faster than humans can travel: indeed, those about the words written above enraged the top ranks of the IrAF to a degree where they began plotting a coup against Saddam. From their standpoint, it was not only that the strongman in Baghdad was 'squandering billions' for an aircraft type considered 'too vulnerable to combat damage', but it foremost appeared as if Saddam was enriching himself with every one of the air force's losses. What they needed was evidence, and this was available only in the form of the middleman in question. Therefore, his trip – by aircraft from Paris to Kuwait City, and then by car to Baghdad – was closely followed: he was arrested at the border and never seen again.

The documentation collected by Jakowitsch over the years has revealed another spicy detail: it was already in February 1982 – and not only years later, as usually reported – that Iraq had placed an order for not only 50 much more advanced Dassault 2000 fighter-bombers, but also an entirely new generation of weapons systems for them. Paid for by Saudi Arabia on behalf of heavily indebted Baghdad, it was this contract that resulted in the emergence of an entirely new generation of French high-technology weapons. Moreover, the combination of information provided by Sadik and that by Jakowitsch, has pointed at another fact: the story of Iraqi Mirages is not only that of aircraft, pilots, and ground crews, but also one of Iraqi electronic warfare, during the war with Iran and beyond – which is a topic usually declared as a 'non-story' by nearly all of the experts in this field.[4]

Rather unexpectedly, the final impetus for this project was provided by a discussion related to the emergence of what is known as the Littoral Combat Ship (LCS), developed for the US Navy (USN) in the 2000s in reaction to experiences from involvement in multiple 'small/low-intensity wars' around the Globe. In the course of the research and development work on this class of vessels, a USN officer was given the task of researching about world-wide experiences in defence from attacks by anti-ship missiles. Like so many other US military officers in similar positions, he was sent to Israel with the task of working himself through the local military archives. In turn, the Israelis provided him with what they described as, 'precise details on Iraqi combat experiences', stressing these included exactly *50 combat firings* of AM.39 Exocet anti-ship missiles. Rather surprised by this figure, and as somebody considering it as 'well-known' that the Iraqis had fired about ten times as many Exocets in combat against Iran, co-author Cooper was naïve enough to challenge the content of the Israeli reports. What came in response was a statement in style of, 'They are Israelis and my friends. I stand by my conclusions and data'.

From that moment onwards, it was certain: there is an urgent need to research about the air-naval warfare between Iran and Iraq – especially what is colloquially known as the 'Tanker War' – otherwise this was likely to remain a largely unknown element of that conflict. Furthermore, there was a question to what degree was the Iraqi aerial onslaught upon Iran's economy, and its oil industry in particular – run foremost, but not exclusively, by the Iraqi Mirages – actually effective in denying the Iranian oil exports? Indeed: considering that even the latest Western accounts of the 'Tanker War' are still bristling with descriptions of the related Iraqi efforts running the entire range from 'lacking aggressiveness' and 'incompetent' to 'effective' and 'devastating', the question is also if all the famed operations by the Iraqi Mirages were really able to 'defeat' Iran's war machine? Were they a factor directly, or at least indirectly, pushing Tehran into the acceptation of the United Nations Security Council's Resolution 598, and thus ending the war – as regularly claimed? And if, then how did they achieve that?

While our efforts in regards of this massive undertaking are still going on, this book – 'Iraqi Mirages' – can be seen as one of its first results. By now it is clear that the cooperation between one of the 'superpowers' and Iraq played a crucial role in the further development of the militaries and defence sectors in both countries. The availability of the Iraqi Mirages above the battlefields of the Iran-Iraq War did provide the IrAF with a tool to counter superior Iranian interceptors, but – away from Iraqi claims – remains an unknown quality in the overall context. Indeed: the state of affairs in Iraq is such that even the majority of details about their success, or failures, can only be reconstructed with help of Iranian sources. This is even more valid in regards of the so-called 'Tanker War', the story of which – thanks to extensive research by Nadimi – turned out to have been part of an entire 'Oil Campaign' run by Iraq: while generally considered to be one of the best-known and –documented aspects of that war (even though not 'public knowledge'), it transpired that this was actually one of its most misunderstood aspects.

We doubt this project is going to offer precise answers to all of the questions, and are sure that it is going to contain a few mistakes. However, it is at least going to be the first ever to provide an insight into the full background and extent of not only the operational history of Mirage F.1s in Iraq, but – and foremost – the full impact this and associated fighter-bomber types *actually* had upon the build-up of the Iraqi Air Force, and the flow of the Iran-Iraq War.

While our related research had begun already back in the mid-1980s, and went through several crucial periods over the intervening time, we cannot but express our utmost gratitude for all the help, advice, and patience of Brigadier-General Ahmad Sadik. We owe much to *Ing.* Günther Jakowitsch, for his trust and cooperation over the years, as well as to Ali Tobchi, our dear Iraqi friend, supporter and translator, and would like to express our special gratitude to both of them. Thanks to Farzin Nadimi, his unique work with help of the Iranian archives, provision of his PhD thesis, and plenty of advice, we became able to cross-examine the results of often famed air strikes by 'Iraqi Mirages'. At least as helpful were numerous visitors of the ACIG.info forum that helped collect plentiful pieces of the giant puzzle about the aerial warfare between Iran and Iraq over time, including Javad A. and Sander Peters. Our thanks go to Hugues De Guillebon, a diligent researcher from France, who did a lot to unearth the French part of the story on the Franco-Iraqi cooperation with regards to further development and working-up of Super Etendards and Mirage F.1s. Two successive – and always friendly and helpful – editors of the *Fana de l'Aviation* magazine in France, Michel Benichou and Alexis Rocher, have supported this project over more than a dozen years with additional information, photographs, and contacts to sources. Alfredo André has provided additional information from Brazil, while Albert Grandolini and Jacques Guilleme provided very rare photographs and precious assistance, too. Dr. David Nicolle, from Great Britain, and Tom Long and Doug Dildy from the USA, have supported our work in every meaningful fashion over the years, and there is never going to be a way to express our gratitude to all of them in any sufficient fashion. Last, but not least we would like to thank our beloved wives – Pia, and Lenka – for their endless patience, love, and selfless support all the while through this project.

1 PRELUDE

The usual story about 'Iraqi Mirages' starts with the observation that Iraq had already attempted to obtain Dassault's Mirage fighters from France in the late 1960s, but the related negotiations remained fruitless until around 1975. As so often before and after, the reality was dramatically different – and was related to the complex history of Iraq.

CRADLE OF THE CIVILISATION

There are plenty of good reasons why Iraqis like to call their country the 'cradle of the civilisation': the oldest traces of inhabitation and culture found on this territory date back to times around 65,000 BC. While the Arabic name 'al-Iraq' has been in use since before the 6th Century, and means 'deeply rooted', 'well watered' or simply 'fertile', it is probably of Sumerian origin. Over the last 8,000 years, this area was either the centrepiece or at least under the control of such magnificent civilisations as the Sumerian, Akkadian, Assyrian, Canaanite, Amorite, Babylonian, Persian, Hellenic, Roman, Sassanid and Arab. The powerful Abbasid Caliphate made Baghdad their capital in the 8th Century, developing it into the leading metropolis of the Arab and Muslim world, the largest multicultural city of the Middle Ages, and the centre of learning and culture for centuries. The area – including the precious library of Baghdad, with countless historical documents – was ruined by repeated Mongol invasions of the 13th Century, and then fell under the Ottoman control in the 14th and 15th Century. After a period of rule by a Mamluk dynasty of Georgian origin, and two Persian invasions, the Ottomans recovered Iraq in the 19th Century and imposed their direct control on what was meanwhile a wasteland: while the population of Iraq was estimated at 30 million in the Year 800, at the start of the 20th Century it counted barely 5 million people.

Modern-day Iraq was carved out by the pens of British and French imperialists through the notorious Sykes-Picot Treaty of 1916, which 'regulated' the partition of the Ottoman Empire after the end of the First World War – resulting in the creation of the Middle East as we know it today. Correspondingly, the former Ottoman provinces of Mosul, Baghdad, and Basra were joined into one kingdom, administered by the British under a League of Nations mandate, and its links to the areas further west (Syria) and south (Transjordan, later Jordan) cut off arbitrarily in complete disregard for local history, traditions, and relations. Almost instantly, the British found themselves facing a widespread popular uprising of Arab nationalists: finding no other solution, in 1920 they enthroned Faysal ibn Husayn of the Hashemite dynasty – son of the Sherif of Mecca and ruler of the short-lived Arab Kingdom of Syria – the king of Iraq. Moreover, by recruiting Sunni Arab officers with Ottoman military backgrounds and Shi'a tribal elements, they established an Iraqi Army in the same fashion they constituted the entirety of Iraq: as a society in which the Sunni minority dominated the Shi'a majority, the Kurds and everybody else.

Although Iraq was released into independence and admitted to the League of Nations in 1932, British military forces remained in the country, and British officials continued dominating domestic and foreign politics. Combined with the explosive mix of a power struggle between the Sunni and the Shi'a, a Kurdish uprising in the north and a Yazidi revolt in Jabal Sinjar, and the general anti-British sentiment, this resulted in endless political instability. As the best-organized institution in an otherwise weak political system that had few pluralist traditions, the Iraqi military gradually crystallized as the dominating political factor. Between 1936 and 1968, a relatively small group of top Sunni officers instigated more than 25 coups d'état or extra-constitutional transfers of power, all of which had one aspect in common: they were a direct consequence of insurmountable differences between diverse ethnic and religious groups, landlords and tribes, but also cliques within the military, each solely preoccupied with its own and often diametrically opposite political aims.

POLITICAL AIR FORCE[1]

Established in 1931 and thus considered the oldest of all Arab air forces, the Iraqi Air Force (IrAF) was always a mirror image of the situation in the country. Originally founded as the flying branch of the army, and with the intention of operating against 'dissident tribesmen' of northern Iraq, the IrAF grew relatively quickly in the late 1930s, but was de-facto destroyed by the British when it turned against them in 1941. Re-built with significant support from

The Royal Iraqi Air Force was officially established on 22 April 1941, upon arrival of first five pilots and the first five de Havilland DH.60 Moth training aircraft in Iraq. (Tom Cooper Collection)

British influence was strongly felt within the IrAF well into the late 1960s, by when the service was dominated by British-trained officers most of whom used to fly Hawker Hunters. (Albert Grandolini Collection)

London, by 1955 it was virtually an appendage of the Royal Air Force (RAF): its structure and training, as well as nearly all of its aircraft, were British; its pilots were trained in Great Britain; and all of its personnel wore uniforms closely resembling those of the RAF. British influence remained strong even after the Hashemite Dynasty and its governments were toppled in the bloody coup of July 1958. Indeed, it regained power after the two coups of 1963 – when air force officers played a crucial role, and although by the time the IrAF's operational units were staffed along political predilections of their commanding officers – into 'republican', 'pan-Arabist/Nasserist', 'communist', 'Ba'athist', and other units.

Over the next two years, successive governments in Baghdad not only purchased 51-52 additional Hawker Hunter fighter-bombers, but also considered acquiring the English Electric Lightning interceptor. Further cooperation with Great Britain was foremost hampered by the lack of offers: as of the mid-1960s, London simply had no fighter-bomber with capabilities sought for by the IrAF. In need of additional and more advanced aircraft due to the ongoing war against Kurdish guerrillas in the north of the country, the Iraqi air force began pressing Baghdad into finding alternative sources: in 1966, Iraq thus placed an order for 50 MiG-21F-13s and MiG-21FLs in the Union of Soviet Socialist Republics (USSR, also 'Soviet Union'), followed – less than a year later – by an order for 32 Sukhoi Su-7BMK fighter-bombers.

While proving nowhere near as well-armed or pilot-friendly as Hunters, Soviet aircraft were available in large numbers at short notice and were cheaper to acquire, simpler to maintain and operate, and more survivable of combat damage. Unsurprisingly, they left lasting impressions upon the IrAF, further splitting the force into two major schools of thought: the British-trained officers continued favouring Western aircraft, while the continuously increasing number of officers trained in the Soviet Union and Czechoslovakia preferred Soviet-made aircraft, and – internally – became known as the 'Sukhoi Clique'.

THE FIRST MIRAGE DEAL[2]

The viewpoints of both groups were challenged during the June 1967 Arab-Israeli War (also known as the 'Six Days War'), when the Israeli Defence Force/Air Force equipped with delta-winged Dassault Mirage fighter-bombers of French origin, severely defeated three major Arab air forces, of which two were entirely equipped with Soviet-made combat aircraft. After this experience, and with the Iraqi military still proving unable to suppress the continuous Kurdish uprising in the north, the government of President (and Major-General of the Iraqi Army) ar-Rahman Arif found itself facing massive public pressure to significantly expand the army and air force and bolster them through the acquisition of modern arms. Arif acted quickly: after ordering the establishment of ten additional divisions of the army, on 25 September 1967 he sent a delegation of top officials to Paris. Following months-long negotiations, France first publicly announced an economic agreement with Iraq and then, in December of the same year, its preparedness to supply aircraft and military equipment. In the light of this development, Baghdad rushed a military mission to Paris: on 6 April 1968, the French government then announced that it had signed a contract for the supply of 54 Mirage 5s, 46 Sud-Est (later Aerospatiale) SE.316C Alouette III helicopters, and AML-60 and AML-90 armoured cars to Iraq.

The realisation of this deal was spoiled by numerous factors. In France of 1967-1970, there was a wave of sympathy for the Kurdish cause: Kurdish activists led by insurgent leader Mullah Mustafa skilfully exploited this opportunity to write a letter to President Charles de Gaulle, requesting him *not* to supply military material to Iraq 'until the Kurdish problem had been addressed' – to their satisfaction. Already overbooked by a mass of orders for Mirages and other equipment it received from elsewhere after the June 1967 War, the French industry saw little incentive: unsurprisingly, Paris soon had second thoughts about the deal. The opposition within the IrAF was growing, too: while an internal study of the air force's High Command concluded that the Mirage would provide the capability to support ground troops more accurately, while carrying heavier bomb load over extended ranges in comparison to Soviet-made aircraft, and that it could still protect itself against enemy interceptors – an increasing number of officers opposed the idea of having to build-up the necessary support infrastructure. Others declared the Mirage not only 'excessively costly' in comparison to Soviet aircraft, but objected to both the protracted delivery schedules and the long training required for pilots and ground personnel. Finally, Soviet representatives in Baghdad did their best to dissuade the government from buying French aircraft.

The final nail in the coffin of the first Iraqi Mirage deal was delivered by the next – bloodless – coup d'état in Baghdad: this was launched on 17 July 1968, when Major-General Ahmed Hassan al-Bakr and C-in-C IrAF, Hardan at-Tikriti, brought the local branch of the Arab Socialist Ba'ath Party to power. Already dominated by al-Bakr's deputy – and younger relative – Saddam Hussein at-Tikriti (who was no military officer), the Ba'ath applied extreme violence to impose itself upon all elements of Iraqi society, foremost the military. In a series of purges, all of which were declared to be 'in the interest of consolidating the Ba'ath' but actually served the purpose of securing his position, Saddam systematically cleansed the top ranks of Iraqi political officials and military commanders: by 1970, even Hardan at-Tikriti was forced into emigration. Meanwhile, President Bakr ordered the army into a major offensive against the Kurds in the north, while intensifying its expansion through huge orders for additional aircraft in the USSR and Czechoslovakia instead. In the light of these developments, Paris quickly cancelled the part of the deal related to the Mirages: all that was left of the Franco-Iraqi arms deal from 5 April 1968 were deliveries of Alouettes.

THE SECOND IRAQI-KURDISH WAR[3]

Despite the failure to acquire Mirages in 1968, and large-scale acquisition of MiGs and Sukhois, the idea of acquiring the French-made deltas soon experienced a sort of a renaissance. Indeed, and as in several other Arab air forces of the late 1960s and 1970s, it developed into something of an obsession: the more they studied the Arab-Israeli War of June 1967, the more officers of the air force, but even those of the army became convinced of the notion that this particular aircraft was the key to the Israeli success and that, if it would be acquired, the 'gates to the victory would be wide open'.[4]

This school of thought became influential enough to spoil the next major Soviet-Iraqi deal: in 1972, the Soviets presented their brand-new Sukhoi Su-20 fighter-bomber to an IrAF delegation visiting Kubinka Air Base (AB). However, obsessed with the Mirage, the Iraqis considered it 'crucial' to convince their top political leaders to get that type instead. A suitable opportunity presented itself during the October 1973 Arab-Israeli War: at the time, the USSR was in the process of delivering a total of 14 Tupolev Tu-22 supersonic bombers to Iraq. However, these arrived without any of the massive FAB-3000, FAB-5000 and FAB-9000 bombs (3000kg, 5000kg and 9000kg, respectively) explicitly demanded by Baghdad: Moscow refused to deliver any for the duration of the conflict. Instead, when Baghdad issued an official protest, the Soviets literally dumped a batch of ten Su-20s upon the IrAF: these arrived on board ten Antonov An-12B transports that landed at Rashid AB mid-way through the October 1973 War – without Baghdad ever placing an order for them. Although Moscow subsequently delivered eight additional Su-20s, and the type proved highly popular in service with No. 1 Squadron, commanders of the Iraqi air force felt mistreated enough to express interest in acquiring another Western type instead: the SEPECAT Jaguar.[5]

Related negotiations were still going on when Iraq became embroiled in the next war. After an attack by Iraqi ground units on the Iranian border town of Mehran, on 10 February 1974, which reportedly left 41 soldiers and gendarmes dead, the Imperial Iranian Air Force (IIAF) hit back with McDonnell-Douglas F-4 Phantom II fighter-bombers, and then flew a massive power demonstration deep within the Iraqi airspace: as impressed by 'mighty' F-4s as by the Mirages, the IrAF failed to raise to the challenge. Furthermore, on 11 March 1974, a force of 25,000 Kurdish insurgents led by Mullah Mustafa Barzani launched a new uprising – also known as the Second Iraqi-Kurdish War. In a matter of a few weeks, they brought most of Iraq's border to Turkey and Iran under their control, and put the provincial capital of Zakho under siege. The Iraqi army counterattacked and retook most of the areas adjacent to the Turkish border: as a mass of up to 130,000 Kurds fled to Iran, Tehran deployed its regular military units inside Iraq, including at least one Rapier and one MIM-23 HAWK SAM-site. The IrAF – which was providing crucial air support for ground troops, but had no means for electronic countermeasures (ECM) – was the first to feel the consequences: by early 1975, the Iranians claimed up to 18 of its aircraft shot down, including at least one Tupolev Tu-16 bomber, two Hunters, a Su-20, and several brand-new MiG-23BNs. Left without a choice, the Iraqis reacted by deploying their supersonic Tu-22 bombers. Dropped from high altitude and speed, 'area weapons' like FAB-9000s tended to obliterate entire sections of insurgent positions: indeed, they proved crucial for enabling at least a slow, even if costly advance of the Iraqi ground forces. The intensity of Tu-22 eventually reached such a scale, that the two units operating them – No. 18 and No. 36 Squadrons – ran their stocks of Soviet-made bombs dry. When Iraq requested a re-supply, Moscow flatly refused and stopped deliveries of all types of ammunition.[6]

THE MIC

Once again left without choice, Baghdad agreed to negotiate under Algerian mediation and Saddam Hussein – meanwhile in the role of the Vice-President and Foreign Minister of Iraq – signed the Algiers Treaty with Iran, on 6 March 1975. Under that accord, the international border along the length of the Shatt al-Arab waterway was demarcated along the thalweg line. Three months later, on 15 June 1975, both sides signed a follow-up agreement regulating their mutual border, pledged the return of some disputed territory to Iraq, and agreed to discontinue supporting armed opposition to the other side.

For Saddam, the major lesson from these experiences – which he latter described as 'a shame' – was that Iraq was in need of an alternative source of arms, even more so considering that Iran had meanwhile placed an order for 80 of the powerful and brand-new Grumman F-14A Tomcat interceptors (of which Saddam was an

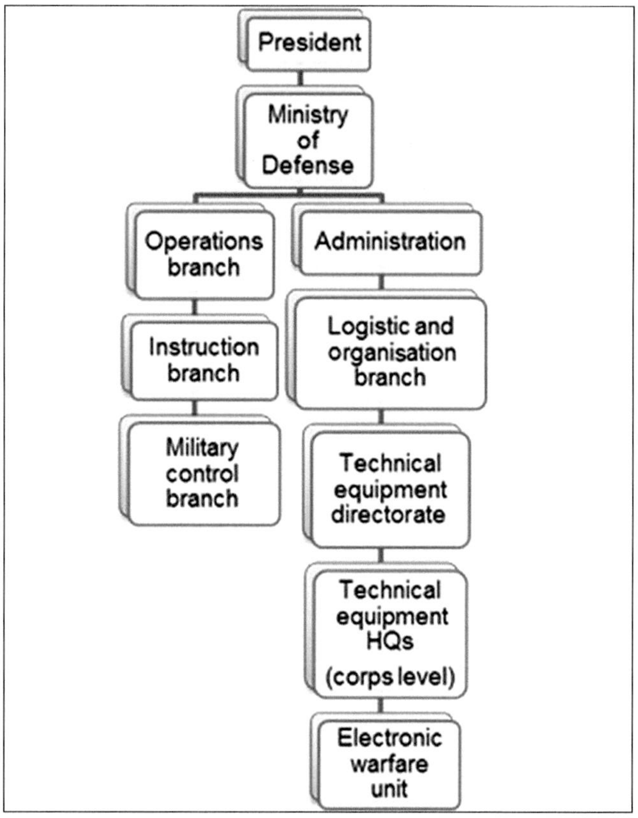

Organisation of the operational branches and the Logistics and Organization Branch of the Iraqi military, part of which – elevated to the corps level over the time – was the Technical Equipment Directorate, which in turn was responsible for the control over electronic warfare units. (Diagram by Milos Sipos)

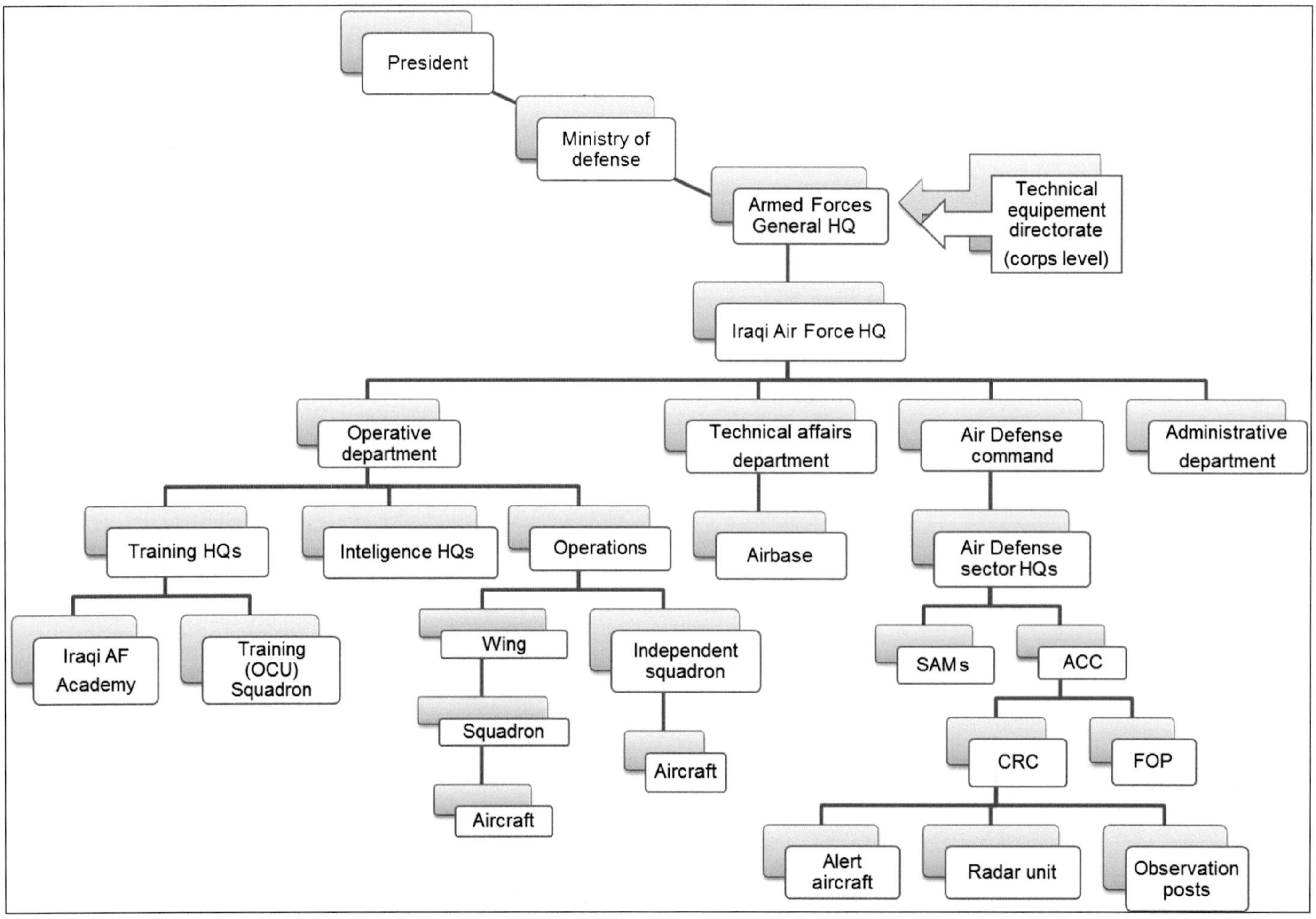

Organizational structure of the Iraqi Air Force in the 1970s and 1980s. (Diagram by Milos Sipos)

avid fan). Moreover, already during the same year, Saddam took care to establish the Military Industrialization Commission (MIC, also known as the Directorate of Military Industries) and for this to become a major contributor to the Arab Organization for Industrialization (AOI) – an Egypt-based Arab military organization established during the same year in Cairo, and co-sponsored by the Kingdom of Saudi Arabia (KSA), the United Arab Emirates (UAE), and the Emirate of Qatar, with the intention of supervising and coordinating the collective development of the pan-Arab arms industry.[7] How important this decision was for the Iraqi strongman also demonstrates the fact that right from the start, two of Saddam's closest, yet also very young confidantes, played a crucial role in the further development of the MIC: Hussein Kamel Hassan al-Majid and Amer Mohammed Rasheed al-Obeidi. Their task was to develop the national defence industry sector to minimize the dependence upon, and vulnerability to, external factors, but also as a leading edge for military training and development of skills for the civilian sector, and to lower foreign exchange expenditure and dependence. Over time, related activities by Majid and by Rasheed resulted in the emergence of a huge network of research centres, state enterprises, front companies, and dual-use factories capable of producing both civil and military goods.[8]

ENTER THE MIRAGE F.1

During the late 1960s, the French defence sector went through a period of reforms and reorganisations in the course of which less successful enterprises were systematically bought up by profitable companies; other companies entered close cooperation with investors from the USA thus securing not only their own survival but also an influx of know-how; while the survival of the few non-profitable but technologically important enterprises was safeguarded through their nationalisation. In order to better coordinate the work of the entire sector, in 1965 the government in Paris established the Ministerial Delegation for Armament (*Délégation Ministérielle pour l'Armement*, DMA). The DMA proved its worth already when the French Air Force (*Armée de l'Air*) began setting up requirements for a new generation of combat aircraft: although uncertain about the outcome, the air force used the DMA to issue basic guidelines to the aircraft industry, so that this could start researching and developing necessary technologies 'on time'. With the Groupement Avions Marcel Dassault establishing itself as the leader in the French aviation industry after assimilating the Louis Breguet company in 1967, all of the related work resulted in four projects run by what was now the Avions Marcel Dassault – Breguet Aviation (AMD-BA): Mirage IIIT, Mirage IIIF, Mirage IIIG/IIIG8 and Mirage IIIV. Although derived from the Mirage IIIE, all were big and complex tandem cockpit designs which actually led nowhere. Realizing this in time, the AMD-BA promptly suggested a different option: in 1965, it proposed a Mirage IIIE-sized aircraft, equipped with the same avionics and the well-proven Atar 09K engine, but with a shoulder-mounted cropped delta wing. The resulting 'Mirage F1C' flew for the first time on 23 December 1966 and showed performances that were promising enough for the AdA to re-write its official requirement around it. Series production was launched in 1971, and it entered operational service with the AdA a year later under the designation Mirage F.1C, as a medium-altitude interceptor armed with Matra R.530 missiles and two 30mm DEFA cannons.[9]

THE DIA

Meanwhile, the DMA established the Direction of International Affairs (*Direction des Affaires Internationales*, DIA) as its office for export business. While usually operating in great discretion, and often becoming involved in affairs of a rather dubious nature, the DIA enjoyed the full official support of Paris and thus proved far more effective and influential than comparable organisations abroad. Until 1974, the boss of the DIA was General Hughes de l'Estoile: although replaced by Paul Assens in same year, he was subsequently appointed the responsibility for the export of the Mirage F.1. L'Estoile and the DIA pursued a very aggressive sales policy for the Mirage F.1. As well as getting the new type involved in the contest for a multirole fighter-bomber sought by the Belgium, Denmark, Netherlands and Norway to replace Lockheed F-104G Starfighters, Northrop F-5A Freedom Fighters, and North American F-100D/F Super Sabres – the so-called 'Sale of the Century' – they managed to sell it to numerous countries either considered 'pariahs' (especially by the governments in Washington and London) and thus subjected to arms embargoes, or at least those requests which were turned down on diverse political grounds. The net result was that Mirage F.1 became a major export success.[10]

Under the prevailing circumstances in France and Iraq, the interests of the two governments – and their defence sectors – thus had to meet, sooner or later.

PROJECT BAZ

The lengths to which the DIA was ready to go with its marketing shows the fact that only months after securing the first export order for F.1s – from Kuwait in April 1974, and that in a deal that was prompted by a shallow invasion by Iraqi forces and a series of border clashes in 1973 – the same type was offered to Baghdad.[11] Over the following months, top French politicians, the DIA, and top military and industrial representatives continued courting Saddam, the Minister of Defence of Iraq, Adnan Khairallah, representatives of the MIC, and the C-in-C IrAF, Major-General Nima'a ad-Dulaymi with a series of related briefings and presentations – with success. By September 1975, the Iraqis were convinced and – although the Mirage F.1 had lost out in the 'Sale of the Century' to the General Dynamics F-16A – once the French expressed their preparedness to help establish depot-level maintenance and engine-overhaul capability in Iraq, it was the primary contender for a sale to the IrAF.[12]

Henceforth, there was no holding back: a month later, a team led by Lieutenant-Colonel Adel Suleiman was invited to test-fly the F.1 and the Jaguar at Istres AB, in France. The resulting report was submitted to Saddam Hussein on 21 November 1975 with quite a clear conclusion: the Mirage F.1 was a winner. Baghdad thus decided to open related negotiations.[13]

What followed was a period of intensive and rather protracted talks, primarily because of the MIC's requirement for France to deliver not only its most advanced combat aircraft and the associated armament, but also a full transfer of some of the most advanced high-technologies France was able to offer, and that together with full technical support. Demanding that the DIA run the entire project as though it was for the French military, the Iraqis requested the development of an essentially entire new generation of high-tech weapons. Negotiations were concluded only on 3 July 1977, when the representatives of the Iraqi government and a consortium of the involved French companies signed the contract for *Project Baz* ('Falcon' in Arabic).[14]

Amongst others, *Project Baz* stipulated the deliveries of 4 Mirage

F.1BQ two-seat conversion trainers; 16 Mirage F.1EQ; 16 slightly improved Mirage F.1EQ-2s; their avionics, engines, and underwing pylons; two flight simulators, and a huge assortment of air-to-air and air-to-ground weaponry. While Iraq was to start transferring related payments in December 1977, roll-out of the first Mirage F.1 manufactured for the IrAF was expected for spring of 1979, with deliveries to follow a year later.[15]

THE F.1EQ

As in the case of all the Mirages manufactured for export customers, the Mirage F.1s manufactured for Iraq received unique suffixes to their designation: EQ stood for 'Electronique' and 'Iraq'. Usually presented in public as multi-role fighter bombers, the first 16 Mirage F.1EQ single-seaters were considered 'just the first step' in the cooperation between France and Iraq, and originally equipped with an avionics suite only minimally advanced in comparison to the Mirage IIIE and Mirage F.1C. Therefore, all were to be upgraded to the F.1EQ-2 standard before delivery. The centrepiece of the same was the slightly improved navigational system, and a weapons system centred on the Thomson-CSF Cyrano IVQ/C Ramadan airborne interception radar, compatible with the then brand-new Matra Super 530F semi-active radar homing missile.[16]

All the Mirage F.1EQ-2s also had their wing-tip stations wired for the carriage of Matra R.550 Magic infra-red homing air-to-air missiles. Furthermore, the original Thomson-CSF TMV-011 BF radar warning receiver (RWR) was replaced with the slightly modified variant custom-tailored to IrAF's requirements.[17] In addition to Super 530F-1s and R.550s, within the frame of the *Project Baz*, the French were to deliver eight COR-2 pods equipped with reconnaissance cameras, six Dassault Aviation CC.420 gun pods, Matra F1 and F4 pods for 68mm unguided rockets, general-purpose bombs like the SAMP Type 25 (400kg) and Type 21 (200kg) and Thomson-Brandt BAT-100 anti-runway bombs. Another sub-contract was specifying the development of two highly sophisticated weapons, both made by Matra: the BGL-250/400 series of laser-homing bombs, and the sophisticated battlefield dispersion cluster package designated BLG.66 Belouga, containing three types of grenade-type submunition designed by Thomson-Brandt.[18]

BREAKTHROUGH

While the Mirage F.1EQs were the most obvious result of *Project Baz*, from the standpoint of the Iraqi military – and the MIC in particular – at least as important was the French support for the development of Iraqi electronic warfare capabilities. As described above, during the war with Israel in October 1973, and then the Second Iraqi-Kurdish War, the Iraqis became painfully aware of that

The Mirage F.1BQ serial number 4000: the first of its kind manufactured for Iraq, as seen on finals during pre-delivery testing. (Tom Cooper Collection)

The second Mirage F.1BQ, serial number 4001, as seen in February 1981. (Dassault, via Tom Cooper)

fact that they possessed no capabilities in this regard at all. Thus, as soon as he took over as the new Commander-in-Chief IrAF, in 1976, Major-General Hamid Sha'ban ordered the establishment of a related branch of the air force, designated the Directorate of Technical Equipment.[19]

Initially, the IrAF had only a bare minimum of related equipment, consisting of Soviet-made Type P pods for electronic intelligence (ELINT) carried by four MiG-21Rs operated by the Rashid AB-based No. 70 Squadron. This pod used the oldest and hopelessly obsolete technique of converting light marks on a moving strip of photographic film, with the help of which it recorded the location of detected enemy radars with an accuracy of 'several kilometres', and determined their working frequencies. Although IrAF's MiG-21Rs flew dozens of reconnaissance sorties along the Iranian border during the second half of the 1970s, the resulting image of the Iranian radar network remained 'hazy' at best. Therefore, during negotiations for *Project Baz*, Sha'ban went to great extents to secure the delivery of such electronic warfare systems as the Thomson-CSF TMV-002 Remora (a self-protection jammer) and Thomson-CSF TMV-004 Caiman (a broad-band, offensive stand-off jammer), Matra Sycomor chaff and flare dispensers, and Thomson-CSF TMV-018 Syrel ELINT pods. The results of lengthy negotiations were summarized in the contract for *Project Baz-AR* ('Falcon, anti-radar') signed on the same day as that for *Project Baz*.[20]

As of 1977, nearly all of the systems in question existed on paper only: they took years of research and development – and massive Iraqi funding – to be realised. Indeed, the Iraqi order contained an element of challenge for the French, and the promise of catching up with the USA in this field: while their existing systems were all made to counter Soviet-made air defence systems, the companies involved had to deliver equipment capable of countering US, British, and Israeli-made equipment.[21]

The DIA's agreement to provide sensitive technology to Iraq prompted an outright avalanche of offers from diverse other foreign companies over the following years. For example, in 1978 Moscow agreed to deliver Mikoyan i Gurevich MiG-23MF and MiG-25P interceptors, and also MiG-25R/RB reconnaissance fighters equipped with a custom-tailored reconnaissance suite, and ground-based stations for communications intelligence (COMINT), signals intelligence (SIGINT), and electronic support measures (ESM). Combined with the training of Iraqi personnel abroad, this bolstered the further development of the Directorate of Technical Equipment where this was raised to the corps level and subjected to the direct control of the Logistics and Operational Branch of the General Headquarters (GHQ) of the Iraqi Armed Forces: this is why the story of Iraqi Mirages is also that of the Iraqi electronic warfare.[22]

ROLL-OUT

The first single-seat Mirage F.1EQ – serial number 4004 – was rolled out in early 1979. Instead of being delivered straight to Iraq, after making its first flight on 11 April that year at the Flight Test Centre (*Centre d'essais en vol*, CEV) at Cazaux, and together with the second example – serial number 4005 – it was used for extensive testing of all the different weaponry ordered by the IrAF. Thus, even after officially accepted by Iraqi representatives, on 10 April 1980, both aircraft remained in the country.[23]

The first group of IrAF pilots to undergo conversion to the type arrived at Mont-de-Marsan AB in France in June 1980. Led by Lieutenant-Colonel Ali Raji, this included Major Magdi Alladin Yousef, and Captains Abdul Karim Mukhalad, Ryadh Abdul Majid at-Tikriti, Salah Ismail Nasser, and Wallid Hussein. By this time, Mirage F.1BQs with serial numbers 4000 and 4001, as well as F.1EQs 4006, 4007, 4008, 4009, and 4010 were rolled out and were ready for flight training run by a group of experienced French instructors. While two Iraqi pilots were washed out after six months (one for health-related reasons), the others completed their course late the same year. The second group – including Abdul Ghani Nuwaidis, Idris Hassan al-Ammari, Mahmoud Hamid, Amer Dareb, Salah Ismail Nasser, and Khalid Jihad ad-Dahy – arrived in December 1980, and were trained on Mirage F.1EQs with serial numbers 4011, 4012, 4014, 4015 and 4017. The third group – consisting of new pilots that underwent training in Italy, and were recalled by French sources only as Kafah Muhammad Ali, Hafez, Sa'ad Abed, and Amad – followed in February 1981.[24]

Training of Iraqi personnel in electronic warfare began in 1979 at the Higher Electronic Warfare School (*École Supérioeure de Guerre Aérienne*, ESGA): as soon as the first group completed its course, in May 1980, it was quickly replaced by another: once back in Iraq, they began working-up a number of battalion-sized specialized assets, which usually received such simple designations as Unit 114 (COMINT), or Unit 128 (SIGINT).[25]

Meanwhile, the construction of an entirely new home-base for the Mirages was launched in northern Iraq, 20 kilometres west of

The Mirage F.1EQ/EQ-2 serial number 4008 as seen in France in February 1981, while being used for conversion training of the first group of Iraqi pilots. (Dassault, via Michel Benichou)

This fine study of the Mirage F.1EQ/EQ-2 serial number 4010 was taken on the same occasion. Notable is the application of the national insignia on top wing surfaces. (Dassault, via Tom Cooper)

Home of the Mirages: Saddam AB (better known in the West as 'Qayyarah West') was the principal hub of Iraqi Mirage operations. (Photo by Martin Rosenkranz)

Qayyarah, a town about 350 kilometres north of Baghdad. Planned to include an extensive support infrastructure and 33 hardened aircraft shelters, this facility – eventually named the Saddam AB – was envisaged to serve as a home base for three squadrons, but also as a logistics and technical hub for the Mirage-fleet.[26]

WOES OF THE BAZ-AR

Project Baz-AR stipulated the development of a custom-tailored version of the Matra/Hawker Siddeley Dynamics AJ.168/AS.37 Martel anti-radar missile (ARM). The work of Matra and Electronics Marcel Dassault came forward relatively quickly, despite the 'issue' with the original missile being anything other than user friendly, and containing technology of British and US origin. The AS.37 required three different, interchangeable seeker-heads to target radars working in three different bands of frequencies. In France of the late 1970s, the development of the analogue technology was reaching its peak, while digital was still in its infancy: inertial guidance systems capable of guiding a missile to specific geographic coordinates were non-existent. An anti-radar weapon thus required a 'cooperative' target: one that continued to emit throughout the missile's flight, or the seeker-head would lose the target and the ability to guide the missile. In order to keep the development costs low, the French used the airframe and aerodynamic configuration of the existing weapon: nevertheless, the Baz-AR missile received an entirely new, broadband passive seeker designated ADAR ('*autodirector anti-radar*') that could not only be pre-set to search for specific frequency before the take-off, but also adjusted by the pilot once the aircraft was airborne. Although much underestimated until today – foremost because it was overshadowed by contemporary US and Soviet progress in the same field – the work on the Baz-AR also resulted in a missile with an exceptional range and a deadly warhead (largest in the World for any anti-radar missiles).[27]

Flight-testing of the Baz-AR began in February 1980 (using the F.1EQ-2 serial number 4004). The first powered test-flight was undertaken on 7 November 1980, while the first test-firing from an F.1EQ-2, took place on 27 November. Finally, the first telemetry test – using a missile with live seeker-head but without a warhead – was undertaken on 21 April 1981, and concluded successfully. Following further refining and two additional test-shots, the Baz-AR was declared operational in November 1981, and the first shipment of 30 missiles to Iraq took place by the end of the same year. The second shipment of 30 missiles was planned to follow in 1982. For the first time in its history, the IrAF was thus in possession of technologically superior weapon in comparison to its primary enemy – the Iranian air force.[28]

Mirage F.1EQ-2 serial number 4004, as seen while equipped with one of the Baz-AR test rounds. (Dassault, via Michel Benichou)

The work on the Baz-AR in turn resulted in the development of the ARMAT – an advanced variant designed for service with the AdA, one of which is visible in this official photograph. (Matra)

SADDAM'S FALCON

The French were still busy preparing diverse orders from *Projects Baz* and *Baz-AR* when, on 16 July 1979, Saddam Hussein staged a 'palace coup' and forced President al-Bakr to resign. Immediately after, he mercilessly purged all of the potential rivals within the Ba'ath party, and then embarked on shaping the country – and its military – according to his ideas: correspondingly, one of his first decisions was to advance in rank numerous officers that were members of the Ba'ath Party, irrespectively of their merits. As a consequence, by 1980 the IrAF was once again well on the way to becoming a top-down, politically dominated force. Furthermore, because Saddam sought for ways to position himself as a great Arab leader and represented the standpoint that such leaders are only remembered by their military victories, and such needed advanced armament, he opened negotiations for an acquisition of additional Mirages.

Thanks to a meanwhile very close relationship between the boss of the DIA, General René-Pierre Audran, and Amer Rasheed of the MIC, related negotiations were concluded rather quickly. On 16 December 1979, representatives of the French and Iraqi governments finalized the deal for *Project Baz-2* (contracts for which were designated in the BAZ-221x-series). This stipulated the delivery of the first truly 'Iraqi' variant of the Mirage F.1: the Mirage F.1EQ-4 multi-role fighter, still equipped with the Cyrano-IVQ/C Ramadan radar, but now having a new, Thompson-CSF VFT-150 radar scope, a centreline hardpoint stressed to carry RPL.201 Irakien drop tanks with capacity of 2,200 litres of fuel, and compatibility with the new reconnaissance pod, designated Harold, eight of which were to be manufactured for Iraq.[29]

Table 1: Overview of *Projects Baz*(-1) and *Baz-2*, 1977-1979						
Contract designation	Date of Order	Number of Aircraft	Version	Serial Numbers	Roll-Out Dates	Acceptance Dates
Project Baz(-1)						
BAZ-121x [30]	3 Jul 1977	4	Mirage F.1BQ	4000-4003	18 Jul 1980 – 22 Jul 1981	27 August 1980 – 28 July 1981
BAZ-121x	3 Jul 1977	16	Mirage F.1EQ	4004-4019	9 Apr 1980 – 14 Jan 1981	26 Aug 1980 – 14 Oct 1981
BAZ-121x	3 Jul 1977	16	Mirage F.1EQ-2	4020-4035	9 Apr 1981 – 24 Feb 1982	9 Apr 1981 – 10 Mar 1982
Project Baz-2						
BAZ-221x	16 Dec 1979	4	Mirage F.1EQ-4	4500-4503	31 Dec 1982 – 2 Mar 1983	31 Dec 1982 – 11 Jul 1982
BAZ-221x	16 Dec 1979	2	Mirage F.1BQ	4504-4505	14 Apr 1982 – 27 Jul 1982	15 Apr 1982 – 27 Jul 1982

2
WAR WITH IRAN

When Shah Reza Pahlavi of Iran was toppled by what subsequently became known as the 'Islamic' Revolution, in February 1979, Iraq sought an accommodation with the new authorities in Tehran. However, another of Saddam's early actions once he established himself in power was to order the arrest (and then the execution) of Muhammad Baqir as-Sadr, one of Iraq's leading Shi clerics – on suspicion of fomenting unrest with Iranian support. In retaliation, Tehran broadcasted repeated calls for the overthrow of Saddam's regime. Enmities between Persians (predominantly members of the Shi'a branch) and Arabs (most of whom are members of the Sunni branch of Islam) are centuries old, but mutual wars relatively rare: by late 1979, they were replaced by politically-motivated violence as both sides began providing material and financial support to each other's dissidents. Indeed, by early 1980, Baghdad and Tehran were running terrorist operations against the other's officials. After foreign ministers of both countries narrowly survived assassination attempts, in April 1980, Iraq supposedly registered ten violations of its airspace, and thus concluded that a 'Persian aggression was in the making'.[1]

Who exactly could have violated the Iraqi airspace at that time remains unclear because of what was formerly the mighty IIAF, but meanwhile officially the Islamic Republic of Iran Air Force (IRIAF), was in tatters and out of condition to do so: paralyzed during the revolution, subsequently it had all of its top commanders either arrested or executed, and most of its air bases occupied by diverse groups of armed civilians and non-commissioned officers (NCOs). Amid an almost complete collapse of order and discipline, and a de-facto civil war that raged in Iran between 1979 and 1983, the IRIAF was in no condition to operate effectively even against the relatively small Kurdish uprising in north-west of the country.[2] The situation only worsened after the failed coup attempt organized by a group of about 400 officers of the air force and the army at the Tactical Fighter Base 3 (TFB.3), outside Hamedan, in June 1980: this resulted in another, sweeping purge of mid-ranks. By July 1980, the air force that used to total about 100,000 officers and other ranks was down to 30,000; all the training flights stopped; all the maintenance activity ceased, and the mass of the IRIAF's aircraft were stored – or left to rot wherever parked. Therefore, although it is perfectly possible that some of the border accidents were caused by over-zealous officers or local Iranian clergy – often out of eagerness to attract favours from the new strongman in Tehran, Ayatollah Sayyid Ruhollah Musavi Khomeini – there is little doubt about who attacked whom in September 1980.[3]

Indeed, after monitoring the wholesale collapse and disorganisation of the Iranian armed forces for a while, and concluding that the Iranians would be easy opponents, Saddam made the decision to invade Iran during the meeting of the Ba'ath party leadership in Abu Ghraib on 6 July 1980. As a pretext, on 4 September 1980, Baghdad accused Tehran of shelling the vicinity of two villages which Iraq was supposed to receive from Iran in accordance with the Algiers Treaty, and which its army required as a springboard for its attack: when Tehran – preoccupied with the post-revolutionary chaos – ignored demands for their handover, the Iraqi Army, supported by Mil Mi-25 helicopter gunships of the Iraqi Army Aviation Corps (IrAAC), seized both places, three days later.[4]

The complete absence of an Iranian reaction then encouraged Saddam to order further, similar actions: by 10 September 1980, Iraqi troops had taken six border posts in the central sector of the border, and then captured a forward COMINT-station of the Iranian military intelligence, killing dozens of Iranians in the process. When Tehran attempted to order its military to stop Iraqi attacks and incursions, it was forced into a realisation that there was very little left of the same – except for a few squadrons of the air force. Thus, the Iraqi armed forces were left free to continue occupying one Iranian border post after the other. When the IRIAF was finally ordered into action, on 8 September 1980, it quickly lost two McDonnell-Douglas F-4E Phantom II and three Northrop F-5E Tiger II fighter-bombers to Iraqi and own ground fire. All the Iranians managed in return was for one of their F-14A Tomcat interceptors to hit an Iraqi Mi-25 with gun fire, mortally wounding its pilot, while two others shot down one each of Iraqi MiG-21Rs and a Su-22 out of many that were meanwhile moving freely inside Iranian airspace.[5]

FROM THREATS TO THE WAR

The Iraqi military launched the invasion of Iran during the afternoon of 22 September 1980 in quite some confusion: many of its officers were convinced they would be involved in a 'pre-emptive' attack, designed to 'prevent a Persian aggression'. Moreover, based on an underlying assumption that this would result in a quick and easy victory, the invasion was undertaken without a clear strategic goal or aim. The IrAF did its best to follow its much belated orders for the opening air strike, and bombed nine Iranian air bases and one civilian airfield, but before long found that it lacked the necessary aircraft, armament, training *and orders* to keep even the much-weakened IRIAF under serious pressure. Similarly, the Army trundled into the

Khuzestan province while even lacking up-to-date maps – but in hope that something might turn up.[6]

Instead of turning and running away, united by the challenge of an aggressor on their soil, the Iranians put up fanatical resistance. Within just two weeks, the main prongs of the Iraqi advance were stopped by severe casualties. The IRIAF reacted almost instinctively: using emergency plans prepared well before the war (indeed: before the revolution of 1979), it went into action by bombing Iraqi air bases for two days, before re-directing its effort into a devastating offensive against the Iraqi oil-industry: by the end of October, the latter stopped all Iraqi oil exports and forced Baghdad into importing fuel from Kuwait. Although the IrAF did achieve some success in defence, such remained scarce: the general impression was that the IRIAF was ranging wide and far over Iraq to bomb whatever it wanted to bomb. Furthermore, whenever the Iraqi air force was ordered to provide close air support (CAS) for ground troops, it experienced the next surprise: because it consistently failed to target the seven base-level maintenance facilities available for Iranian F-4s, F-5s, and F-14s, it also failed to constrain the IRIAF's ability to sustain its operations. This was to prove a particularly deadly mistake because, the longer the war went on, and despite losses, the more the IRIAF proved capable of keeping its aircraft operational. Whatever any of the surviving Iraqis are ready to admit nowadays, or not, by the end of 1980 the Iranian Tomcats ruled the skies over the battlefield, and the IrAF lacked both the means and ideas on how to counter them.[7]

In a country where there is a native penchant for ignoring uncomfortable facts, like Iraq, all of this was anything other than good news. Nevertheless, the combination of unexpectedly high casualties, and the Iranian refusal to give up, eventually made Saddam reluctant to continue the adventure. Correspondingly, he ordered the army to dig itself into elaborate defensive positions and the air force to conserve its surviving assets. His new idea was to wait for the Iranians to sue for peace. Unsurprisingly, such expectations proved unrealistic: on the contrary, even if their first counteroffensives all ended in costly failures, during the following months the Iranians had succeeded in establishing a psychological advantage in the field. Between September and November 1981, they were to score their first significant victory and thus turn the tide: Iraq began to lose the war with Iran.

MIRAGES IN IRAQ

It was against this backdrop that Baghdad began pressing Paris to start deliveries of Mirages even though the necessary support infrastructure was still far from being complete, although – contrary to original intentions – no French advisors were present, and despite French reluctance to deliver heavy arms to a country that was at war. Massive pressure from Baghdad – which arguing that by early 1981 it was nearly 3 1/2 years since the contract for *Project Baz* was signed, but that not one of the Mirages has reached its destination – but also from Cairo, Amman and other Arab capitals eventually prompted the French government to grant the necessary permission.[8]

Run under the pretext of 'delivery to Jordan', and supported by an Ilyushin Il-76 transport painted in colours of the Jordanian Alia Airlines, the transfer of the first four F.1EQ-2s took place between 27 and 31 January 1981, along the route from Mont-de-Marsan, via Solenzara on Corsica, Kalamata in Greece, and Larnaca on Cyprus, via Turkey to Saddam AB. The second transfer of Mirages – this time along a simpler route via Solenzara and Tanagra AB in Greece – took place between 5 and 6 March 1981. The first team of French advisors – including a technical assistance team from Dassault, and Captains Aimé Marion and Jean Andrieu (two pilots contracted by the Dassault Aero Services) – arrived a month later. What they found at Saddam AB was rather 'dramatic': the base was still under construction and expected to become completed only in April 1984; most of its facilities were still non-existent; the runway was improperly cleaned and full of construction debris and dust; there was a total absence of organization on the flight line; aircraft received no servicing after returning from a sortie; their maintenance log-books were unusable, and only one out of four Mirage F.1BQ two-seaters delivered in the meantime was still operational. A 'confidential' report sent to Paris cited:

> The good will of some technicians is drowned by the incompetence and ignorance of the majority of the staff. Technical officers are boasting around, but never feel responsible; NCOs speak no English; there is no circulation of information…the wing command is aware of problems, but unable to find a solution.

Overall, the first task of the French advisors was to reorder all the activities, instruct and train the Iraqis with help of ground courses and simulator sessions – and then, gradually, train pilots and ground personnel to a level where these could run combat operations. Simultaneously, they took care to help construct clean spaces necessary for the maintenance, and flight-test the new aircraft. Much to their dismay, this process was to experience frequent interruptions by the war, unfavourable weather in winter, and excessive heat in summer. Unsurprisingly, it was only in September

A pre-delivery photograph of the first four Mirage F.1EQ-2s prepared for transfer to Iraq. (Dassault, via Michel Benichou)

Before its arrival in Iraq, the Mirage F.1EQ-2 serial number 4011 was used for training of the second group of Iraqi Mirage-pilots. (Dassault)

Mirage F.1EQ-2 serial number 4012, as seen on arrival at Saddam AB, in 1981. (Ahmad Sadik Collection)

1981 that No. 79 Squadron – commanded by Lieutenant-Colonel Ali Raji – was officially declared as operational and ready for action.[9]

ARMAMENT

The first tasks assigned to No. 79 Squadron were air defence and photo-reconnaissance with the help of the COR-2 pod. With the IRIAF aerial offensive against the Iraqi oil industry largely over, the squadron found itself with very little to do within Iraqi airspace. Therefore, and knowing that the Iranians were preparing further counter-offensives in western Khuzestan, the General Headquarters (GHQ) in Baghdad assigned it the task of fighting for aerial supremacy over that part of the battlefield. For air combat, the Mirage F.1EQ-2s carried three types of weapon, the most important of which was the Matra Super 530F. Equipped with a Dassault Electronique Super AD26 semi-active seeker head, and capable of carrying its 30kg (66lbs) fragmentation warhead at speeds up to Mach 4.6 over a maximum range of 40km (25 miles), this was one of the most advanced air-to-air missiles of its time. The principal reason was its 9,000m (29,530ft) 'snap-up' capability, but also the reported ability to pull 20gs at an altitude of 17,000m (55,780ft) or 6gs at 25,000m (82,020ft): this made it the most versatile contemporary air-to-air missile.[10]

The secondary weapon was the Matra R.550 Magic (later Magic Mk.1): this short-range air-to-air missile had an infra-red seeker head that permitted rear-aspect engagements only, a warhead of 13kg, 90kg launch weight and a range from 300 to 3,000 metres. The first R.550s were delivered to Iraq by the summer of 1980: a few were promptly adapted to several MiG-21MFs and the resulting combination then tested in combat. According to Iraqi reports, the Magic quickly proved shorter-ranged than the US-made AIM-9 Sidewinder (the primary short-range air-to-air missile on the Iranian side), but also more reliable and – even if less likely to score a direct hit in combat against a manoeuvring target – quite a surprise. Correspondingly, it scored at least two confirmed kills against IRIAF's F-4s and F-5s in October 1980.[11]

Finally, each Mirage F.1EQ-2 was equipped with two well-proven and highly successful DEFA 553, single-barrel, gas-operated 30mm revolver cannon, with a capacity of 135 rounds apiece, and a firing rate of 50 rounds per second.[12]

All the IrAF's intercept operations of the time relied on ground

The F.1EQ-2 serial number 4008 demonstrating the installation of the COR-2 reconnaissance pod. (Dassault, via Tom Cooper)

control, which used Soviet-made P-35 long-range/early warning radars (ASCC/NATO-code 'Bar Lock') supported by PRV-11 height finders (ASCC/NATO-code 'Side Net'). In order for Mirages to be recognized by these as friendly, all the F.1EQ-2 were adapted for the use of Soviet-made SRZO-2 IFF-transponders/interrogators.[13]

TOMCAT MENACE

While nearly all available Iraqi sources remain insistent that their primary opponent in the skies over Iran were Iranian ground-based air defences, there is little doubt that as of 1980-1981 the main opponents were still the IRIAF's F-14A Tomcats. The first combat aircraft ever to be equipped with microchips, the F-14 was a technological marvel of its times: as well as reaching speeds well above Mach 2, or the ability to remain airborne for up to 4 hours (or up to 12-13 hours with help of multiple in-flight refuellings), it was as manoeuvrable as the much smaller MiG-21. Moreover, the Tomcat was equipped with the powerful AWG-9 radar and weapons system, with a maximum detection range of over 200 kilometres for fighter-sized targets. It could carry up to six AIM-54A Phoenix active radar homing air-to-air missiles, with the range of over 100 kilometres. Iran originally placed an order for 80 Tomcats and 714 Phoenix missiles: by the time relations between Tehran and Washington were interrupted, in April 1979, 79 F-14As and 240 AIM-54s were delivered. However, Iran never received any of the advanced AIM-7F Sparrow and AIM-9H Sidewinder missiles intended to complete the arsenal of its Tomcats and thus for the first six months of the war the type had to serve armed with Phoenixes and internally installed 20mm General Electric M61A1 Vulcan six-barrel cannon. It was only in spring 1981 that the technicians of the IRIAF adapted the fleet to carry rather dated and less reliable AIM-7E-2 Sparrows and AIM-9J Sidewinders. Surprisingly enough, this fact remained entirely unknown to the Iraqis even for years after the war.[14]

Out of about 120 Iranian pilots and slightly less than 100 radar-intercept officers (RIOs) that had completed their training on F-14s by 1979, fewer than two thirds were still serving as of 1981. Nevertheless, each of them had received extensive training in air combat tactics in the USA and at home, and this was refreshed during rushed courses launched following the first border clashes with Iraq in August 1980. As of 1981, the fleet was still organized in the same fashion as before the revolution – in four squadrons: one deployed at the Tactical Fighter Base 7 (TFB.7, near Shiraz), and three at the TFB.8 (outside Esfahan). Cut off from US support and with its support infrastructure in chaos, most of the time the IRIAF was unable to keep more than 12-20 (out of 76 available) Tomcats in fully mission capable (FMC) condition at any time. Still, these were enough to maintain combat air patrols (CAPs) over Khuzestan, Khark Island and Tehran, usually lasting from 0900 in the morning until 1700 in the afternoon.[15]

By autumn 1981, battling Iranian F-14As proved a futile exercise for the IrAF: the available MiG-21MF/bis' and MiG-23MS' were equipped with poor radars and missiles requiring attacks from the rear hemisphere: much too often they would be detected early and either shot down or forced to withdraw. All the IrAF managed in one year of related efforts was for one of its MiG-21 pilots to hit and damage a single F-14A with few shells from its 23mm cannon in the course of a chaotic dogfight over Ahwaz. The situation was even more dramatic for Iraqi fighter-bombers: because their old RWR-systems proved unable to detect emissions of the AWG-9 when this was operated in the track-while-scan mode; and because the AIM-54 flew along a ballistic trajectory and thus attacked its targets from above, dozens of Iraqi pilots were shot down by long-range shots without ever knowing what had hit them. The sole effective method of defence was possible only once the presence of IRIAF Tomcats was visually confirmed – and consisted of fighter-bombers promptly jettisoning their ordnance and beating a hasty retreat.[16]

Unsurprisingly, not only did the GHQ in Baghdad put great emphasis on No. 79 Squadron finding a way to stop the 'Tomcat menace': the commander of the newly-established 3rd Air Defence Division IrAF (responsible for air defence of southern Iraq), Brigadier-General Nagdat an-Naqeeb, insisted on re-deployment of Mirages to one of his bases: together with Marion and Andrieu, who helped develop the necessary tactics, Naqeeb – an enterprising former Hunter-pilot with combat experience from the 1967 War with Israel – was subsequently to prove the driving force for the early success of No. 79 Squadron's F.1EQ-2s.[17]

The Mirage F.1EQ-2 serial number 4015 as seen at Bordeaux in 1981. This aircraft was soon to prove its worth in about a dozen interceptions of Iranian interceptors and fighter-bombers. (Dassault)

INITIAL OPERATIONS

Forward deployed at Wahda AB on order from Baghdad, a detachment of two Mirage F.1EQ-2s from No. 79 Squadron commanded by Major Abdul Karim Mukhalad flew its first operational mission on 1 September 1981. The Iraqis intercepted a pair of Phantoms underway on an interdiction strike against Iraqi ground forces in western Khuzestan and fired at least one Super 530F as soon as one of them established a lock-on – from maximum range: the Iranians did report coming under missile attack, but also that the Iraqis disengaged as soon as the lead F-4E fired a single AIM-7E-2 in return. A similar situation followed on 4 September 1981, when another pair of Mirages intercepted a pair of Phantoms, and claimed one of these as shot down by a single Super 530F fired from maximum range again. The IRIAF is not known to have lost a single F-4E during that month, although units from TFB.3 (Hamedan) and TFB.6 (Bushehr) flew over 100 combat sorties in support of Operation *Samene-al-Aeme*, which resulted in lifting the Iraqi siege of Abadan, later in September 1981. Another intercept attempt by Mirages from Ali Ibn Abu Talib AB was spoiled on 17 September 1981, when the mere presence of two escorting F-14A Tomcats was sufficient to discourage two F.1EQ-2-pilots that attempted to catch the McDonnell Douglas RF-4E Phantom II reconnaissance fighter flown by Major Mohammad Reza Atayee.[18]

Never discussed by any available Iraqi sources, the reasons for unimpressive results of these early operations by their Mirages can be found in US intelligence assessments and the recollections of French advisors involved in working up No. 79 Squadron. Since 1 October 1980, the US Air Force (USAF) maintained a detachment of four Boeing E-3A Sentry aircraft and 200 ground personnel from the 552nd Airborne Warning and Control Wing (AWACW) at Riyadh, in Saudi Arabia. Designated European Liaison Force One (ELF-1), this operation primarily served the purpose of protecting the Saudi airspace, but also in following the developments on the battlefields of the Iran-Iraq War. Because both the IrAF and the IRIAF began operating at medium altitudes during 1981, with their 400-kilometres-range AN/APY-1 radars, the E-3As had a very good insight into what was going-on on the other side of the Persian Gulf. Reports by the ELF-1 were short but to the point, and resulted in the conclusions that that the IrAF's Mirage operations were always tightly controlled by the ground control; that the aircraft were usually approaching their targets head-on while underway at low altitudes and maximum speeds with their radars on stand-by; that the pilots would power up their radars when ordered to do so by the ground control, then quickly achieve a lock-on and fire Super 530Fs from maximum range – thus offering their opponents plenty of time to recognize and avoid their attacks. As soon as they observed any kind of a detonation approximately in the direction of the target, the Iraqis would promptly return to the base, without attempting to re-engage or inspect the damage they had caused. Classic 'dogfights' – including manoeuvring air combat at close range – were something the pilots from No.79 Squadron did their utmost to avoid. On the contrary, a mere lock-on by an Iranian F-4E or F-14A would inevitably cause them to jettison their drop tanks and return home, even when odds were in their favour.[19]

THE EMPIRE STRIKES BACK

For a full understanding of what happened next with the Iraqi Mirages, it is necessary to look back at the developments from a few months earlier. Keen to replace the USA as a major ally of Iran, Moscow strongly disagreed with the Iraqi invasion and imposed a complete arms embargo upon Iraq, on 22 September 1980. Correspondingly, deliveries of such types as the MiG-23MF and MiG-25s were all stopped: the aircraft that were already in Iraq were stored, and involved IrAF personnel returned to operational units. Within just a few months, the Soviet stake in arms deliveries to Iraq thus declined from 95% of the total to less than 60%.[20]

Deeply disappointed, Baghdad scrambled to acquire replacements for Soviet-made arms and equipment from elsewhere: amongst others, they found them in diverse countries of Eastern Europe, but foremost in Egypt. Isolated from all members of the Arab League because of President Anwar el-Sadat's decision to make peace with Israel in 1979, Cairo was happy to provide support to Baghdad – and in turn earn handsomely from lucrative orders for arms manufactured by the AOI.[21]

However, as the months-long and intensive Soviet efforts to court Tehran ended nowhere, and France then began delivering

Mirages, Moscow had second thoughts. Indeed, only days after the second transfer of F.1EQ-2s to Iraq, it started making overtures to Baghdad: a month later an agreement was reached to lift the arms embargo: deliveries of MiG-23MFs and MiG-25s were resumed in May 1981, and over 1,000 Soviet advisors and technicians arrived in Iraq to help work-up related units.[22]

In attempt to recover its influence and prestige in Baghdad, Moscow added several 'bonuses'. The first of these arrived in form of six KKR-1TE/2MK reconnaissance pods, associated equipment, and a team of experts sent to the Firnas AB, outside Mosul, to convert four Su-22Ms of No. 5 Squadron into reconnaissance fighters. Another Soviet team arrived at the Tammuz AB to help work-up the 12 MiG-25RBs and 12 MiG-25PUs delivered to Iraq in the summer of 1980, but stored ever since. The MiG-25RBs were of particular importance then as, in addition to a reasonably advanced ELINT suite, they carried a set of excellent reconnaissance cameras. Combined with their operational altitude of 20,000 (and more) metres, and their capability to operate at speeds above Mach 2, they were capable of simultaneously running photo-reconnaissance and ELINT-gathering operations. Due to the urgency caused by the situation on the battlefield, the GHQ rushed them into operation and for most of the second half of 1981 and all of 1982, their pilots flew three reconnaissance sorties a day – on average. One of the results was that they detected about 50 operational MIM-23B I-HAWK SAM-sites of the IRIAF, most of these deployed for the protection of Tehran, Esfahan, Shiraz, Bandar-e Imam Khomeini and Khark, but also some near Abadan.[23]

NISSIN-28

Another of Moscow's 'bonuses' followed in autumn 1981, when the Soviets delivered a batch each of Kh-28C and Kh-28E (ASCC/NATO-code 'AS-9 Kyle') anti-radar missiles and the Myetel guidance pods necessary for their deployment. These arrived together with a team of technicians that modified six additional Su-22Ms of Firnas-based No.5 Squadron to the standard locally known as 'Su-22M-2K'. The Soviet representatives in Baghdad then encouraged the IrAF to press the new combination into combat against MIM-23B I-HAWK SAM-sites of the IRIAF: not only in their's, but also in the opinion of the Iraqis, these were the most powerful air defence weapon in Iranian hands.[24]

Originally designated the MIM-23 Hawk, the MIM-23B I-HAWK ('Improved-Homing All the Way Killer') was an improved variant of a SAM-system that had already proved highly effective while deployed by the Israelis in combat against Egyptian and then Syrian air forces in the period 1969-1973. As described above, the Iraqis had their own, rather unpleasant experience with Iranian MIM-23Bs already in 1975: by 1981, the system became known within the IrAF as the 'Death Valley'. With Soviet help, they identified the high power illuminator (Doppler) radar (HPIR) of the I-HAWK as the centrepiece of the system and the Kh-28E – which became known as the 'Nissin-28' in Iraq – was developed especially for targeting the same.[25]

The modified Su-22M-2Ks flew the first attack with Kh-28s on 27 October 1981. Although releasing their weapons from as far as 70 kilometres away, one of the Sukhois involved was promptly shot down by Iranian F-14As. Nevertheless, this attack came as the first major surprise for the IRIAF in this war and resulted in the confirmed destruction of six Iranian HPIRs. Taken aback by the first deployment of ARMs, the Iranians reacted by ordering commanders of their MIM-23B SAM-sites to stop emitting continuously: instead, these were to keep their radars on stand-by, and power up only when explicitly ordered to do so. Furthermore, the IRIAF took

A dusty Kh-28/AS-9 anti-radar missile (left, foreground) next to an Iraqi Su-22M-2K, as captured by US Army troops at the Ali Ibn Abu Talib AB in March 1991. (US DoD)

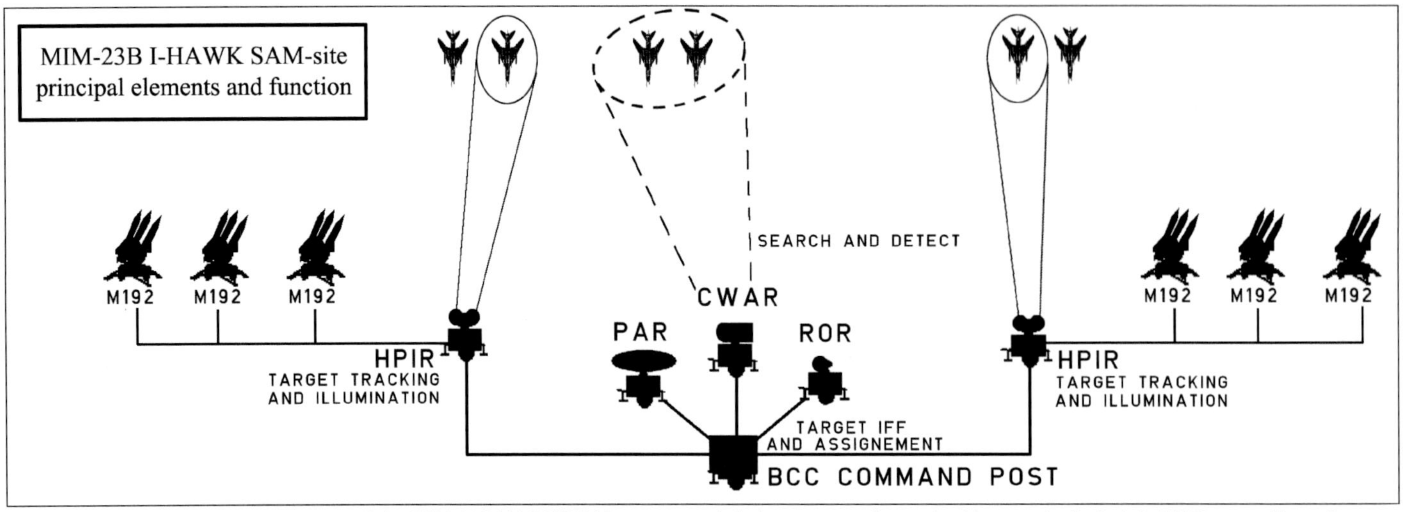

Diagram showing major components of the MIM-23B I-HAWK SAM-system and their purposes. A standard battery included six M192 towed launchers with three missiles each. These were supported by one AN/MPQ-50 pulse acquisition radar (PAR), one AN/MPQ-48 continuous wave acquisition radar (CWAR) – and two AN/MPQ-46 high power illuminator (Doppler) radars (HPIRs), each of which served one group of three M192 launchers. The IRIAF frequently operated its HAWK SAMs in 'assault mode', where one site would be broken into two elements, each of which consisted of one HPIR and three M192s. (Diagram by Tom Cooper)

care to return to operational service its two Lockheed (E)C-130H Khoofash SIGINT-gatherers. These leftovers from *Project Ibex* – run in cooperation with the Central Intelligence Agency (CIA) and National Security Agency (NSA) of the USA in the 1970s – were equipped with powerful, even if inauspicious COMINT and SIGINT systems capable of reading and decrypting Iraqi military communications in real time. Henceforth, Khoofashs were expected to provide timely warnings of incoming Iraqi air strikes.[26]

SUCCESSFUL GIRAFFES

While the Kh-28-attack on the Iranian I-HAWKs in late October 1981 was successful, early performance of Iraqi Mirages remained anything but impressive. The IRIAF thus continued its intercept operations over Khuzestan in same style as before. Continuously pushed by Brigadier-General Nagdat an-Naqeeb, and supported by their French instructors, the pilots of No. 79 Squadron worked hard on improving their tactics before the detachment at Wahda AB re-launched its operations. Reportedly, these resulted in 'two additional kills' by the end of October: according to the currently available information, both remain unconfirmed. Similar is true for Iranian claims to have shot down an Iraqi Mirage F.1 – supposedly the first ever – during a nocturnal engagement near Ahwaz, on 5 October 1981.[27]

As the IRIAF's F-14As on CAP-station north of Ahwaz continued causing losses to its fighter-bombers, in early November, the High Command IrAF ordered No. 79 Squadron to reinforce its detachment at Wahda AB to 10 aircraft. On order from Naqeeb, henceforth every Iraqi airstrike would be preceded by a pair of Mirages and MiG-23s that attempted to at least distract the Tomcats. Late on the morning of 15 November 1981, a pair of MiG-23MS' from No. 39 Squadron approached the Tomcats on station north of Ahwaz to attract their attention. As the Iranians moved to intercept, a pair of Mirage F.1EQ-2s led by Major Mukhalad sneaked upon them at very low altitude from the other side. When the two low-flying interceptors were within 20 kilometres from their targets, the ground control issued the pre-determined code-word – 'Giraffe!' – advising the pilots to climb and power up their radars. The two Iraqis established a lock on and then fired at least two Super 530F, this time from about 10 kilometres range. Taken by surprise, the Iranians were left with too little time to react. The F-14A piloted by Captain Gholam-Reza Nezam-Abadi – with Lieutenant Fahollah Jalal-Abadi as the Radar Intercept Officer (RIO) – received at least one direct hit, which forced the crew to eject. For the first time ever, the IrAF has scored a confirmed kill against an F-14A Tomcat.[28]

Emboldened by this success, Brigadier-General Naqeeb ordered No. 79 Squadron into a major effort on 24 November 1981. Two Giraffe operations – so-called due to their flight profile – were run that day, both again in coordination with MiG-23MS' from No. 39 and MiG-23MFs from the newly-established No. 67 Squadron, and both along same pattern as the first, successful, one. However, in their excitement the Iraqi pilots always targeted just one F-14A: thus, they just hit one in each attempt. Late in the morning the aircraft flown by Captain Jafar Bahadoran and Lieutenant Yadollah Hosseini was shot down, and in the afternoon another F-14A, flown by Major Abolfazl Hooshyar with RIO Lieutenant Ahmad Roustaei (both Iranian crews ejected safely).[29]

This was a major success that forced the IRIAF into a grudging realisation that the Iraqis have found a way to counter its F-14-force: from the Iranian point of view, this situation was intolerable because they needed aerial dominance over the battlefield in order to support coming operations for the liberation of Khuzestan. Correspondingly, the Deputy Operations of TFB.8, Lieutenant-Colonel Mohammed Hashem All-e-Agha, promptly devised a counter-strike. The plan was risky and included a complete ban on all other aerial activity of Iranian aircraft and helicopters over the Khuzestan sector, except for interceptors – including Tomcats, and Northrop F-5E Tiger IIs from the TFB.4, outside Dezful. While theoretically leaving the Iranian ground forces exposed to Iraqi air strikes, and without helicopter support, the measure enabled Tomcat-crews to operate free of the usual problem with sorting out their own from enemy aircraft, while F-5Es flew low-altitude barrier combat air patrols (BARCAPs) with the aim of blocking the approach of the Iraqi Mirages. The plot worked almost perfectly: when two MiG-23MFs attempted to repeat the feat of their colleagues from No. 79 Squadron, on 25 November 1981, both were claimed as shot down by a single AIM-54. Worse yet, with the MiGs out of the way, and Mirages forced to withdraw after being detected on time by low-flying Tiger IIs, the IRIAF's Tomcats had a field day: by sunset their pilots claimed five additional kills against MiG-23BNs and Su-22s, effectively sweeping the skies free of the Iraqi Air Force.[30]

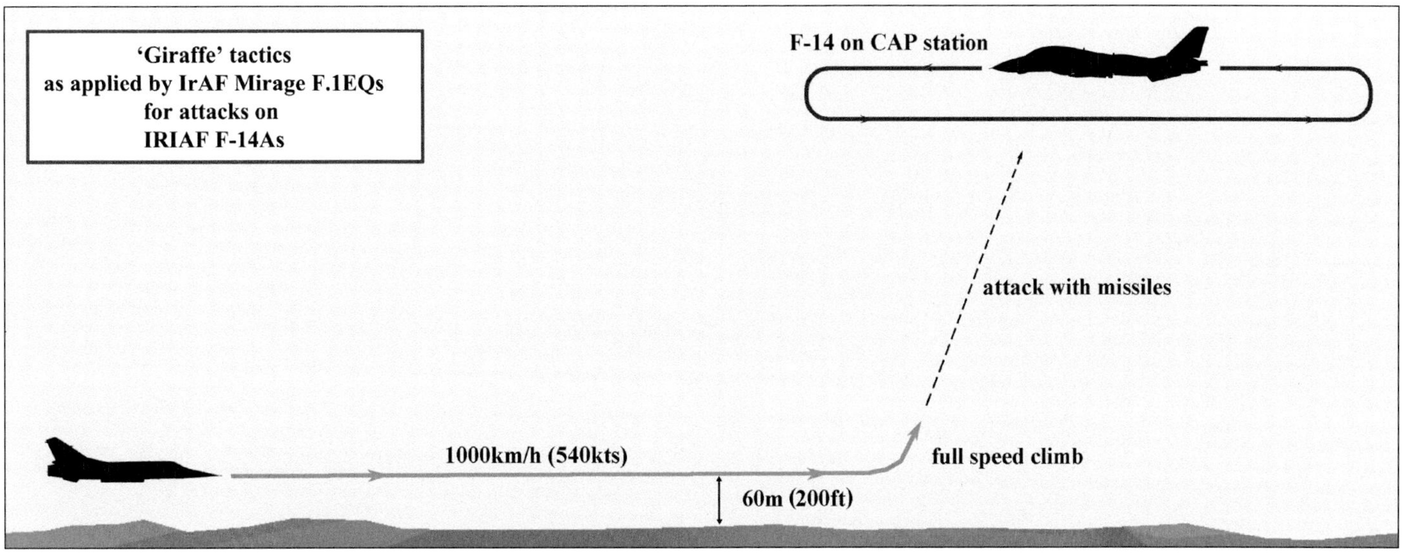

A diagram illustrating the flight profile of the IrAF's Mirage F.1EQ-2s for 'Griraffe' tactics. (Diagram by Tom Cooper)

IRIAF'S REVENGE

On 29 November 1981, the Iranian ground forces launched Operation *Tariq al-Qods* with the aim of liberating the town of Bostan, in northern Khuzestan. Well supported by air strikes, this push caused sufficient urgency in Baghdad to prompt the GHQ into ordering Mirage-pilots from Wahda into renewed Giraffe operations. However, with help of timely warnings from the (E) C-130H Khoofash, the low-flying F-5E BARCAPs spoiled two attempts on 29 November: each time, the Mirages beat a hasty retreat as soon as they detected the Tiger IIs. An attempt including a pair each of Mirage F.1EQ-2s, MiG-23MS' and MiG-23MFs, launched on 30 November, was spoiled in the same fashion, and ended with the IRIAF Tomcats claiming three kills against MiGs and two against Mirages. Similarly, on 2 December 1981, the approaching Iraqis were detected early and this time one of the MiG-23MS' involved was shot down by Captain Assad Adeli (RIO Mohammad Massbough), and its pilot captured by the Iranian ground forces. Moreover, the following formation of Su-22s first lost one aircraft due to pilot error, and then had to jettison all of its ordnance and beat a hasty retreat. All the Iraqi Mirage-pilots could show in return was an unconfirmed claim of downing of two F-4Es by Captain Salah Ismail Nasser.[31]

A day later, on 3 December 1981, All-e-Agha went a step further and set up a trap for the Mirages: instead of deploying a pair of F-14As on their usual CAP station north of Ahwaz, he arranged for two F-4Es from TFB.6 to operate there – as usually protected by a low-flying BARCAP of F-5Es from TFB.4. In turn, the four Iranian fighter-bombers were shadowed by a pair of F-14As from TFB.8 that orbited at low altitude well to the rear, undetected by the Iraqis. When a pair of Mirages appeared to attempt another Giraffe operation, the F-14As powered up their AWG-9s and fired one AIM-54A each. According to the Iranians, both Mirages were shot down and one of their pilots captured by the troops of the 92nd Armoured Division. The Iraqis confirmed only one loss.[32]

Launched on 4 December 1981, the IrAF's attempt to extract revenge remained unsuccessful: as Major Mukhalad and 1st Lieutenant Haytham Khatab Omar attacked two F-4Es on a CAP over Ahwaz, and the leader of the Iraqi pair fired two Super 530Fs from a range of 18 kilometres, the Iranian Phantom-crew was left with enough time to recognize the attack and break left, causing Mukhalad's radar to lose the lock-on and both missiles to miss. Contrary to the usual practice, the Iraqi leader then pressed home his attack, cut the range and fired a single R.550: however, the missile detonated behind the F-4E, only causing it to distance while leaving a trail of smoke. Mukhalad and Haytam disengaged to avoid a pair of counterattacking Tomcats.[33]

Despite the early success of No. 79 Squadron against IRIAF's Tomcats, the IrAF thus proved unable to establish itself at least in possession of aerial dominance over the battlefield: indeed, an Iraqi intelligence report prepared later the same month concluded that, 'the Persian enemy's combat capability for current and future [operations] should not be underestimated'. Unsurprisingly, continuous pounding of the Iraqi ground forces in the Bostan area eventually prompted Saddam Hussein into ordering the 224th Missile Brigade into action: on 18 December 1981, this unit fired about a dozen R-17E (ASCC/NATO-code 'SS-1c Scud-B') ballistic missiles at Dezful and Ahwaz, killing at least 21 civilians and injuring over 100. Even so, there was little doubt that Operation *Tariq al-Qods* ended in the first clear-cut Iraqi defeat of this war.[34]

AMBUSH OVER KERMANSHAH

As the emboldened Iranians continued exercising pressure upon demoralized Iraqi ground forces, the GHQ in Baghdad ordered No. 79 Squadron to deploy another detachment of Mirage F.1EQ-2s to the Abu Ubaida AB, outside Kut, and attempt distracting the IRIAF through intercept operations over the central section of the front. However, related communications were intercepted by one of the IRIAF's Khoofashs and the 82nd TFS at TFB.8 was put on alert for operations in this sector. Once again operating along the plan devised by Lieutenant-Colonel All-e-Agha, on 12 December 1981 the Iranians deployed a pair of F-4Es from TFB.3 into a high-altitude CAP between Zarand and Ghilan-e-Gharb, in the Kermanshah province. As usual, these were protected by a BARCAP of F-5Es, and a pair of low-flying F-14As. The Iraqis promptly swallowed the bait: the pair of Mirage F.1EQ-2s dispatched in this direction thus ran straight into an ambush and the aircraft flown by 1st Lieutenant Idris Hassan al-Amari was shot down by one AIM-54A fired by All-e-Agha. The pilot ejected safely but was captured by the Iranian ground forces.[35]

The mood within No.79 Squadron certainly did not get better two days later, when six F-4Es from TFB.3 bombed two power stations in Baghdad. When all but one of the participating Phantoms were damaged by the ground fire, their crews requested help, in turn prompting a pair of F-14As from the 82nd Tactical Fighter

A dramatic photograph taken by an RF-4E of the IRIAF on 14 December 1981, and showing one of two Mirage F.1EQ-2s that briefly caught up with the Iranian reconnaissance bird, but failed to bring it down. (Farzin Nadimi Collection)

The Mirage F.1EQ-2 serial number 4017 as seen in Bordeaux, in early 1981. By the end of the year the aircraft was in Iraq and flown in combat against Iran. (Jacques Guillem Collection)

Left hand view of the serial number 4017, and another example from the same batch, as seen at the start of their delivery flight to Iraq, at Solenzara AB on Corsica. (Albert Grandolini Collection)

Squadron (TFS) to violate the standing order prohibiting them from flying into Iraqi airspace. The Tomcats not only proved faster than the four IrAF interceptors scrambled to intercept the egressing Phantom formation, but their sheer appearance proved sufficient to prompt all four Iraqi pilots to turn away. Minutes later, another pair of Mirage F.1EQ-2s was scrambled to intercept a McDonnell-Douglas RF-4E that flew post-strike reconnaissance. In the course of a high-speed chase, the Iranian crew forced the Iraqi to overshoot, taking photographs of the interceptor with their reconnaissance cameras. Less lucky was the crew of the RF-4E that flew post-strike reconnaissance after an airstrike on targets in the Basrah area, on 27 January 1982. Major Moukhalad was scrambled from Ali Ibn Abu Talib AB to intercept the Phantom flown by Major Mohammad Shokuhnia (RIO 1st Lieutenant Mohammed Esmaeli Peyrovan). Approaching from nearly head-on, Moukhalad fired one Super 530F: this hit the front cockpit, instantly killing the Iranian pilot. The badly injured RIO managed to eject safely only seconds before the burning wreckage hit the ground.[36]

3

SAVING PRIVATE SADDAM

As the year 1981 turned into 1982, dramatic events took place well away from the frontlines of the Iran-Iraq War. With hindsight, the affairs in question can be described as 'crucial', even if having a long-term impact only upon the flow of the war between Iran and Iraq.

AN ARAB ALLIANCE

As of early 1981, the Iraqi oil industry was still recovering from the blows it received from the IRIAF in October and November 1980. Lacking the necessary heavy industry, Baghdad had to import most of the equipment necessary to repair it and re-start its oil exports, and even once these began to flow, the pipeline to the Syrian port of Banias on the Mediterranean coast was shut down by the increasingly hostile government in Damascus. Although thus left without its major source of income, Baghdad continued spending lavishly for development, rapidly drawing down reserves accumulated before the war. By the end of the year, the country was unable to continue paying its debts, and became dependent on credit from its allies. Driven by the growing suspicion over Iraq's ability to prevent a spill-over of the war with Iran, and – because of their sizeable Shi'a populations – always sensitive of Tehran's threats to 'export' its 'Islamic Revolution', in February 1981 six Arab countries of the Persian Gulf arrived at the decision to form the Gulf Cooperation Council (GCC). Established by Saudi Arabia, Kuwait, Bahrain, Qatar, Oman and the United Arab Emirates, the GCC was officially to serve the means of pooling resources and safeguarding stability – and thus became involved in supporting the Iraqi war effort against Iran – directly and indirectly: by the end of the year, Riyadh and Kuwait City each granted loans worth US$6 billion to Baghdad. This decision was indirectly 'confirmed' on 1 April 1981, when the IRIAF flew a spectacular air strike on the al-Wallid AB (better known as 'H-3' in the West), in western Iraq, and then on 7 June 1981, when an Israeli air strike destroyed the construction site of the Osirak reactor, outside Baghdad. To the strongmen in Riyadh and Kuwait City, it appeared as if Baghdad was slowly but certainly losing control of the conflict it had provoked – and then at the time the new government of President Francois Mitterrand in Paris was proving anything other than enthusiastic to continue supporting Iraq.[1]

Perfectly aware of their ability to manipulate Western decision-makers through offering prospects for lucrative arms deals, the rulers of the GCC went into action later the same month. When the US Congress rejected a Saudi order for five E-3 Sentry AWACS, Riyadh 'retaliated' – by opening negotiations with France, (West) Germany, and the United Kingdom on behalf of the GCC, but also the AOI. Related talks advanced very quickly and resulted in a number of major arms contracts signed between late 1981 and through 1982. Egypt made the first step by signing an order for Mirage 2000s in December 1981. Originally planned to be concluded around the same date, Iraqi negotiations lasted longer than expected: one reason was the need to arrange an offset deal for future oil purchases; another that the Iraqis insisted not only on an

First ordered instead of the still-born Mirage F.1EQ-3 within *Project Baz-2* in December 1979, the F.1EQ-4 was the first sub-variant equipped for in-flight refuelling, compatible with the massive Irakien drop tank with a capacity of 2,200 litres, and capable of carrying diverse advanced electronic warfare systems still undergoing development in France. Highly satisfied with this version, the Iraqis eventually acquired 28 examples. (Dassault)

The Mirage F.1EQ-5 was envisaged as the first significantly upgraded variant of the original, including compatibility with AM.39 Exocet anti-ship missiles (visible in this photograph), and AS.30L laser-homing missiles. (Ahmad Sadik Collection)

extremely careful evaluation of their new aircraft, but on the highest possible sophistication of the weapons system mix that would be provided.[2]

A solution was found only when the Saudis agreed to pay for additional Iraqi aircraft through deliveries of crude oil: for all practical purposes, and together with Kuwait City, Riyadh now began financing the Iraqi war effort against Iran. The contract for *Project Baz-3* was thus signed only on 16 February 1982: it stipulated an expansion of the original option for 18 Mirage F.1EQ-4s to 24, and then an order for 20 additional aircraft of an entirely new and much more advanced variant, the Mirage F.1EQ-5. Moreover, an even more important contract was signed on the same day related to the Iraqi order for Mirage 2000s.[3]

MIRAGE 2000

The IrAF was carefully monitoring the development of the next generation of the Mirage from at least 1979, and Lieutenant-Colonel Ali Raji is known to have test-flown the two-seat variant at Istres, sometime within the following two years. However, the Iraqis were disappointed by the type because its original radar – designated the RDM, and installed into Mirage 2000Es ordered by Egypt – proved only slightly improved in comparison to the Cyrano-IV. The situation changed dramatically when Ali Raji was permitted to evaluate the attack variant of this type. Originally known as Mirage 2000P, later Mirage 2000N, this was to be equipped with the Dassault Electronique/Thomson-CSF Antilope 5 radar and slated to become the primary carrier of the new stand-off nuclear weapon then under development by Aerospatiale and known as the 'Air-to-Ground Medium Range' (*Air-Sol Moyenne Portée*, ASMP). This 5.38m long, 900kg, rocket/ramjet-powered weapon was usually equipped with the TN80 nuclear warhead with a yield of 150 kilotonnes, or the TN81 with double that.[4]

Contrary to entirely unsupported claims spread by Israel and its allies in the West, Iraq was not working on the development of a nuclear weapon as of 1981. Instead, the IrAF and the MIC developed a keen interest in acquiring a sub-variant of the Mirage 2000N equipped with a conventionally armed version of the ASMP and such guided weapons as the Aerospatiale AS.30L, which the Iraqis wanted to manufacture under licence.[5]

Other than that a contract for an order for 60 Mirage 2000s was signed on 16 February 1982, very little is known about what happened afterwards. Sadik explained:

> The order for Iraqi Mirage 2000s was a strategic decision and the logical evolution to upgrade the F.1-fleet… but also used to pressure the French … The Iraqi Mirage 2000IQ had nothing to do with its French counterparts: upon our requests, it was so much modified that it resembled the French variant no more. The order was never cancelled: [instead,] related talks continued until 1990.[6]

Indeed, from the rather poor copy of the contract in question left behind by the chief Iraqi negotiator, it appears that in addition to AS.30Ls, the Iraqi Mirage 2000s would have been equipped with a conventionally-armed variant of the ASMP – but also with the 'Interception, Combat and Self-Defence Missile' (*Missile d'Interception, de Combat et d'Autodéfense*, MICA). As such, it would have been quite different from the 70 Mirage 2000Ds acquired by the AdA in late 1980s. The reasons why this order was never realized were quite complex:

- Despite loans from Riyadh and Kuwait City that enabled the financing of *Project Baz-3*, Baghdad was de-facto bankrupt by 1982 and unable to pay its dues. Unsurprisingly, even top officials of the DIA began experiencing growing problems while trying to convince the decision-makers in Paris to permit additional arms sales: because of its rule not to deliver armament to a country at war, France was already very reluctant to continue deliveries of Mirage F.1EQ, ordered before the Iraqi invasion of Iran, not to mention honouring the new Iraqi order for Mirage 2000s.[7]
- The contract for *Project Baz-3* should have contained a clause according to which the French were obliged to pay US$10 million to Saddam Hussein's private account in Switzerland for each Mirage shot down by the Iranians. Reportedly, this Iraqi request was motivated by the Iraqi suspicion that the French might not deliver their 'most advanced' equipment. Whether this was truth or not, related rumours provoked the top ranks of the IrAF into accusing Saddam of enriching himself whenever Iraq was losing the war and threatening to launch a coup against him. Saddam reacted by issuing a standing order

for the IrAF to avoid even 'reasonable risks' in order not to lose its aircraft, and – according to Sadik – 'allocated US$1 billion for additional development of IrAF's electronic warfare capabilities'. For the time being, the strongman in Baghdad could thus not proceed with the acquisition of Mirage 2000s without raising suspicion amongst 'his' generals.[8]

- Before long, the governments of France, Germany, Great Britain, and the USA realized that the Saudis were playing them off against each other in order to get the best deal for E-3 Sentries. Thus, while selling additional F.1EQ-4/5s to Baghdad, the French refused to grant a licence for production of Mirage 2000s in Egypt or Iraq; instead, they only agreed to help establish an AOI-run factory in Helwan, in Egypt, necessary for the assembly of Dornier-Dassault Alpha Jet trainers from knock-down kits delivered by France.[9]
- The British then attempted to exploit the opportunity and made serious offers for their BAe Nimrod airborne early warning aircraft, Panavia Tornado interdiction-strike fighter-bomber, and a ground-attack variant of the BAe Hawk jet trainer to Baghdad. This resulted in intensive talks between representatives of the MIC, British Aerospace, Marconi Avionics, and Rolls Royce, and a 'protracted evaluation'

Table 2: Overview of Project Baz-3, February 1982

Contract designation	Date of Order	Number of Aircraft	Version	Serial Numbers	Roll-Out Dates	Acceptance Dates
BAZ-2210	16 Feb 1982	18	Mirage F.1EQ-4	4506-4513	7 Apr 1983 – 24 May 1985	10 Jun 1983 – 26 May 1985
BAZ-321x	16 Feb 1982	6	Mirage F.1EQ-4	4514-4529	6 Jan 1984 – 11 Jul 1984	6 Jan 1984 – 11 Jul 1984
BAZ-321x	16 Feb 1982	3	Mirage F.1BQ	4556-4558	8 Jun 1984 – 14 Dec 1984	9 Jun 1984 – 14 Dec 1984
BAZ-321x	16 Feb 1982	20	Mirage F.1EQ-5	4560-4579	19 Dec 1983 – 28 Feb 1985	19 Dec 1984 – 28 Feb 1985

PIRANHA

The continuous Iraqi search for alternative sources of arms resulted in Baghdad establishing relations with Brazil where it bought armoured cars and artillery rockets. However, with Saudi and Kuwaiti funding, in late 1981, the MIC became keen to expand related cooperation through its involvement in the development of the MAA-1 Piranha air-to-air missile – which the Iraqis considered for installation on their Mirages.[11]

The weapon – roughly comparable in shape and size to the AIM-9 Sidewinder, but expected to be faster – had been in development since 1976, but advanced very slowly due to the lack of funding and the necessary know-how, and then a severe economic crisis and an US arms embargo. Of critical importance was the technology for the seeker head, which no foreign companies were ready to supply – at least not at prices acceptable to the Brazilians. However, when a trade delegation visited Baghdad in November 1981, it quickly found out that the Iraqis were highly interested in funding the further research and development of the MAA-1.[12]

The Iraqi – i.e. Saudi and Kuwaiti – funding not only saved the Brazilian project: it enabled the establishment of Órbita – a state-owned company responsible for further development of the Piranha – and the acquisition of the necessary high-tech, either from France or somewhere else. As a result of this enterprise, the D. F. Vasconcellos company (which was manufacturing night-vision binoculars, but also telescopic sights for Cascavel armoured cars) was contracted with the development of the seeker-head. By 1984, the Piranha was thus 'back on track', and the first test-firing took place just two years later. By 1988, the project reached an advanced stage and a team of Brazilian rocket scientists was deployed in Iraq to help setting up local production facilities.[13]

It was the Iraqi invasion of Kuwait of August 1990 and the following, total arms embargo imposed by the UN that delivered the proverbial 'nail in the coffin' of the idea to complete the development of the Piranha and set up its production in Iraq. Baghdad had to stop financing the project, the Brazilians were sent back home, and further development of the missile slowed down to a crawling pace – resulting in the MAA-1 becoming outdated and de-facto cancelled. In the 1990s, the Brazilian air force opted to buy Israeli-made Python-3 missiles instead. It was more than ten years later that the project was re-launched under the designation MAA-1B, and then with some help from South Africa. Exactly how many Piranhas were ever manufactured, and if they really entered service with the Brazilian Air Force remains unclear.[14]

A MAA-1 Piranha as seen installed on an F-5E Tiger II fighter-bomber of the Brazilian Air Force. (Photo by Henrique L Martins, via Alfredo André)

of at least the last two types. Related negotiations reached an 'advanced stage' by March 1982. However, by the time Baghdad was about to make its decision, in June 1982, it became known that Tornado was at least 12 months behind its development schedule, that Nimrod was facing 'insurmountable problems', and that the British were refusing to sell a licence for production of the Hawks to Iraq. Therefore, while the MIC was initially capable of exploiting negotiations with the British to *de-facto* blackmail the DIA into accepting the order for Mirage 2000s, when no orders for Tornados, Hawks, or Nimrods materialised, the French had no incentive to deliver.[10]

VITAL INTELLIGENCE

Early 1982 thus found the IrAF in the process of acquiring and pressing into service ever larger quantities of French and Soviet weapons: indeed, in the middle of a period during which Moscow and Paris were in an outright race to outpace each other's deliveries. The number of Mirages meanwhile flown to Iraq, and the number of Iraqi pilots converted to fly them grew sufficiently to establish a second unit: the Saddam AB-based No. 89 Squadron, initially commanded by Major Magdi Alladdin Yousef. Like No. 79 Squadron, this unit was primarily tasked with air defence. Nevertheless, it was also assigned most of the two-seat conversion trainers, and – supported by Marion and Andreu – served as an Operational Conversion Unit (OCU).[15]

Meanwhile, the GHQ in Baghdad was busy collecting intelligence about future Iranian intentions. The GMID's and the IrAF's picture about the Iranian air defence network was greatly bolstered in late September 1980, when the army captured the Dehloran early warning radar site west of Dezful. Amongst the items found there was a 400-page thick folder prepared by US specialists in the late 1970s, containing a detailed description of every major radar site in Iran, the areas they were covering, and the gaps in their coverage. Unknown to even the few officers informed about this 'treasure trove', this find was to have long-lasting consequences for the rest of the war. Another intelligence coup took place in autumn 1981, when an Iranian army officer defected to the Iraqi side bringing with him a Crypto C-52 electro-mechanical enciphering machine. Thanks to technical assistance provided by the Committee for State Security of the USSR (*Komitet gosudarstvennoy bezopasnosti*, KGB), the GMID used this machine to start cracking Iranian military codes used for tactical communication.[16]

In a top-down, heavily centralized military like that of Iraq in the early 1980s, the intelligence collected in this fashion, and that obtained by reconnaissance sorties of IrAF's MiG-25RBs and COR-2 equipped Mirage F.1EQ-2s, was vital for the work of the GHQ. It resulted in the development of very precise planning not only for fire support missions for the artillery, but also for interceptor and fighter-bomber operations of the IrAF, all of which were expected to play a crucial role in the defence of ground troops entrenched in Khuzestan. Having collected extremely detailed information on enemy units facing them and their intentions, the Iraqi generals de-facto prescribed the coming battle, phase by phase, and expected to easily overpower whatever came their way.[17]

However, the Iranians operated in an entirely unpredictable fashion: although their Operation *Fath ol-Mobbin* was expected by Baghdad, simple infiltrations by Iranian commandos and infantry took the local Iraqi commanders by surprise and forced them to withdraw from Bostan and Dezful in late March 1982. Worse yet, on 29 April 1982, the IRIAF hit several headquarters and major communication centres of the Iraqi Army, thus opening Operation *Tariq al-Qods*: during the following days, the Iraqi resistance collapsed and by 4 May 1982 the Iranians began converging upon its centre in Shalamcheh.[18]

SURPRISE IN THE FOG

Due to the rain and resulting fog, the IrAF flew relatively little during the Iranian Operation *Fath ol-Mobbin*. When the clouds cleared, it found itself facing a well-positioned integrated air defence system (IADS) of the IRIAF covering the battlefield in Khuzestan. Designed by Colonel Bahram Houshyar (the IRIAF commander for this enterprise), this was initially centred on two forward-deployed MIM-23B I-HAWK SAM-sites: the 'Khyber' was covering the northern side of the battlefield, and the 'Tabuq' the southern part and the city of Abadan – and both were changing their positions every night, thus keeping the GHQ in Baghdad on its toes. Furthermore, IRIAF's F-14As were now flying CAPs at altitudes of 40,000ft (12,192m) or higher – partially in order to improve their radar coverage, but also to keep any Mirages or MiGs that might attempt a 'Giraffe' attack upon them, at distance. The Tomcats were now operating in coordination with the SAM-sites: the HAWK-crews kept their HPIRs on standby, waiting for incoming Iraqi air strikes to approach to less than 20 kilometres: at that point in time, the IrAF formations would suddenly find themselves confronted by SAMs and by F-14s.[19]

Unaware of all of this, the Iraqis reacted with sending MiG-25RBs into reconnaissance of Iranian positions. However, their attempt on 10 March 1982 was spoiled by a combination of F-14s and HAWKs. An attempt by Mirage F.1EQ-2s from No. 79 Squadron to run a COR-2 mission was spoiled by F-14s on 14 March. According to Iranian sources, while both Iraqi fighters dived in attempt to evade the Phoenix missiles fired at them, one failed to recover from a steep dive, and hit the ground: it was last seen distancing in a western direction while on fire.[20] By 21 March, the IRIAF's combination of high-flying F-14s, low-flying F-5Es, MIM-23B I-HAWKS, extensive use of UAVs to 'waste' Iraqi SA-6 SAMs, and repeated Iranian air strikes began overwhelming the IrAF's ability to cope. When the Iraqis attempted to counterattack, they did so in easily predictable fashion: in the form of an ARM-attack which aimed to open the way for fighter bombers. On 27 March 1982, six Sukhois from the Wahda-based No. 109 Squadron – recently upgraded to the Su-22M-2K standard by the Soviet 'Kh-28 team' – attacked the known positions of the IRIAF's SAM-sites with a total of six Nissin-28s. While the Iraqis declared this attack as a 'total success', it achieved exactly nothing: warned about the incoming strike by a Khoofash, the Iranian commanders turned off their HPIRs on time. When their troops reported nearby detonations of Kh-28s that had missed, they powered them up again and went into action, claiming one Iraqi fighter-bomber after the other. Indeed, it seems that the GHQ in Baghdad promptly understood that this attack was a major failure, and no further air strikes by its fighter-bombers were reported for the next few days. On the contrary, the IRIAF was left free to subject the Iraqi 12th Armoured Division alone to more than 180 air strikes, while the Iranian ground forces then completely annihilated the Iraqi pocket between Dezful and Susangerd, liberating the ruined Dehloran early warning radar site in the process.[21]

DEATH VALLEY

Whatever is known about the activity of IrAF's Mirages over the following three months can only be reconstructed on the basis of

The Mirage F.1EQ-2 serial number 4020 was the first from the second batch of 16 aircraft ordered within *Project Baz(-1)*, in 1977: it reached Iraq on time to take part in air combats of early 1982. Notable is that the first batches from a total of 1,000 drop tanks ordered by the IrAF were all left in their 'bare metal overall' colour. (Dassault)

Iranian sources. When finding no other solutions for the IRIAF's HAWKs, the Iraqis deployed their long-range artillery to shell the Khyber SAM-site, on 20 April, and then the Tabuk SAM-site, a week later. While the former site lost some equipment, at least one of its HPARs and several launchers survived this ordeal, and the latter site escaped any damage. On 28 April 1982, Su-22M-2Ks from No. 109 Squadron flew another Kh-28 strike, and knocked out the HPAR of the Khyber SAM-site: not only was the unit repaired within the next 24 hours, but the number of IRIAF MIM-23B systems covering the battlefield subsequently grew to five sites, as additional SAM-systems were deployed at Dezful, Sarbandar and Omidiyeh. When the IrAF attempted to hit Iranian ground troops involved in Operation *Tariq-ol-Qods*, on the morning of 30 April, Iranian SAMs claimed six Iraqi fighter-bombers as shot down.[22]

Forced to stay out of the combat zone, for the rest of this battle the Iraqi Mirages were limited to intercepting those Iranian formations that flew interdiction strikes on rear Iraqi positions. It was in this fashion that on 2 May 1982, a pair of F.1EQ-2s from No. 79 Squadron caught a formation of three F-4Es from TFB.6 on return from attack on enemy positions in the Kushk area, and shot down the Phantom flow by Captain Manoucher Rawadgar and 1st Lieutenant Jahangir Engheta. Four days later, on 6 May 1982, a formation of eight F-4Es from TFB.6 was caught by another pair of Mirages while bombing Iraqi positions west of Shalamcheh, and the Phantom flown by Captain Hassan Taleb-Mehr and 1st Lieutenant Cheragh Ali Amjadiyan was shot down. Finally, late in the morning of 8 May 1982, an F-4E from TFB.1 flown by Captain Hossein-Ali Zolfaghari and 1st Lieutenant Mohammad-Ali Azami may have been shot down by an Iraqi Mirage during another air strike on the Iraqi troops in the Shalamcheh area.[23]

I SHOT AND SAW AN EXPLOSION!

One of very few available accounts about Iraqi Mirage operations during this period is dated 2 June 1982. Correspondingly:

> Major Mukhalad, meanwhile Deputy Commander of No. 79 Squadron…was vectored by the ground control to intercept two Iranian aircraft high above Ahwaz. While approaching at low altitude, they powered their radars up, and the HUD began showing the first sign of their targets, approaching from the left. After obtaining a lock-on from a range of 25 kilometres, Mukhalad visually acquired his target and steered his aircraft on a collision course. Recalling the advice of his French instructor, he

Still lacking advanced electronic warfare equipment undergoing development in France, the Iraqi Mirages found themselves hard-pressed to fight back at the IRIAF that was in full swing as of early 1982. Serial number 4021 was an F.1EQ-2 from the second batch of 16 ordered within *Project Baz(-1)*. (Jacques Guillem Collection)

In the opinion of most of the Iraqi pilots, and according to some Iraqi post-war analyses, the MIM-23B Improved-HAWK surface-to-air missile was the most dangerous air-defence weapon in the hands of the Iranians. The system proved very hard to jam, hard to hit with anti-radar missiles, and caused enough problems to become known as the 'Death Valley' within the IrAF. (Farzin Nadimi Collection)

held his fire until the range decreased to 17 kilometres. Entering a shallow climb, he then fired the first Super 530F.

Switching his attention from the mesmerising trail of white smoke left by the missile, Mukhalad took a look at the panel of his BF RWR: this was showing no indication of a missile launch warning. The Iranians failed to react. But, when taking a look back at his target, he noticed that one of the Phantoms was now turning left. Mukhalad was not concerned, though, then he knew that the target was meanwhile inside the no-escape zone of his missile. Indeed, when the time-to-target counter showed 0, there was a white puff in the air, and his wingman shouted, "Enemy aircraft down! It's burning!"[24]

According to available Iraqi sources, the pilot of the downed F-4E was subsequently captured, while the RIO perished when the missile hit his cockpit: however, the IRIAF is not known to have suffered such a loss. According to Brigadier-General Sadik, this was little surprising:

> By the end of June 1982, Major Mukhalad claimed a total of 14 kills – all against F-4s and F-14s and by Super 530Fs. His claims caused quite a controversy in the HQ of the IrAF, because they all took place over Iranian-controlled territory east of Ahwaz and north of Bandar Mahshahr, and because the Air Force Intelligence proved unable to corroborate them with the information obtained from Iranian prisoners of war. Thus, the High Command ordered the gun-camera-films of all his claims to be brought to Baghdad for study by General Amer Rasheed (still Deputy Commander IrAF for Technical Affairs), a group of Iraqi engineers, and a representative of Matra. We all wanted to know the truth. Their analysis could confirm only one kill: Mukhalad was credited correspondingly, and that's it. However, since he was the deputy commander of No. 79 Squadron, he meanwhile painted 14 kill markings on his favourite aircraft. While never an ace, he is memorized by many officers as one until today. Although never a brilliant pilot or officer, Mukhalad subsequently rose in rank to that of a Lieutenant-General because he was one of only four pilots to complete the first conversion course in France.'[25]

While many former IrAF officers and Mukhalad's family continue insisting until today that he really shot down 14 Iranian aircraft, the French informed about this affair came to conclusions similar to those of Sadik: amongst them, the Iraqi became known by his favourite statement, 'I shot and saw an explosion'. Certainly enough, this did not damage his career: thanks to his 'high score', in March 1983 Mukhalad was promoted in rank to that of a Colonel and appointed the deputy commander of Saddam AB; in April 1984, when Colonel Ali Raji was transferred to the Operations Directorate of the IrAF in Baghdad, Mukhalad was appointed the command of the Mirage Wing.[26]

THE SOVIET CHALLENGE

Successful Iraqi interception operations remained much too few to change the flow of the battle. By the time the Iranians launched their next offensive – Operation *Beit-ol-Moqaddas* – the IrAF stopped

The Mirage F.1EQ-2 serial number 4014 as seen prior to delivery to Iraq, in Bordeaux, in 1981. (Jacques Guillem Collection)

A right-hand view of the 4014. This aircraft became the favourite mount of Major Mukhalad, who went on to claim 14 aerial victories with it – and then decorate this jet correspondingly (for details, see the colour section). (Jacques Guillem Collection)

its attempts to challenge the IRIAF in the skies over Khuzestan. This Iranian offensive thus resulted in the biggest defeat the Iraqi army experienced in this war and the liberation of the city and port of Khoramshahr, on 23 May 1982. After losing over 50,000 troops, over 300 tanks, more than 1,000 other armoured vehicles, and over 500 artillery pieces, the Iraqis were forced to withdraw to the international border.[27]

Desperate to distance themselves from the catastrophe, and still under pressure because of the affair related to *Project Baz-3*, Saddam, Khairrallah, and top Ba'ath Party officials court-martialled most of the responsible military commanders: between 3 and 12 were sentenced to death, while up to 300 were demoted or dismissed. Furthermore, Saddam severely restricted the individual initiative not only of all of the army's divisional commanders, but also all the base and squadron-commanders of the IrAF: amongst others, henceforth only corps commanders were granted permission to request, and

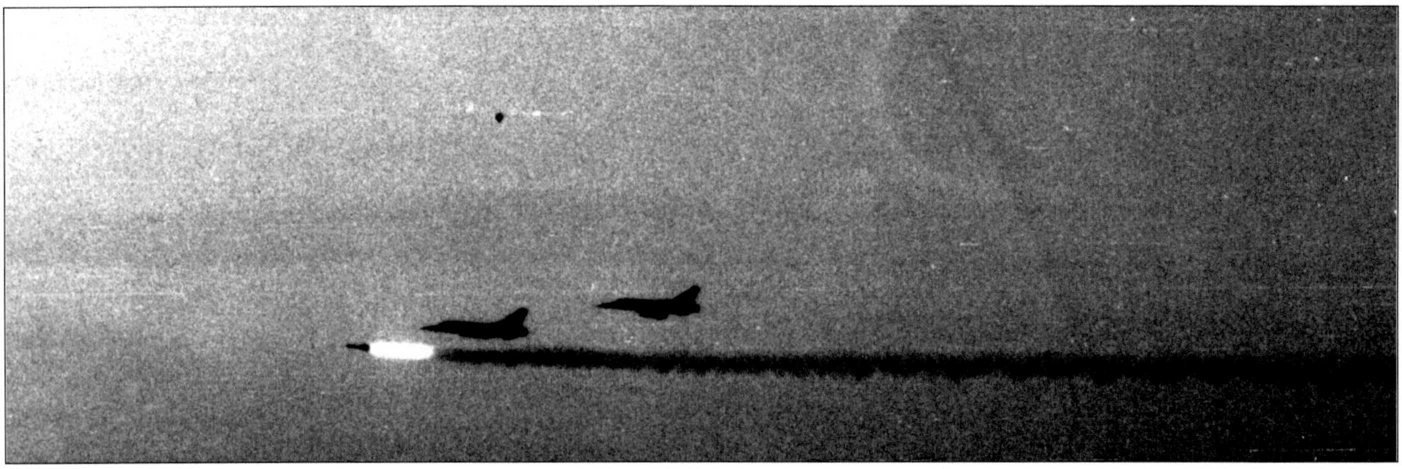

Mirage F.1EQ-2 serial number 4033, flown by Lieutenant-Colonel Ali Raji (left), and serial number 4013, flown by Major Henri de Waubert (right), seen while test-firing a Baz-AR missile in Iraq on 30 October 1982. (Ahmad Sadik Collection)

only the GHQ in Baghdad could authorise, reconnaissance missions of Mirage F.1EQ-2s equipped with the COR-2 pods.[28]

Next, the strongman in Baghdad turned his attention upon the IrAF: while the GHQ in Baghdad had neither forgotten nor forgiven the Soviet tergiversations over resupply of armament and ammunition in the opening months of the war, the 'Sukhoi clique' was still emphasising the 'immense success' of the Kh-28, and began questioning the purpose of further spending for expensive French Baz-AR missiles that after nearly five years of development were still not in service.[29]

In an attempt to demonstrate the efficiency of the system, Lieutenant-Colonel Ali Raji set up and ran two test-firings – both of which failed. Baghdad promptly complained to Paris and demanded the 'problem to be rectified', thus initiating an affair that was to last for months: issued in May 1982, related threats were sufficient for General Audran to order the entire stockpile of Baz-ARs to be airlifted back to France, where it was subjected to extensive testing on the ground, and one test-firing of a live missile, a month later. One way or the other, the missile proved nowhere as simple to use as the Soviet-made Kh-28: in order to enable its batteries to warm-up and its gyroscopes to spool-up, it had to be powered up at least five minutes before release. Any firing before that procedure was completed was automatically resulting in a failure. Although the Iraqis were advised correspondingly, their next test-launch – undertaken on 6 August 1982 – was unsuccessful again. Uncertain if the IrAF was following prescribed procedures, Audran then pulled all the strings to make sure the fault was not on the part of the French – including subjecting Matra's production line to special supervision, and a series of test-flights at Cazaux to verify the proper function of the ADAR on each missile before delivery. Finally, Matra not only developed new pre-flight test-tools, but the chief-test pilot of the CEV, Commandant Henri de Waubert, wrote a new operational manual.

By the time it was undertaken, the third – 'ultimate' – test of the Baz-AR in Iraq was monitored by an entire 'mission' of the DGA, Matra (including all of that company's project managers), the CEV, and the AMD-BA, and lasted two weeks, starting with 14 October 1982. Each of 24 sorties flown over the following week included six simulated firing passes by Lieutenant-Colonel Ali Raji, Lieutenants Muhalab Hussein Sabri (son-in-law of the CO Saddam AB, Colonel Khaldoun K Bakir), Mowaffak and Khalaf Ahmed Hussein al-Jabouri. Using four aircraft – including recently delivered 4033 and 4035 (plus 4013 and 4018) – this not only proved highly successful, but also resulted in emergence of new tactics for deployment of the Baz-AR. As now usual, this was developed by Commandant de Waubert, who recommended the attacks to be flown by two aircraft, with the wingman/Number 2 flying five minutes ahead of the leader, and both aircraft tracking the same target. When the leader fired his Baz-AR, it was on the wingman to monitor the work of the target with help of his missile's seeker head: if the targeted SAM-site turned off its HPIR at the calculated time of impact, there was a high probability that the missile had scored a hit. If not, then the wingman was to repeat the attack. Furthermore, de Waubert taught the Iraqis to deploy their Baz-ARs from low altitude, thus narrowing the electromagnetic horizon of the missile: while the firing aircraft was thus less likely to be detected by the enemy, the ADAR was also less likely to get distracted by the wrong targets.[30]

De Waubert was subsequently ordered to remain in Iraq and help set up an actual attack on Iranian HAWKs. With Syrel ELINT pods still not being available, during several reconnaissance sorties flown between 18 and 20 November 1982 he used training Baz-AR rounds to track down IRIAF's SAM-sites – including a previously unknown one positioned in the hills only 120 kilometres east of Baghdad. On the basis of data collected in this fashion, on 25 December 1982 Lieutenant-Colonel Ali Raji and three other pilots from No. 79 Squadron flew the first Baz-AR combat sortie ever. After launching from Ali Ibn Abu Talib AB, they operated as trained by de Waubert – in two formations of two aircraft in trail each – and then released their missiles from 70km range and an altitude of 7000 metres. According to the Iraqis, the success of this attack was 'total': a COR-2-equipped Mirage F.1EQ-2 that flew post-strike reconnaissance on 27 December 1982, came back with photographs that showed that:

> all missiles spent have scored hits, detonating at between 8 and 12 metres above the ground, and blowing antennas of Iranian radars out of their place. The wreckage of white radomes was clearly visible, as well as the remnants of the antennas and various structures supporting them[31]

While no Iranian accounts of this attack are currently available, a US intelligence report described the mission as follows:

> Two to four MiG-23 aircraft flew as decoys for a single ARM-carrying Mirage flying in trail. The MiG-23 flew at ranges up to 40nm (64km) from the I-HAWK site. Although Iran developed countermeasures to the ARM for its target acquisition radars, Iraq experienced success with this tactics.[32]

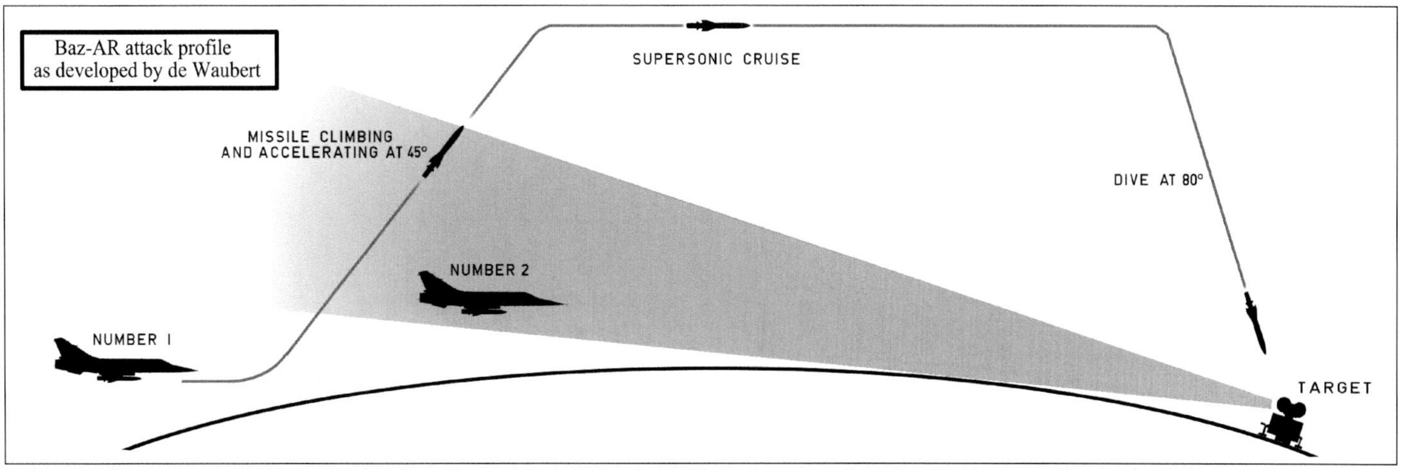

A diagram illustrating the ARM-tactics developed by de Waubert for the IrAF's deployment of the Baz-AR. Correspondingly, the wingman (or 'Number 2') of the formation flew five minutes ahead of the leader and used the seeker-head of his missile to monitor the work of the targeted HAWK SAM-site. (Diagram by Tom Cooper)

Project Baz-AR was thus saved from cancellation and the system entered service with the IrAF. In practice, no technology transfer ever took place and the IrAF never went beyond acquiring 60-80 missiles. In comparison, between 1981 and 1983, it imported 115 Kh-28s, of which no fewer than 104 were fired in combat by 1988.[33]

NEW DIRECTIONS

By mid-1982, the Iranians had set up the pattern of how the Iran-Iraq War was to continue for years. Their victories in Khuzestan forced the Iraqis into a rushed retreat to the international border, in turn gaining the strategic initiative for Iran: now it was on Tehran to make the choice between ending the war or launching a counter-invasion of Iraq. In a vain attempt, on 10 June 1982, Saddam offered a unilateral ceasefire – supposedly in order to enable Iraqi and Iranian forces to fight off the Israeli invasion of Lebanon – and then announced the withdrawal of his troops from all of Iran. However, on 21 June 1982, Khomeini publicly announced the war would continue until Saddam Hussein's regime had been toppled.

Taken in complete disregard for the condition of the regular Iranian military, this decision was to have grave consequences: it not only extended the bloody and pointless war for years to come; while the IrAF was in the process of being reinforced through an unprecedented influx of combat aircraft from France, the Soviet Union, and the People's Republic of China, the IRIAF was completely exhausted, in need of rest, maintenance and replacement aircrews and aircraft. Still deeply distrusted by the new government in Tehran, the morale of the force was further shattered by renewed purges and resulting defections. Eventually, the top ranks were left without a choice but to withdraw their aircraft from the bloody battle of attrition and concentrate on the task of protecting strategically important installations inside Iran. Henceforth, IRIAF fighter-bombers flew only sporadic sorties in support of ground offensives, while F-14s ceased flying CAPs near the battlefield: instead, the ground forces were to be protected by IRIAF's MIM-23B I-HAWK and Roland SAMs, and anti-aircraft artillery only. To the 'hawks' in Tehran, and commanders of the IRGC in particular, this didn't matter: they were convinced that the religious zeal of their infantry was sufficient to overcome any obstacles. The IrAF thus won the battle for battlefield air superiority not because its Mirage-pilots claimed 25 kills by January 1981, and 36 (including up to 12 F-14s) in total by mid-1983 – but *by default*, because the IRIAF ceased challenging it.[34]

OPERATION RAMADAN

Two hours after the midnight of 14 July 1982, the Iranians launched their invasion of Iraq, Operation *Ramadan* – an offensive with the aim of conquering Basra. The second largest city in Iraq was excellently protected on the ground, while Iraq Army's air defences included two 2K12 Kub (ASCC/NATO codename 'SA-6 Gainful') SAM-sites, for which the IRIAF lacked suitable countermeasures. In order to enable its fighter-bombers to provide at least sporadic support for ground troops, the Iranians saturated the two Iraqi sites with numerous UAVs that acted as decoys, and then hit them with high-altitude air strikes. The first such operation was launched early on the morning of 14 July 1982 and took the Iraqis by surprise: protected by ECM-pods and escorted by a pair of F-14As, the four involved F-4Es dive-bombed and destroyed one SA-6 site. Late in the morning of 15 July, the Iranians launched their strike on the second position. This time, at least eight Iraqi interceptors were scrambled in time to engage the incoming formation that was underway at an altitude of more than 30,000ft (9,144m). In the ensuing missile exchange the F-14A flown by Captain Hassan Harandi, with Captain Mohammad Roustaie as RIO, was hit by one of several Super 530Fs fired by the Iraqis, while claiming one of the IrAF interceptors in return. The crew was forced to abandon their badly damaged Tomcat after returning to Iranian airspace.[35]

The Iraqi Mirages achieved their next success later the same day. According to Iranian sources, a combat team of the Islamic Republic of Iran Army Aviation (IRIAA), consisting of three Bell AH-1J Cobras and a Bell 214A flown by Major Jamshid Pour-Azad and Captain Abbas-Zadeh, involved in Operation *Ramadan*, came under attack of two Iraqi 'MiGs'. The forward air controller of the IRIAF promptly issued a call for air support and a pair of F-4E Phantoms led by Major Ali-Reza Yassini – one of the Iranian top fighter-bomber pilots – engaged the Iraqi interceptors in air combat. Several missiles were fired by both sides in the course of one of only a handful of 'dogfights' of this war before a MiG burst into flames and withdrew towards Iraq trailing smoke. The Iranian joy did not last long: only seconds later, a pair of Mirages joined the fray and hit Yassini's Phantom with a Super 530F. With the rear fuselage of its aircraft on fire, the IRIAF crew was forced to eject: it was recovered shortly later by Pour-Azad's and Abbas-Zadeh's Bell 214A that was still in the combat zone. Finally, the Bell 214A was forced into a hurried withdrawal due to the appearance of two Mil Mi-25 helicopter gunships of the Iraqi Army Aviation Corps (IrAAC).[36]

The final known aerial clash of this period that might have involved Mirages took place on 19 August 1982, when either a pair

A row of F.1EQ-2s and F.1BQs used for conversion training of additional Iraqi pilots in France. By mid-1982, nearly all of these aircraft were at Saddam AB. (Albert Grandolini Collection)

of MiG-23MFs or a pair of F.1EQ-2s (perhaps both of these) was responsible for the downing of the RF-4E flown by Lieutenant Fariborz Ghani-Nejad and Captain Masoud Koorosh: while Ghani-Nejad ejected safely and was subsequently recovered, Koorosh was killed.[37]

INSTITUTIONALIZED PROBLEMS

Next to nothing is known about combat operations of the Iraqi Mirages during the fall/autumn of 1982 – or if, then only from the Iranian sources. Reasons were multiple: starting with Saddam's standing order not to lose aircraft and preoccupation with the requirement to save the Project Baz-AR, another was the poor overall technical reliability of the fleet: a British intelligence report from 1983 cited an overall serviceability rate of F.1EQ-2s as, 'seldom reaching 40%'. Indeed, poor technical reliability is known to have robbed Iraqi pilots of at least half a dozen opportunities for aerial victories over the following months, including at least once in May 1983, and again in June 1983. In both cases, multiple attempts to launch Super 530Fs and R.550 Magics from almost ideal intercept positions were unsuccessful due to failures in the firing circuit boards.[38]

The IrAF faced a host of other, institutionalised problems. As unlikely as it might sound, even at the times of the greatest distress following the defeat at Khorramshahr, there was no trace of alarm at the various headquarters in Baghdad. The HQ IrAF, especially, went on with business as usual, continuing to be as preoccupied as before with plans for acquisitions of new equipment and development of the force 'after the war'. This complacency dominated the air force even when the Iranians ran several offensives in the central and northern part of the frontlines, some of these only 120 kilometres from Baghdad, and – certainly – well within the range of Saddam and Abu Ubaida ABs.[39]

More troublesome was the need to bring the two existing units up to operational status: while the introduction of new aircraft and equipment had given the IrAF the potential necessary to develop and improve its capabilities, it still lacked skilled personnel. Thus, the air force was in need of time necessary to consolidate. Instead, it was constantly supplied with more and more sophisticated equipment: for most of the 1982-1983 period the IrAF – and its Mirage-equipped squadrons in particular – possessed more capacity than capability.[40]

Other reasons remained related to Saddam's continuous micromanagement of the air force. After realizing that Tehran would not stop the war, and failing to impress the Iranians through air strikes on their urban areas, the strongman in Baghdad re-directed the IrAF to target the Iranian capability to continue waging the war, i.e. its oil industry, as described in the next chapter. While it could be expected that the IrAF – designed, equipped and trained to support ground forces – would have excelled in this discipline, it failed to do so precisely because of the constant political interference: the tightly centralized control of all operations not only impaired the air force's performance, but also minimized its cooperation with ground forces. The reluctant strategy was further supported by Saddam who began rewarding pilots with medals, money, and cars regardless of their performance, or without actually being informed about the same. While such measures had helped improve the morale within the IrAF that – after its failure to prevent the IRIAF from providing decisive support during the Khorramshahr campaign – felt humiliated, they proved counterproductive. Almost ironically, the IrAF's officers are not known to have questioned the operational and political restrictions imposed upon them: this was especially the case with pilots that grew rich from cash and other awards presented to them for their service, who had no interest in jeopardizing their position by questioning Saddam and his decisions. Lower ranks were aware of the resulting problems, but not in a position to influence any changes.[41]

A bi-product of this process was Baghdad's increasingly virulent rhetoric towards Iran: while early during the war the Iraqi military communiqués were models of factual reporting, strict censorship was imposed as soon as the going became rough, and content ruthlessly distorted. Over the following years, the propaganda machinery went to extremes in regards of de-humanising the Iranians. While generally following the ancient tradition of declaiming one's own virtues while denouncing the venalities of the opponent, this resulted in the creation of several fatal legends – not only by the Iraqi mass media, or within the armed forces, but even by the Iraqi military intelligence services. The myths ranged from claims that it was the Iranian air force that provoked the war by 'air strikes on Iraqi cities, including Baghdad on 4 September 1980', via a 'victorious withdrawal' and a 'rearward reorganisation' at Khorramshahr of 1982, to the story that the IRIAF as a whole was de-facto non-existent, at least barely operational, its F-14s non-operational and their crews hopelessly incompetent.[42]

EXPANDING CAPACITY

Saddam's order that the IrAF should compensate for the army's defeats through airstrikes on 'highly visible targets' prompted the air force into requesting its French advisors to train Mirage-pilots in air-to-ground operations: the first related course was started in February 1982. In turn, and in relation to Saddam's order to avoid losses, this required the introduction in to service of new equipment including Syrels, Caimans, and Sycomors, necessary for operations in high threat areas. Obviously, each new piece of equipment required additional training of pilots and ground personnel.[43]

Saddam providing an interview to the media while surrounded by IrAF's pilots. His standing order for the IrAF to avoid even risking aircraft in combat, and subsequent micromanagement of air force's operations, while also continually making new acquisitions – and thus the necessity to train additional personnel – resulted in minimal combatactivity being recorded for the Iraqi Mirage-squadrons through late 1982 and early 1983. (Tom Cooper Collection)

With hindsight, it can be said that the Syrel was the most important single element of the entire *Project Baz*. This was an electronic reconnaissance pod capable of detecting all types of radars within about 250 kilometres around it, processing and sorting these out, and reporting their position to associated ground stations deployed on a north-south axis along the borders to Iran. Using Thomson-CSF TFH troposcatters, Thomson-CSF TFH 150 line-of-sight equipment, and a network of electro-optic cables laid down by the Swedish company Ericsson, the latter were feeding collected intelligence directly into the main computer of the KARI IADS/ATMS, installed in the Air Defence Operations Centre (ADOC) of the IrAF, in Baghdad. Correspondingly, for the first time ever, the Iraqis not only obtained the technical capability to precisely track the work of the Iranian IADS in real time, but also for the officers at ADOC to instantly analyse the tactical situation and arrive at corresponding decisions. The related 'introductory course' for the IrAF took place at Saddam AB in November 1982, and was led by a French officer whom Sadik described as, 'no kidding, the best French specialist for ESM'. The first test-flight of a Mirage F.1EQ-2 equipped with Syrel in Iraq took place on 11 December 1982, while the first operational sortie was flown on 3 January 1983. Once No. 79 Squadron and the crews of all the associated ground stations worked up on this system, Syrel operations were to be run at high intensity: by 1984 Mirages equipped with Syrels were to accompany every single strike package launched by the IrAF, regardless if this was performing close air support, battlefield interdiction (BAI), anti-ship, or strike operations deep inside Iran.[44]

While next to no data on Caiman operations was released by Iraqi sources, US intelligence reports indicate that early trials of these were not entirely successful and required additional development work. As of November 1983, an E-3A Sentry of the ELF-1 tracked two Iraqi Mirages underway at an altitude of 34,500ft (10,515m) and 1111km/h, and on a bearing of approximately 300 degrees from the targeted SAM-site in south-western Khuzestan. The F.1s proceeded inbound to the HAWK with a four-minute interval between them. About 120 kilometres away from their target, they commenced jamming, and continued to within 55 kilometres, before turning away short of entering the SAM-range.[45]

Nevertheless, after necessary improvement and refinement, the Caiman developed into the major stand-off jammer system of the IrAF. Each pod included two jammers, each with its own receiver, and fore-and-aft receiver antenna. Power output from each of the two jammers was 250 watts in the I-band (8-10GHz), or 1kW in the L-band (50GHz). The system had three modes of operation: 'manual' enabled the pilot to select any one of three predetermined frequencies at will; 'fully automatic' automatically activated the jammers when predetermined signals were received, and the 'semi-automatic' mode alerted the pilot of an incoming transmission, enabling him to take the appropriate action.[46]

Based on experiences from the earlier Phimat, the Sycomor was a passive system capable of jamming threat radars and infra-red homing missiles by ejecting clusters of suitably cut chaff, and flare cartridges, respectively. While much more complex and heavier than diverse chaff and flare dispensers that appeared subsequently, its primary advantage was its sophistication: it possessed the capability to adapt the length of the chaff to the wavelength of the radar it had to jam.[47]

Overall, by late 1983, there was no doubt that the IrAF was continuously expanding its capacities. In the words of a contemporary US intelligence report:

> The IrAF has developed, with Soviet and French assistance, a good and improving electronic warfare capability. Since early-to-mid-1983, the IrAF has consistently displayed ECM and ESM capabilities not previously credited to them. For example, the IrAF has conducted airborne electronic jamming missions against various types of threat radars in support of strike operations and electronic reconnaissance missions designed to provide intelligence elements with the local of Iranian radar sites.[48]

A Syrel-equipped Mirage F.1EQ-2 serial number 4028 returning from a mission in early 1983. The introduction to service of the Syrel pod was one of the crucial moments in the Iran-Iraq War: thanks to its connection to an entire network of ground stations, this system enabled the commanders in Baghdad to follow the air war in real time. (Ahmad Sadik Collection)

Another crucial new piece of equipment introduced to service with the Iraqi Mirages in late 1982 and early 1983 was the Thomson-CSF TMV-004 Caiman offensive stand-off jamming pod, one of which is seen under the centreline of this prototype F.1, photographed in France. This powerful system was eventually developed to a degree where it played a crucial role in blocking the work of the Iranian MIM-23B I-HAWKs. (Dassault)

THIRD MIRAGE SQUADRON

As soon as the seventh class of (seven) pilots converted to the Mirages in France had completed its training and their instructors graded all of them as 'excellent', in January 1983 the Iraqis requested France to accept additional cadets – not only for Mirage-conversion courses, but also for elementary and advanced flight training. The DIA reacted by setting up a special training centre for them in February of the same year: by 1988, up to 200 Iraqi pilots were trained there. Through the same period, in addition to providing continuation training to qualified Mirage-pilots, the team of the Dassault Aero Services working with No. 79, and then No. 89 Squadrons at Saddam AB – since October 1983 reinforced through the addition of a third French pilot, Captain Henri Leroy (specialist for electronic countermeasures and reconnaissance) – also completed the conversion of 84 pilots to the Mirages.[49]

The immediate result of all these efforts, and deliveries of Mirage F.1EQ-4s that began in June 1983, was that a third Iraqi Mirage unit came into being, in September of the same year: the Saddam AB based No. 91 Squadron, which in turn replaced No. 79 Squadron re-deployed to Abu Ubaida AB. Overall, by 1984, France delivered 64 Mirage F.1EQ-2/EQ-4 and F.1BQ to Iraq, of which five were written off. Simultaneously, 84 pilots were converted to the type in the course of 13 courses held in France, and 64 of these were still serving at Saddam AB.[50]

Table 3: Structure of IrAF's Mirage-Units, 1983-1984				
Unit	**Base**	**Commander**	**Deputy Commander**	**Notes**
No. 79 Squadron	Abu Ubaida	Major Mukhalad	Major Salah Ismail Nasser	Mirage F.1EQ-2/EQ-4; ground attack, reconnaissance with COR-2 and HAROLD, Baz-AR, Syrel and Caiman operations; detachment at Ali Ibn Abu Talib AB
No. 89 Squadron	Saddam	Major Riyadh	Major Wallid	Mirage F.1EQ-2, Mirage F.1BQ; OCU, air defence & ground attack; detachment at H-2/Sa'ad AB and H-3/Wallid AB
No. 91 Squadron	Saddam	Lt.-Col. Munir Bashar Hassan		Mirage F.1EQ-4; ground attack

Including the ability to cut chaff to the required length before dispersing it, the Matra Sycomor chaff (and flare) dispenser was one of most advanced systems of its kind as of the mid-1980s. (Matra)

This 'family photo' came into being after US troops captured the Saddam AB in 2003, and shows a pair of Sycomor dispensers (foreground), four Caimans (background), and a single Remora jammer with its own pylon (left upper corner). Notable is that the Caimans and Remoras were painted in the same colour as the undersides of Iraqi Mirage F.1EQ-2s and F.1EQ-4s. (US DoD)

Table 4: Deliveries of Mirage F.1EQ-4s to Iraq[51]		
Transfer Number	Date	Serials
10	7-10 Jun 1983	4503, 4506, 4507, 4510
11	8-9 Jul 1983	4502, 4511
12	12-17 Sep 1983	4504 & 4505 (BQs), 4004 (EQ-2), 4512
13	25-29 Oct 1983	4508, 4509, 4514, 4513, 4515, 4516
14	22-24 Nov 1983	4024 (EQ-2), 4517, 4520
15	13-14 Dec 1983	4518, 4519, 4521
16	10-11 Jan 1984	4015 (EQ-2), 4501, 4524
17	14-16 Feb 1984	4500, 4522, 4525
18	29-30 Mar 1984	4526, 4527
19	11-12 Jul 1984	4523, 4529

In 1983, the sprawling Abu Ubayda AB, outside al-Qut in central eastern Iraq, became the second major Mirage-base in Iraq. (Photo by Martin Rosenkranz)

PILOT TRAINING IN THE IrAF

While good pilot training is essential for every air force, in the case of the IrAF this aspect is so massively ignored by all researchers that, although this air force played a key role in a number of conflicts over the last 50 years, there are more unsubstantiated legends about the training of its pilots, than about any other aspect of its operations.

As in most other air forces, pilot training in the IrAF of the 1970s and 1980s was a three-phase process. It began with selection of applicants by their physical and psychological fitness, though also on basis of their ethnic, religious and political backgrounds: while there is no dispute that it included many successful Shi'a, Kurdish, and Christian officers over time, the IrAF was always dominated by the Sunni. With Saddam's ascent to power, membership in the Ba'ath Party became important, although not decisive. Finally, the IrAF Academy always welcomed volunteers that graduated the Army's Military College. As of the 1979-1980 period, annual intake averaged about 200 new cadets, about half of whom were scheduled for combat aircraft – but at least 50% of whom were washed out by the end of their training.[52]

Next, cadets would report for three-years training at the IrAF Academy at the expansive as-Sahra AB, outside Tikrit, constructed in the early 1970s. Contrary to never-ending reports abroad, the Air Force Academy was largely dependent on instructors provided by the Indian Air Force for the training of its pilots and ground personnel. On the other hand, and with the exception of operations of one type (see below), Soviet advisors were next to non-existent in Iraq of the 1970s and 1980s: at most, some technical instructors were present within the base repair organisations.[53]

The first stage of the pilot training at the Academy included six months of basic military training: those meeting top physical and pilot aptitude requirements were then inducted into the basic pilot training program, lasting one year, during which cadets learned to fly Czechoslovak-made Zlin 326 basic trainers, Aero L-29 basic and Aero L-39 advanced jet trainers. After graduating this stage, pilots selected for flying combat aircraft would be assigned to one of the advanced flight training units equipped with MiG-21s or Chinese-made Shenyang F-7Bs. During the last six months of their third and final year at the academy, and on the basis of not only their proven performance and individual qualification but also their relation to the Ba'ath Party, cadets would then be selected for operational conversion to specific types of combat aircraft: MiG-21s were used as lead-in trainers for diverse MiGs, and Su-7BMKs, Su-7UMs and Su-22UMs as lead-in trainers for diverse Sukhoi types. Flight training at all levels was heavily reliant on foreigners for instruction and technical support, thus limiting improvements in its quality. Furthermore, in the period 1986-1989, the Academy was forced to shorten the elementary and basic training courses to only two years, to replace losses from the war with Iran. After completing their conversion training – by when they usually clocked around 400 hours – pilots would be finally assigned to operational units.[54]

Future Mirage-pilots were selected from the 'best' cadets of each class, and then sent to France for conversion courses. Certainly enough, the Americans assessed the French flight training as 'tougher and more thorough than that of the Soviets', and observed that the Iraqi pilots washed out of training in France often got their wings while flying Soviet-made aircraft. However, there are next to no studies about the influence of the language barrier: indeed, hardly any of the related reports even mention the fact that next to no foreign instructors working in Iraq spoke Arabic. On the contrary, it is generally ignored that all the Iraqi pilots (and ground personnel) had to learn the English, French or Russian language, regardless if undergoing training only at home in Iraq, or conversion courses abroad.

In another of the paradoxes of the Iran-Iraq War, no matter if Indian, French, or Soviet, with few exceptions most foreign instructors tended to assess the skills and training of Iraqi pilots negatively and often rated them as 'poor fliers'. How much of this was based on the language barriers or little more than prejudice, perhaps even racism, is hard to gauge; the authors' interviews of Iraqi pilots and officers have left little doubts over their tactical and technical competence. Indeed, US intelligence reports from the mid-1980s pointed out that once assigned to an operational unit, novice pilots frequently found themselves constrained by the conservative tactics dictated by the GHQ. By 1986, this resulted in complaints from pilots that found their skills had deteriorated because they had to fly tactics that not only varied from their training – no matter where provided – but often made no sense to them. The reason for this was that the GHQ dictated not only the target, but also the number of aircraft to use, what pilots were to fly the mission, the ordnance to be used, the altitude to fly the entire mission, and the exact coordinates where pilots were to make turns. The precise reasons for such stringent control – especially between 1982 and 1986 – are explained elsewhere; as subsequent developments were to show, there is no doubt that such behaviour of the top Iraqi commanders placed undue stress on Iraqi pilots' capabilities, and had largely negative consequences.[55]

4
THE OIL CAMPAIGN

One of the primary targets assigned by Saddam to the IrAF in 1982 became the Iranian oil industry. Certainly enough, the same was repeatedly targeted since the start of the war, but related efforts transformed into an outright Oil Campaign very slowly. For a full understanding why, it is necessary to take at least a superficial look at an entire plethora of details about the structure and technology of the industry in question.

IRANIAN OIL INDUSTRY

The Iranian oil industry, most of which was concentrated in Khuzestan province and the city of Abadan, was booming already in the 1920s. Due to the country's geographic isolation, its exporting capacity was heavily dependent on tankers, which by the 1940s grew in size to a degree where they could not operate within the confined Shatt al-Arab waterway. This prompted the construction of a major deep-water exporting terminal near Mahshahr – originally called Bandar-e Shahpour, but renamed Bandar-e Imam Khomeini in 1979, and colloquially known as the 'BIK' to the Iranian seamen – which included not only major oil-loading facilities, but also the biggest modern, general-purpose port in the Middle East. Thanks to its railway connection to Ahwaz, Abadan and beyond, this port could forward huge volumes of oil, fuel, general cargo, and also troops and supplies with minimum delay. As the Iranian oil industry continued to boom, in the 1960s a new major oil export terminal was constructed on Khark Island – a pair of rocks some 42 kilometres off Iran's coast, 44 kilometres southwest of Genaveh and 60 kilometres northwest of Bushehr. To serve these three facilities a massive multi-line pipeline was constructed connecting them with Abadan and 24 oilfields with 304 producing wells, and 60 production, treatment, and booster units. At its southern end, this giant system of pipelines joined at the Gorreh pumping station, before proceeding for the Genaveh manifold – both on the coast of the Persian Gulf: one of the most powerful in the World, the Gorreh pumping station consisted of three separate facilities (simply designated A, B, and C) equipped with a total of 17 pump/turbine units with a total output of 130,800 horse-powers, and a throughput of 9 million of barrels per day (bpd). Directly or indirectly connected to nearly all of the crude oil production from inland and offshore oilfields in Iran, the Gorreh pumping station was considered the 'heart of Iran's oil industry': it required so much electric power that it became the principal reason behind the Iranian decision to launch the construction of a nuclear powerplant outside Bushehr, in mid-1970s. Similar was valid for the Genaveh manifold, positioned just 4.5km northwest of the port of Genaveh. This facility served as the starting point of six 38-kilometre-long submarine pipelines to Khark, some of which were laid at a maximum depth of 46m. The sole purpose of existence for the Genaveh manifold was to control the flow of the crude to Khark.[1]

After passing the Gorreh pumping station and the Genaveh manifold, and then the undersea pipelines, oil would first reach the Flow Control Station at Khark: this controlled the distribution into the local tank farm that included 41 crude oil storage tanks with a total capacity of 24.5 million barrels. From there its further flow was controlled with the help of large, motor-operated valves: due

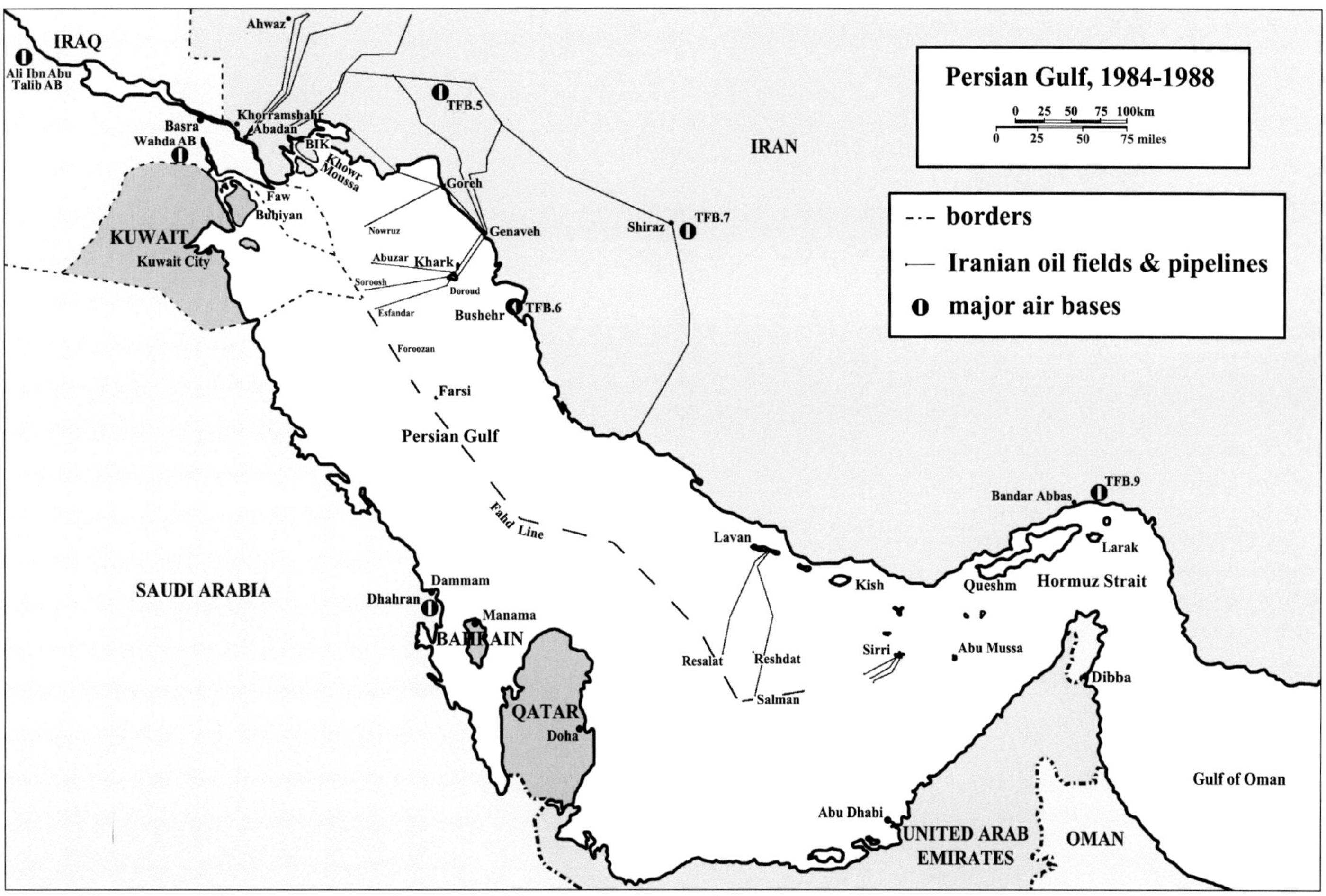

A map of the Persian Gulf – the main scene of the IrAF's Oil Campaign in the period 1984-1988 – with the most important Iranian oil fields and pipelines, and major air bases. (Map by Tom Cooper)

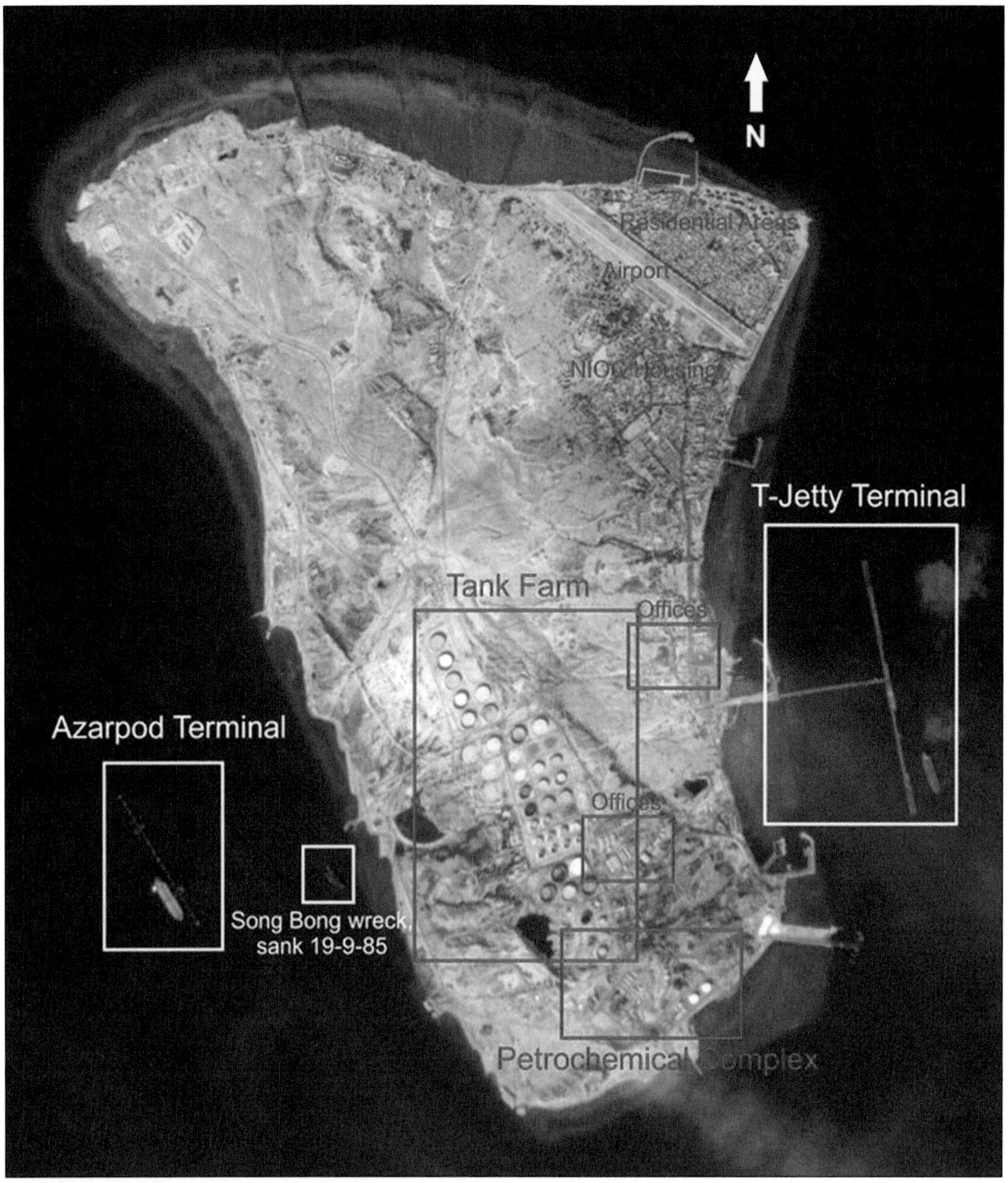

US satellite image of the Khark from late 1980s, with description of most important installations. (Tom Cooper Collection)

to the island's high elevation above the sea surface, loading into berthed tankers was run with help of gravity only. The crude could be loaded on tankers via three terminals: the original *Ten-Berth-Jetty* (or 'T-Jetty') on the eastern side of the island, could accept ships up to 250,000 tonnes and load them at rates up to 3.6 million bpd. The smaller, but newer, 1,100 metres long, four-berths *Sea Island Terminal* (renamed *Azarpod*) on the western side could support the largest tankers available, loading them at rates up to 5.5 million bpd. The third crude export facility on Khark Island was the *Daryush Terminal*: this included a tank farm on the southern side of the island, with a total storage capacity of 5.5 million barrels, and was exporting crude via a single, conventional buoy mooring system with a capacity of 300,000 bpd, located approximately 2km south of the T-Jetty. In between the Daryush Terminal and the southern coast of the island was the *Khemco Terminal*, with a single jetty berth, used to export crushed sulphur and liquid gas. Overall, the oil facilities on Khark were offering an export capacity of 9-10 million bpd. However, this capacity was not used even during the best times of the Iranian oil industry, back in 1977: on the contrary, for most of the period 1980-1983 average exports from Khark were at only about 1.6 million barrels a day.[2]

As well as major facilities like those in Abadan, Gorreh, Genaveh, and on Khark, the northern Persian Gulf was also crowded by man-made elements of the oil industry: foremost amongst these were oil exploitation platforms (or 'rigs') constructed with the purpose of exploiting oil and gas from fields under the bottom of the sea, including those at Abuzar, Bahregansar, Dorud, Foruzan, Hendigan, Sorus and Nowruz. Thus, the area the Iraqi Mirages were about to enter in 1984 was vast in its geographic dimensions, but by no means empty. On the contrary: the geographic isolation of Iran from the oil markets and the lack of an oil pipeline exporting system meant that the country was over-reliant on its loading terminals and the security of sea lanes in the Persian Gulf for exporting its oil. Indeed, in order to be able to finance its increasingly costly war effort, Iran had to resort to a policy of maximal oil production – which is why its oil industry began playing an as important role in the war.[3]

Obviously, the war not only caused critical damage to this industry: what is less-well-known is that due to the loss of refineries of Abadan and Kermanshah early during the war, Iran became a net fuel importer – a matter of fact that was to dawn upon the Iraqis only during the last year of the war. Naturally, this put other Iranian refineries under a massive strain: those in Tehran, Esfahan, Shiraz,

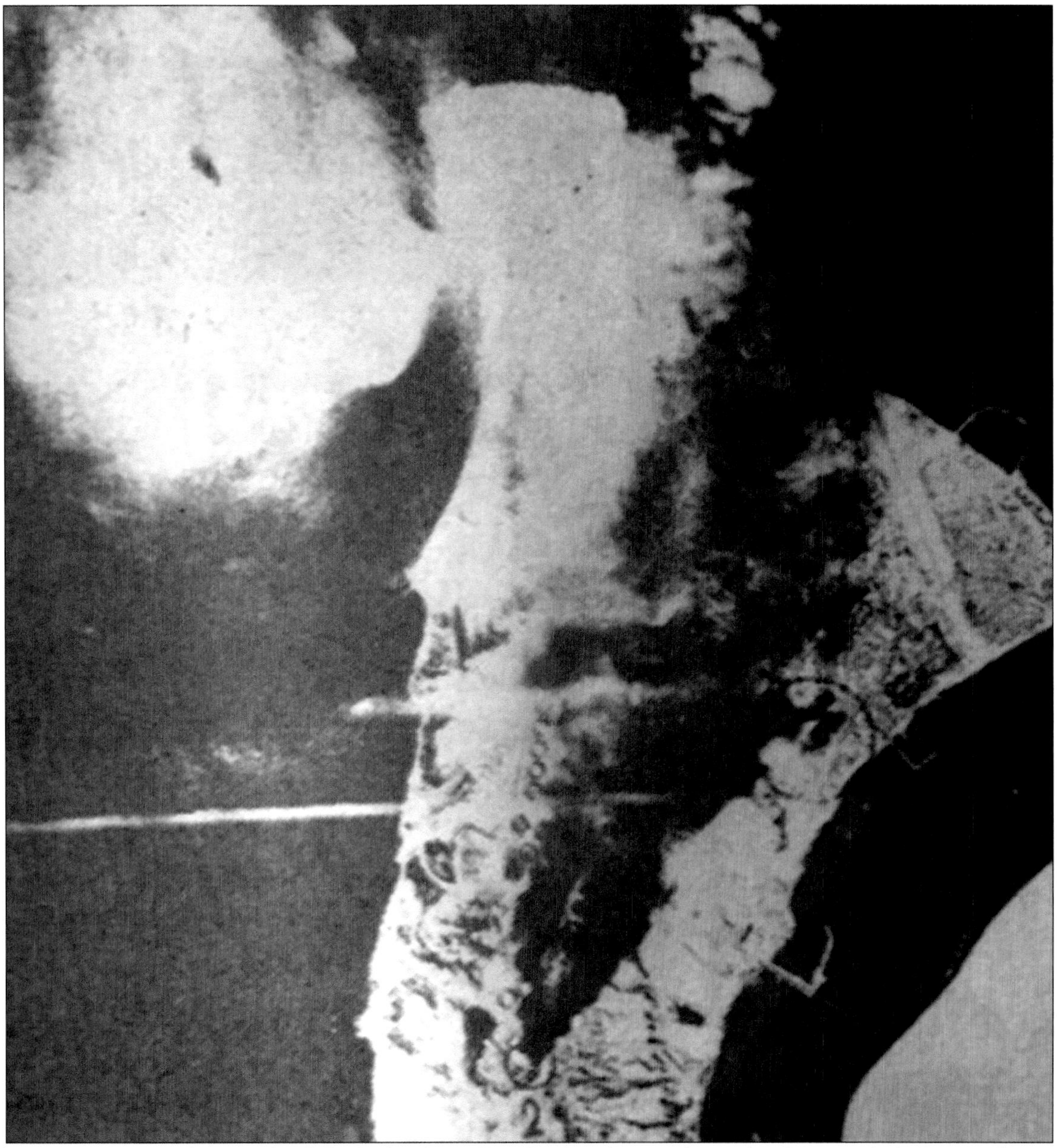

One of the earliest reconnaissance photographs of Khark taken by IrAF's MiG-25RBs, showing the results of an air strike by Su-20Ms from No. 109 Squadron, either in 1982 or 1983, which caused a fire in one of the huge storage tanks. (Ahmad Sadik Collection)

Tabriz and on Lavan Island were under pressure to substitute at least some of the loss by continuously increasing their output. This was possible only through an elaborate and time-consuming expansion of their facilities, and a newly-laid system of pipelines, all of which required a massive effort by the Iranian metal, construction, and transport sectors, but also plenty of imports – the majority of which was run via the ports of BIK and Bushehr. Another solution was to export the crude to the refinery of Aden, in the then Southern Yemen, and return it in the form of derivates to Iran. Overall, at least in theory, the Iraqi strategy for the Oil Campaign was similar to the German strategy of the *U-Boot-Krieg* in the Atlantic of the Second World War, where the Germans sought to inflict attrition upon Allied merchant shipping that would surpass the capability to replace losses: in the case of the Iraqis, the strategy was to suppress Iranian oil exports to 750,000 barrels a day or less, and keep it there.[4]

Parallel to this, the entire Iranian war effort was heavily dependent on the ability to move large amounts of goods, troops and supplies by ship to BIK, from where these could be distributed to the southern – crucial – battlefields of the war with Iraq. As much as the oil-exporting tankers were the 'lifeline of Iran', caravans were the actual 'lifeline of the Iranian war effort'. Therefore, what is usually misreported and misinterpreted as the 'Tanker War' – in sense of a campaign of anti-ship attacks on 'tankers exporting Iranian crude', run on direct orders from Saddam Hussein – was actually a three-fold strategic effort: denial of oil exports, denial of production and fuel imports, but also the denial of the Iranian use of sea lanes for movement of reinforcements and supplies to BIK.[5]

Unsurprisingly, the northern Persian Gulf was the – by far – best protected piece of real estate in all of Iran already as of late September 1980: its importance was such that Tehran preferred to leave its ground troops on the battlefield without sufficient air cover in order to bolster the local defences. By 1982, the area was defended by three major early warning radar stations, three MIM-23B I-HAWK SAM-sites and nine radar-guided Oerlikon anti-aircraft batteries with twin-barrel 35mm cannons, while F-14As from TFB.7 and TFB.8 flew constant CAPs between Khark and Bushehr.

Even then, it might appear as logical to target such an obviously massive system like the Iranian oil industry in south-western Khuzestan with combat aircraft – and easy to knock it out. Indeed, even amongst Iranian oilmen there was a widespread belief early during the war that just one precise hit on Khark – crammed full of gigantic storage tanks, pipelines, manifolds, an airfield, administrative and apartment facilities – was likely to cause the entire island to blow up. As so often, the reality was to prove entirely different.[6]

EARLY EFFORTS AGAINST KHARK, GORREH AND GENAVEH

Despite its strategic importance, Khark was bombed effectively by the IrAF only five times during the first month of the Iran-Iraq War – always by Su-20Ms from No. 109 Squadron. While air raids caused some panic amongst the oilmen, they resulted in minimal damage – while prompting the Iranians to bolster their fire-fighting facilities: before long, the modern, automated fire-fighting system was bolstered through the addition of hundreds of additional spray/sprinkler and foam dispensers, while the workforce was reinforced through the re-deployment of some of the 11,557 workers evacuated form the Abadan refinery. Therefore, Iranian oil operations soon regained momentum and by early 1981 Tehran increased its exports to about 1.1 million of barrels a day.[7]

In attempt to interrupt the flow, Saddam then ordered No. 109 Squadron into attacks on the Gorreh and Genaveh facilities: when operating under high pressure, the pumping station in Gorreh, especially, was extremely combustible, and thus highly vulnerable to air strikes. Over the eight years of war, the IrAF thus targeted this facility no less than 30 times: 26 times with unknown results, and four times with – according to the Iraqis – 'totally destructive results'. Actually, Gorreh booster station was never entirely knocked out: not only that the Iranian engineers went to great extents with regards to installing temporary improvisations in order to bypass damaged or destroyed parts of the installation, but according to its managing director from the times of the Iran-Iraq War, the most the Iraqis managed at different stages of the conflict was to destroy 25% of Gorreh-A, 75% of Gorreh-B, and 55% of Gorreh-C.[8]

Air strikes on the Genaveh facility were even less successful. At least 16 are known to have been flown in eight years of war, without any notable success. Indeed, the Iraqis were soon desperate to a degree where – knowing that the repair of submerged pipelines at war was extremely difficult – on 29 March 1982 the GHQ ordered the involved pilots to carpet-bomb the waters along the whole coastal line with bombs equipped with delayed-action fuses in hope that underwater detonations might cut off the pipelines. While managing to damage the vital mainline (with a throughput of 2.1 million bpd) and temporarily slowing-down Iranian oil-exports – the effects of this attack actually remained unknown in Baghdad. The reason was that the Iranian oilmen not only quickly repaired, but interconnected this pipeline with one of the adjacent lines: thus, whenever one of the two would be cut off, the oil would continue to flow through the other.[9]

CARAVANS

The flow of imports of equipment for the repair and the expansion of the Iranian oil industry, and fuels, but also that of reinforcements for the battlefields in Khuzestan was regulated by the Islamic Republic of Iran Navy (IRIN) and the Iranian merchant navy. Ever since 23 September 1983, these had organized convoys ('caravans' in local vocabulary) of merchant ships between Bushehr and BIK. Run within the frame of Operation *Caravan*, the convoys included cargo ships and tankers averaging about 15,000 tonnes in size, each with carefully trained pilots of the Iranian merchant navy. Never fully understood in Baghdad, this effort remained entirely unknown outside Iran. The reason was simple: because of its sensitiveness and importance, Operation *Caravan* had to be shrouded in secrecy.[10]

Each of the involved cargo ships was armed with at least one

A close-up photograph from the second half of the 1970s, showing the eastern, T-Jetty of Khark, with a total of 10 tankers on its berths. The T-Jetty's construction consisted of a net of steel pylons and pipes, carrying a 'terrace' with a road for the movement of vehicles and loading equipment. This required plenty of direct hits – and lots of explosives – to demolish. (Tom Cooper Collection)

Each of the Iraqi Mirage-squadrons was organized into flights of pilots and aircraft specialized in specific tasks. Prior to delivery of subsequent variants, the Baz-AR flight of No. 79 Squadron was flying F.1EQ-2s 4013, 4018, 4033 and 4035. Illustrated here is the oldest of the four, the F.1EQ-2 serial number 4013, flown – amongst others – by Major Henri de Waubert during the 'ultimate test-series' of Baz-AR missiles, in October 1982. Painted white overall, and with operational rounds having yellow bands to mark a 'live' warhead, the Baz-AR was installed on the LM.058D launcher, and usually wore the title of the manufacturer and – according to different reports – either the designation 'BAZAR' or 'ARMAT'. (Artwork by Tom Cooper)

Certainly the most-photographed and most-famous Mirage F.1EQ-2 ever was the serial number 4014. After being used for training the second and third groups of Iraqi pilots, and then the initial testing of the BGL.250/400 laser guided bombs in France, following delivery to Iraq it became the favourite mount of Captain/Major Abdul Karim Mukhalad – the first deputy commander, and then the commander of No. 79 Squadron. Mukhalad claimed a total of 14 kills with this aircraft (of which the IrAF officially confirmed two), and applied a corresponding total of kill-markings on its front fuselage. The aircraft is shown in the classic intercept configuration for the Iraqi Mirages during the war with Iran: armed with Super 530F and R.550 Magic Mk I air-to-air missiles, and carrying a single RP.35 drop tank under the centreline. (Artwork by Tom Cooper)

All Iraqi Mirage F.1EQ/EQ-2 and F.1BQ were camouflaged in French colours named *Brun Café* (dark sand, FS30475) and Khaki (FS36134) applied following a standardised camouflage pattern on top surfaces (inset) and sides, and light blue grey (FS35189) on undersurfaces. Most pre-delivery photographs show them wearing national insignia in six positions, and fin flashes. These were always removed prior to delivery and often not fully re-applied once the aircraft was in Iraq. The Mirage F.1EQ-2 serial number 4028 was one of at least four used by the electronic warfare flight of No. 79 Squadron for most of the war with Iran. It is shown as equipped with the TMV-004 Caiman offensive stand-off jamming pod, usually installed directly under the centreline of the aircraft. The lower inset shows the COR-2 reconnaissance pod, frequently carried by this and other aircraft from the same flight of No. 79 Squadron. (Artwork by Tom Cooper)

Another of the aircraft operated by the electronic warfare flight of No. 79 Squadron was the F.1EQ-2 serial number 4032. Together with the serial number 4028, this aircraft mostly flew Syrel and Caiman-operations: while rarely eventful, their operations were crucial for good coordination of massive air strikes conducted by the ADOC in the 1984-1988 period. Standard configuration for such flights was as illustrated here: Syrel (or Caiman) pod – both came together with their special adapters installed directly on them – under the centreline; two RP.35 drop tanks installed on Alkan 915B underwing pylons, and two R.550 Magic air-to-air missiles installed on LM.39 wing-tip launch rails. (Artwork by Tom Cooper)

Although the variant bore the brunt of long-range penetration raids into Iran, very little is known about the combat career of the first Mirage F.1EQ-4, serial number 4500. The aircraft is shown in the 'tanker' configuration, including two RP.35 drop tanks installed on Alkan 915B underwing pylons, a pair of R.550 Magic air-to-air missiles on LM.39 wing-tip launch rails, and the Douglas/Intertechnique D-704 in-flight refuelling pod installed on its own adapter under the centreline. Notable is the typical, four-digit serial number applied in the same font and font-size, and in the same position as on F.1EQ-2s, but with more empty space between the individual digits. When last seen (in Iraq), this aircraft was one of several wearing no national insignia at all. (Artwork by Tom Cooper)

Together with the F.1EQ-4 serial number 4510, the serial number 4507 had probably the most colourful career of all the 28 aircraft of this variant. Operated by No. 89 Squadron, it was heavily involved in early long-range raids into Iran. After being damaged in 1984, it was repaired in France: back in Iraq, it may have scored at least one kill against an IRIAF F-4E, some time in 1986 or 1987, before it was shot down during a raid on Farsi Island in August 1987. It is shown in one of the typical configurations for long-range raids flown in 1986 and 1987, including the massive RPL.201 Irakien drop tank under the centreline, an RP.35 drop tank under the inboard underwing pylon (some of which have had large parts pained in dark olive green overall), and a SAMP Type 25 250kg bomb on the CLB.30 outboard underwing pylon (in addition to the usual pair of wing-tip-mounted R.550 Magics). (Artwork by Tom Cooper)

Following necessary training of is pilots, and related testing, the IrAF began deploying its F.1EQs for interdiction strikes and close-air-support operations starting in February 1984. For these purposes, the type deployed a wide range of conventional and chemical-warfare bombs, including: 400kg SAMP Type 21 general purpose bombs (shown installed on underwing pylons), and (insets, from left to right) 200kg SAMP Type 25 general-purpose bomb, SAMP Type 21 (two examples), EXPAL BR.250WP and R-400 chemical warfare bombs. Most of the time free-fall armament was installed directly on Alkan 915B and CLB.30 underwing pylons. (Artwork by Tom Cooper)

Due to awkward enquiries from the Greek authorities, during their transfer flights to Iraq most of the Mirage F.1EQ-4s received their radio call-signs applied on the top of the fin (instead of the fin-flash, which was either not applied or removed before delivery). The last two of the same were usually re-applied below the cockpit. In most of cases, these codes were never removed after arrival in Iraq: a new set of fin flashes was applied atop of those on the fin. The F.1EQ-4 illustrated here is shown as configured with four Matra BLG.66EG Belouga dispensers, filled with anti-personnel bomblets: the bottom pair was usually installed on the CLB.4 'surf board' under the centreline. Insets show other CBUs deployed by Iraqi Mirages, including (from left to right): Cardoen CB.250, Cardoen CB.500, and SCB.470. (Artwork by Tom Cooper)

Because of their compatibility with the AM.39 Exocet, the F.1EQ-5s were originally meant to be used for anti-ship operations. Correspondingly, aircraft with serial numbers 4561 and 4575-4579 were all painted in suitable colours, consisting of *gris marin foncé* (extra dark sea grey, FS36076) on upper surfaces and sides, and insignia white (FS17875 or FS37095) on bottom surfaces. This example (serial number 4577, reportedly one of top scorers of the Oil Campaign) is shown equipped with one of the 'Iraqi Exocets' (introduced to service in early 1985, and always installed on their special pylon under the centreline), and a Remora on its own adapter on the outboard underwing pylon. Notable is that all the Caiman and Remora pods delivered to Iraq were painted in the same light blue grey colour (FS35189) applied on the undersurfaces of most of Iraqi Mirages. Inset is shown the patch of No. 81 Squadron, IrAF: a unit commanded by Major Haythan Khattab Omar and formed around the core group of pilots that flew Super Etendards in 1983-1984. (Artwork by Tom Cooper)

The Mirage F.1EQ-5 serial number 4564 is shown in the armament configuration used for several long-range raids on the Iranian loading terminals near Sirri and Larak, and the Rey oil refinery outside Tehran, including one RPL.201 Irakien drop tank under the centreline and four 250 kilogram Type 25 general-purpose bombs of French origin. An inset shows the unique cover for the rear IFF-antenna as installed between the ventral fins of all F.1EQ-5s. (Artwork by Tom Cooper)

While primarily deployed for long-range air strikes deep into Iran, and for battlefield interdiction and CAS, Mirage F.1EQ-5s did retain air defence as their secondary role, and were repeatedly deployed for interception purposes. By 1986, the standard configuration for air combat included the usual pair of Super 530Fs, but also Remora jammers and Sycomor chaff & flare dispensers, in addition to one RP.35 drop tank under the centreline. A small number of the latter were painted in yellow sand colour, as illustrated here. This example – serial number 4566 – is shown with full radio call-signs applied for the delivery flight: there was a total of six of these (including Y-IREE, Y-IREF, Y-IBLU, Y-IBLV, and Y-IBLW), and they were applied repeatedly on different aircraft. (Artwork by Tom Cooper)

By late 1986, the AS.30L became the primary precision guided weapon of the IrAF. The Mirage F.1EQ-5 serial number 4569 is shown in standard configuration for such operations, including an AS.30L on the LM.762 inboard underwing pylon, the Sycomor chaff and flare dispenser on the CLB.30 outboard underwing pylon (a Remora pod was most often carried on its own adapter under the right outboard underwing station), and the PDL.1EQ Patrick laser designator installed under the centreline – as, for example, during the Sirri raid of 21 April 1988, when it was damaged by an F-14A. Quite unique was the position of the fin flash, applied high up the fin on this aircraft. (Artwork by Tom Cooper)

The Mirage F.1EQ-5 serial number 4570 was the favourite mount of several pilots of No. 81 Squadron, including its CO, Major Haytham Khattab Omar. It was the only F.1EQ-5 ever flown back to France (to be used for training of pilots in use of AS.30Ls, together with 4561, 4562, and the repaired 4507), but also the only one known to have been decorated with two kill markings: one for an F-4E claimed at an unknown date in 1986, and another for a claim from 1987 or 1988. Serial number 4570 was also deployed for the first combat application of the AS.30L, against the IRGC-operated anti-aircraft ship *Iran Sedaghat*, on 4 July 1986. As far as is known, this F.1EQ-5 never received a fin flash after delivery. (Artwork by Tom Cooper)

The Mirage F.1EQ-5 serial number 4572 is shown in the armament configuration used for the final long-range raid of the war, against Larak, on 14 May 1988. This included 1,000 kilogram, Mk.84 general-purpose bombs mounted on an Alkan 915B pylon, Sycomor chaff and flare dispensers installed on CLB.30 outboard underwing pylons, and the RPL.201 Irakien drop tank under the centreline. By this point in the war, camouflage colours of most of Iraqi Mirages began showing the signs of wear and tear. Similar was valid for the transfer radio-call sign applied on this aircraft (reportedly, this was Y-IBLW). (Artwork by Tom Cooper)

The Mirage F.1EQ-6 serial number 4600 was the first of this 'definitive' variant made for Iraq. Certainly the best-equipped sub-variant of the F.1-family ever manufactured in the series, it included numerous major improvements in terms of avionics, which turned it into the linchpin to the much-expected Mirage 2000. The most notable outside differences were new housings for the Thomson-CSF Sherloc digital radar warning receivers, installed high on the leading edge and the rear edge of the fin, and P0 underwing hardpoints for conformal chaff and flare dispensers. The aircraft is shown in one of its typical configurations for interdiction strikes against the Iranian economy flown during the summer of 1988, including the CLB.4 surf-board under the centreline, with four Type 25 general purpose bombs, and a pair of Remora pods on outboard underwing pylons. Inset is shown the Raphael TH reconnaissance pod, the performance of which was found rather disappointing by the Iraqis. (Artwork by Tom Cooper)

All five Super Etendards leased to Iraq in the 1983-1985 period retained their original camouflage consisting of *gris marin foncé* (extra dark sea grey, FS36076) on upper surfaces and sides, and insignia white (FS17875 or FS37095) on bottom surfaces. Their French national insignia, and inscriptions such as 'AMD-BA' and 'Super Etendard' usually applied on the rudder were removed, and replaced by four-digit serials in the range 4665-4669, while the Iraqi fin flash was applied in the usual position, but with a strong inclination. Standard armament consisted of one AM.39, always carried on its right underwing station. The deployment of this missile required the installation of a module with Exocet-related avionics instead of the two DEFA cannons. The left underwing pylon was always reserved for the RP.23 drop tank (1,100 litre), and the fuselage station for the RP.24 fuel tank (600 litre). If used, outboard underwing pylons were occupied by LM.39 launchers for R.550 Magic missiles. (Artwork by Tom Cooper)

YI-ALE

A reconstruction of the '*Suzanna*' (alias '*Yarmouk*') as of mid-May 1987. This aircraft was originally one of five Falcon 50s operated by No. 53 Squadron, a VIP-transport unit, and it used to wear the livery of Iraqi Airways until being returned to France for modifications. When re-appearing at Villaroche on 3 December 1986, it looked as shown here: painted in white overall, with two 'cheat lines' in gold, and without a registration. It remains unclear if the latter was ever applied. *Suzanna* never flew further combat sorties after the attack on USS *Stark*, but was modified to carry the Raphael TH pod in 1988. Inset is shown the size and fonts in which her registration was applied before delivery. (Artwork by Tom Cooper)

This is a reconstruction of the Mirage 2000IQ based on a model put on display at the Baghdad Arms Fair in 1989. As far as can be said, the aircraft was planned to be camouflaged in the same *Brun Café* and Khaki as used on Mirage F.1EQs, applied on top surfaces and sides along a standardized camouflage pattern for this type, and light blue grey on undersurfaces. The centreline hardpoint was to be used for carriage of advanced guided weaponry, like AS.30Ls, a conventional variant of the ASMP, or laser-homing bombs; either the left or the right inboard underwing station was to be reserved for an advanced variant of the PDL.1EQ (similar to the Atlis II targeting pod), while outboard underwing stations were to be used for carrying either Matra R.550 Magic IIs (shown), Brazilian-developed Piranha, or the advanced MICA air-to-air missiles. (Artwork by Tom Cooper)

Most of the squadron-buildings and ready-rooms of Iraqi Mirage-units were richly decorated, often with murals depicting major achievements by their pilots. This one depicted a reconstruction of the Khark raid from 15 August 1985, flown in cooperation between Mirage F.1EQs and Su-22s, and quite accurately showing hits scored on that day. (Ahmad Sadik Collection)

More recently, Iraqi Mirage-pilots commissioned an unknown Iraqi artist to paint an additional series of artworks, depicting their achievements – like this downing of an Iranian F-4E Phantom II by, amongst others, the Mirage F.1EQ-4 serial number 4507. (Ahmad Sadik Collection)

This mural depicted a reconstruction of the raid on Sirri, flown on 12 August 1986, and shows Mirages in the process of bombing Iranian 'mothership' tankers. (Ahmad Sadik Collection)

Another interesting artwork is this reconstruction of an Exocet-attack on Khark by two Mirages painted in 'naval' camouflage pattern. In reality, Exocet-carrying aircraft never approached within visual range of their targets. (Artwork by Tom Cooper)

Another highly interesting mural depicted one of the air raids on the Rey oil refinery, outside Tehran. (Ahmad Sadik Collection)

Map of major air bases and airfields of the Iran-Iraq War (Map by Tom Cooper)

ZU-23 twin-barrel 23mm anti-aircraft gun, manned by IRIN personnel. Later on, ships regularly involved in Operation *Caravan* received teams armed with Strela-2M (ASCC/NATO codename 'SA-7 Grail') man-portable air defence systems (MANPADS), but also chaff dispensers and towed decoys. The starting point for each of about 150 caravan operations run during the war was the port and anchorage of Bushehr. On average, each caravan consisted of 10-15 ships, sailing approximately one nautical mile from each other. Larger convoys were rare: their size was always limited by the number of available merchant pilots skilled enough to navigate ships through the Khowr Moussa waterway. Each caravan was protected by between two and four IRIN warships, usually including two PF-103 class patrol frigates, one or two Combattante-IIB class fast missile craft, and at least one – often more – Mk.III patrol boats. Furthermore, in 1982, the Iranians began deploying a number of requisitioned ships equipped with up to six ZU-23s along the lane connecting Bushehr with Khowr Moussa, which acted as air defence platforms. While having IRIN skippers, their weapons were manned by IRGC-personnel.[11]

The GMID in Baghdad did get wind of such operations and thus, instead of launching a sustained campaign against Khark, Saddam Hussein ordered the IrAF into attacking the port of Bandar-e Khomeini. The first known air strike against local berths – flown by four Su-20Ms from No. 109 Squadron – seems to have been attempted on 29 September 1980. However, the formation led by Major Faysal Habbou was intercepted by F-14As and quickly lost two aircraft, the pilots of which ejected safely and were captured by the Iranians.[12]

With such operations not working, the Iraqis then attempted to curb the passage of the caravans by the means of Navy-operated, Chinese-made CHETA Hai Ying HY-2 anti-ship missiles (ASCC/NATO codename 'CSSC-2 Silkworm'), fired from a base at Ras al-Biseh, on the Faw Peninsula; by drifting mines; and by Navy-operated Aerospatiale SA.321 Super Frelon helicopters of No. 101 Squadron armed with Aerospatiale AM.39 Exocet ('flying fish') anti-ship missiles. Iraq acquired 16 Super Frelons starting in 1976, 12 of which were equipped with the Thomson-CSF ORB.31D Héraclés radar and compatible with 60 Exocets imported by the end of 1981: dozens of such missiles were spent to no effect by the time one damaged the Liberian bulk carrier *al-Tajdar* near Bandar-e Khomeini on 19 October 1981, as she sailed in ballast in a convoy returning towards Bushehr. However, this first ever successful combat deployment of the Exocet remained entirely unknown to the public for the next 15 years.[13]

Although three additional ships were hit and sunk by the end of the same year, by early 1982 it was obvious that the Iraqi efforts at curbing the traffic to BIK were largely ineffective: indeed, the troops and equipment delivered to south-western Iran with help of the caravans played a crucial role in the liberation of Khoramshahr. Moreover, Khark's output of oil exports continued to increase, earning Tehran ever more money. Even a well-planned and flown air strike by No. 109 Squadron on 30 May 1982 – which targeted loading berths for the first time (and, by accident, hit the first tanker damaged during this war, the Turkish *Atlas I*) – had shown only minimal effects, just as did a further air raid by Su-20Ms on 1 June 1982. Japanese shipping companies announced the suspension of

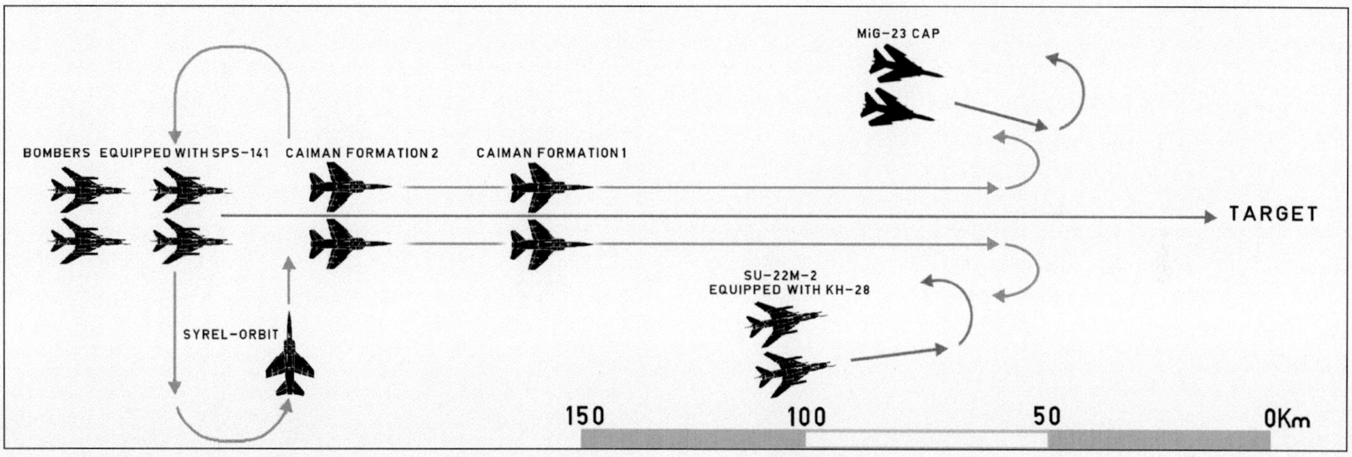

A diagram showing the typical Iraqi CAS or BAI operation as undertaken from the February-March 1984 period until the end of the war:

- 1 F.1EQ-2 equipped with the Syrel pod would monitor the activity of the Iranian air defences from a stand-off range;
- 2-4 Mirages equipped with Caiman pods and in a column formation, with four minutes' separation between two elements, would enter the combat zone about 150 kilometres from the nearest HAWK-site at an altitude of 10,700m and speed of 1,100km/h; they would activate their pods and continue approaching to about 50 kilometres from the SAM-site;
- Caiman-equipped Mirages would be accompanied by 1-3 Su-22M-2Ks equipped with Myetel pods and Kh-28s, which would operate in a racetrack pattern about 60km from the nearest known HAWK SAM-site;
- 2-4 MiG-23MFs flew a combat air patrol;
- if involved, Tu-16 and Tu-22 bombers would deploy a combination of noise and repeater jammers, and chaff, while formations of fighter-bombers were led by examples either equipped with internally installed SPS-141s (MiG-23BNs), or SPS-141s installed in a pod (Su-22s), or Mirages equipped with Remora pods.

Deployed similarly for close air support, battlefield interdiction, anti-ship and for long-range operations against strategic targets deep within Iran, this combination proved overwhelming for Iranian air defences: reportedly, it not only caused the radar displays of F-4Es to turn white, or blocked the acquisition and illuminator radars of HAWK SAM-sites, but was causing problems even for the AWG-9s of Iranian F-14s. (Diagram by Tom Cooper)[35]

trips to Khark, but most of other shippers ignored the threats from Baghdad and by late August at least 14 vessels were loading crude there at once. Indeed, intentionally exaggerated claims about the scale of air raids on 4 September 1982 had diametrically opposite effects to what the Iraqis expected them to achieve.

DECOY GAMES

The reasons for a high percentage of AM.39s fired by Super Frelons missing their targets were manifold. Big and relatively slow, these helicopters were vulnerable to IRIAF interceptors. Correspondingly, their crews tended to operate from stand-off ranges, usually around the Kuwaiti island of Bubyan, from which they had no means of positively identifying their targets: essentially, they fired blindly at anything their radars detected and was at least resembling a ship.[14]

Moreover, the Iranians proved quick in bolstering their defences of the shipping in the northern Persian Gulf. They established a 'war room' at Khark: an authority responsible for coordinating the work of all armed services and the shipping in adjacent areas, equipped with a 'hotline' to the TFB.6, so that it could call-in F-4Es from there, and F-14As that flew CAPs nearby. Moreover, at least according to unofficial Iraqi sources, the Iranians then hired a group of British specialists that helped them design and manufacture a large number of 'floating corner reflectors' – simple decoys for AM.39s. Actually constructed by the Construction Task Force (Jahad-e Sazandegi) of the IRIN and IRGC's al-Hadi Engineering Brigade, these were cylindrical metal buoys, each some 2 metres high and 2.5 metres wide, with a 4 metre tall mast on their top, mounting metal mesh. At least one such decoy was deployed – every two miles – north-west of every single tanker at the anchorage at Khark, and all the way up to Khowr Moussa. Every night, each was re-deployed into a slightly different position by tugboats. Further south, even bigger decoys – some up to 17 metres high, all made of iron alloys and with a radar reflector atop of their construction – were positioned all the way from Khark down to Lavan. These were inspected by Sikorsky SH-3D helicopters of the IRIN, every morning. Finally, ships wrecked during earlier attacks, and several intentionally grounded along sea routes and near anchorage areas, received IRGC-manned ZU-23 anti-aircraft guns, and acted as additional decoys. Such measures had proven highly effective in attracting dozens of Exocets – and this despite the fact that the former officers of the Intelligence Department of the IrAF stress they were in full knowledge about them.[15]

OPERATION SUGAR

Through 1982, Saddam Hussein issued three public warnings for ships in the Persian Gulf to stay away from Khark. All of his threats proved ineffective and there was no reduction in the traffic. In attempt of bringing his point home, the strongman in Baghdad then ordered the 224th Missile Brigade into action: between 18 and 22 August 1982, this unit fired 24 R-17Es at Khark. Nearly all of these missed their target, and less than a handful caused any damage to the oil tanks and pipelines: their only effect was to temporarily lengthen the loading times for a VLCC from 18 to 40 hours.[19]

When Scuds failed to show effects, Saddam ordered the IrAF and the Iraqi Navy into new attacks. However, while a total of 15 ships from the caravans underway to BIK, or returning from there, were damaged and four of these sunk by Exocets through 1982, No. 101 Squadron's stock of missiles was meanwhile down to only 15. Baghdad thus hurried to place an order for further 100, and Paris reacted positively, but announced their delivery would take more than two years.[20]

Left without a choice, the GHQ then ordered No. 109 Squadron into striking oil rigs in the Nowruz, Abuzar and Soroush fields in the northern Persian Gulf in February 1983. However, this unit had meanwhile lost nearly all of its Su-20Ms shot down by the Iranian air defences, and had to be completely re-equipped with Su-22M-3s – which resulted in it being out of action for months. Therefore, the Iraqi Navy was rushed into action: during the night from 1 to 2 May 1983 Iraqi Navy Osa fast missile craft attacked the Abuzar and Nowruz platforms with at least five P-15 Termit (ASCC/NATO-code 'SS-N-2 Styx') anti-ship missiles: two hit decoys, one fell into the water, one was shot down by a .50 calibre Browning machine gun, while one scored a direct hit on the Nowruz rig, killing one person and injuring several others. The IRIN retaliated near-instantly: its Combattante-IIB class fast missile craft IRINS *Shamshir* sunk one of the Osas, leaving 12 survivors of the crew to be picked out of the water by Super Frelons. After this failure, the Iraqi Navy ceased its operations not only against surface vessels underway along the Iranian coast, but also against oil platforms in the northern Persian Gulf.[21]

With Khark remaining safe, Tehran recovered not only the Khuzestan Province but also made a major comeback into the world oil market, and with the IRIAF and the IRIN making all Iraqi efforts in the northern Persian Gulf costly, Saddam concluded that there was a need for a dramatic escalation. The obvious solution was to avoid attacking frontally, and find the means to outflank the Iranian defences north of Khark. Therefore, starting from October 1982 he sent General Rasheed and his Foreign Minister, Tarik Aziz, to Paris to demand the delivery of 20 Super Etendards – the aircraft famed for their performance in combination with Exocet missiles during the Falklands War. Once again, it was General Audran who played the crucial role in convincing the government in Paris to ignore the insolvency of Iraq. A much more significant problem was the fact that the production line for this type was closed, and Dassault was in no position to offer any. Instead, the company offered to modify Mirage F.1EQ-5s with the capability to carry two Exocets. As an intermediate step, the French also cited the option of equipping two Falcon 50 business jets that were short of delivery with AM.39s. While highly satisfied with such offers, the Iraqis remained insistent: they needed solutions right on the spot, without any delays. Eventually, it was the managers of Dassault that came up with the idea: how about Paris 'discretely renting some Super Etendards' to Iraq? Representatives of the Aéronavale – the French Naval Aviation – fiercely opposed the idea, to no small degree because the aircraft were equipped for delivery of nuclear weapons. However, it was President Mitterrand who had the final say: on 26 May 1983, he ordered the Aéronavale to 'rent' five Super Etendards to Dassault, which in turn had the right to do with them whatever it wanted. Only a week later, 6 Iraqi pilots and 30 technicians drawn from No. 79, No.89 and No. 91 Squadrons arrived in France to start their training.[22]

As the IrAF mission completed its conversion courses run at the Naval Air Station Landvisau, 35 kilometres north-east of Brest on the Atlantic coast, in September 1983, the time came to initiate its transfer to Iraq. Run under the codename Operation *Sugar*, this began on the morning of 7 October 1983. Five French military pilots with false passports – and all officially employed by Dassault – flew five Super Etendards (serials 65, 66, 67 68, and 69) from Cazaux to Solenzara, on Corsica. At dawn the next morning, they transferred to the aircraft carrier *Clémanceau*, south of Cyprus: after refuelling, all five were catapulted into the afternoon skies. Upon entering Turkish airspace, they were joined by one Falcon 50, which

Iraqi Super Etendard-pilots and their French instructors in front of the aircraft with serial number 65 – one of five 'leased' to Iraq between 1983 and 1985 – at Landvisau, October 1983. The leader of the Iraqi team, Major Haytham Khattab Omar, is standing first from the left. (Ahmad Sadik Collection)

then led them all the way to Saddam AB – while also delivering a team of seven technicians and one pilot (Jacques de Villars), who had the duty of assisting the IrAF team in the process of working-up on the type.[23]

IRAQ'S 'BOMBER HARRIS'

One of the long-lasting repercussions of *Project Baz-3* was Saddam's decision to replace Major-General Mohammed Jisam al-Jabouri with Major-General Hamid Sha'ban at-Tikriti, in late 1983. Sha'ban was anything other than a novice to this position: a native of Saddam's hometown of Tikrit, trained to fly Hunters in the UK in the late 1950s, and a member of the Ba'ath Party since the early 1960s, he played the crucial role during both of coups in 1963, and the one in 1969, served as commander of Taqqaddum AB during the June 1967 War with Israel, then as the Deputy Commander IrAF for Training, before being appointed the C-in-C IrAF from 1976 until his retirement in 1979. Recalled to service in 1980, he initially served as an adviser to Defence Minister Adnan Khayrallah, before being reinstated as C-in-C IrAF.[24]

Ironically, Saddam's decision to re-appoint Sha'ban to this position was as criticised by many of IrAF officers as in US intelligence assessments. While the former complained about his 'lack of understanding for pilots', and some described him as a 'Sunni extremist', the latter linked Sha'ban's re-appointment with his proximity to Saddam, and argued that he was picked because the strongman in Baghdad was sure Sha'ban would not challenge the regime's handling of air operations.[25]

However, when studying Sha'ban's conduct of aerial warfare against Iran from 1984 until 1988, it is not only his relations to Saddam that require a closer look, but also the fact that he was – just like his predecessor – constantly subordinated to Army officers, most of whom had very little experience in air operations and even less understanding of the capabilities of modern air power. Specifically, through all of the 1980s, the C-in-C IrAF served under the Chief of the Armed Forces General Staff and the GHQ in Baghdad, both of which were almost exclusively staffed by Army officers.[26]

'Iraq's Bomber Harris': Major-General Hamid Sha'ban at-Tikriti in his office at the HQ IrAF, in the late 1980s. (Ahmad Sadik Collection)

Actually, once back in office, and precisely because of his good relations to Saddam, Sha'ban was in a perfect position to initiate a fundamental reform of the IrAF's strategy: understanding that the same was just as governed by political decisions as by capabilities and opportunities, he first decided to study the latter more closely. Therefore, in 1985 he had set up a joint committee consisting of

Brigadier-General Salim Sultan al-Basu: the actual master-mind not only behind Iraq's Oil Campaign, as run in the period 1984-1988, but also most of the long-range operations for which the Iraqi Mirages became famous during this period. (via Ali Tobchi)

his two Deputy Operations – Brigadier-Generals Salim Sultan al-Basu and Hassan Hajj Khudur – and senior experts from the Iraqi Ministry of Oil. Supplied with reconnaissance photographs and intelligence reports, this committee then began advising not only him, but also Saddam – and thus the involved IrAF units – about target selection: precisely this advice was to prove crucial not only for the conduct of IrAF's offensive operations, but indeed that of the entire war against Iran.[27]

Sha'ban and Basu were two of very few Iraqi generals with full understanding of the new technologies meanwhile available to the IrAF. Over the years Sha'ban was the driving force behind decisions to obtain Mirages, and together with Basu he then played a crucial role in acquiring and deploying MiG-25RBs for high-altitude bombing raids, but also in the deployment of Mirage F.1EQs for low-altitude, precision air strikes with the help of AS.30L guided missiles. In comparison, it required not only Saddam but also the majority of other Iraqi generals and Ba'ath Party apparatchiks such bitter pills as the loss of the Faw Peninsula, in February 1986, to finally let Sha'ban run the air war the way he always wanted to do and to orchestrate a truly effective Oil Campaign.[28]

Unsurprisingly, to most of the Iranians in the picture about him, and a handful of well-informed foreign observers, Sha'ban was known as something akin to Iraq's 'Bomber Harris': a commander that not only reformed the IrAF's way of strategic thinking, but the one that launched an aggressive aerial campaign against Iran's centres of gravity – and its oil industry in particular.[29]

SADDAM'S NEW ORDERS

By early 1984, the KARI IADS/ATMS was fully operational. With the help of Syrel-equipped Mirages, the GHQ in Baghdad suddenly realized that the IrAF was free to operate unchallenged by IRIAF's interceptors up to 100 kilometres deep over Iran. Sha'ban promptly began orchestrating operations of ever larger formations drawn from different units and bases, and thus establishing air supremacy over the battlefield – which the IrAF was to maintain until the end of war. Lessons still had to be learnt, and some of the early such operations resulted in failures. For example, on 2 January 1984, the MiG-23s deployed to distract F-14 CAPs covering a caravan underway for BIK remained in the combat zone much too long, and the aircraft flown by 1st Lieutenant Abdul Hussein Hassan was shot down and its pilot killed by an AIM-54A fired by Major Fazlollah Javid-Nia (RIO was Lieutenant Mohammad Oqbaei). In turn, the Super Frelons wrecked the cargo ship *Iran Emamat* with one Exocet.[30]

With reinforcements thus reaching their destination, the Iranians launched their next major offensive, Operation *Khyber*, attempting to cut off the land connection between Baghdad and Basra through an advance over the Howeyzeh marshes on 22 February 1984. Their initial success caused enough panic in Baghdad to prompt Saddam into recalling his order from early 1982 and ordering the IrAF to 'take risks when striking targets'. Simultaneously, the strongman in Baghdad felt compelled into taking special measures in attempt to curb operations of the Iranian F-14s: amongst others, he spread fake rumours about within the circles of the GCC diplomats in Baghdad, to the effect that '...some Iranian pilots wanted to desert with their F-14 aircraft', and that 'arrangements have been made for some of them to seek asylum in Iraq', in the knowledge that these rumours would end up in Tehran, one way or another.[31]

Encouraged by Colonel Kaldoon K Bakir – a veteran Sukhoi-pilot and commander of the Hurriyah AB, initiator of the test-deployment of Belouga-armed Mirages in support of the Iraqi ground troops encircled near the border town of Zarbatya, in July 1983 – Sha'ban reached the decision to deploy Mirages for ground-attacks, too.[32]

The first task assigned to No. 79 Squadron was to strike one of the embarkation points for IRGC troops carried by speedboats to Majnoon Isle. Based on intelligence collected by MiG-25RBs the previous afternoon, this mission was launched on 25 February 1984, and led by Major Salah Ismail Nasser. It included eight Mirage F.1EQ-4s, each armed with four 400kg SAMP Type-21C bombs. Sadik recalled the – much anticipated – post-mission de-brief:

> The formation was protected by one F.1EQ-2 equipped with a Syrel pod, two equipped with Caiman-pods, a pair of MiG-23MFs on a CAP, and four Su-22 armed with Kh-28s, just in case the nearby Iranian SAM-site would switch its radar on. The Mirages came in at an altitude of 6,000 metres, designated their targets with help of the radar, and then dove to attack. The computer of the fire-control system took over and prompted the pilot to squeeze the trigger through symbology on the head-up-display. Bombs were released from an altitude of 4,000 metres, well above the engagement envelope of several 35mm Oerlikon flaks identified bellow. While pulling up and to the right, Salah looked back to see multiple wakes left behind by Iranian boats. As he levelled his aircraft, he could see that others from his formation performed the same manoeuvre as he did. He watched the explosions from all 32 bombs engulfing the area. Subsequent interrogation of Iranian prisoners of war revealed that they've been caught in the open and that a number of buses and speedboats were hit: this attack prevented an entire wave of Iranian troops from reaching the Majnoon Islet on that day.'[33]

What the Iraqis subsequently concluded as a 'total success' was quickly overshadowed the next morning, when the IrAF lost one of its Tu-22 bombers from No. 36 Squadron to IRIAF HAWK SAMs while attempting to hit the same area. Therefore, Sha'aban not only ordered another Baz-AR strike by No. 79 Squadron, but its Mirages to be armed with entirely new tools of the trade.[34]

Spanish-made EXPAL BR.500 bombs filled with chemical agents, as found by UN inspectors in Iraq during the 1990s. (US DoD)

The Iraqis also manufactured their own chemical warfare bombs: designated R-400, based on the design of the SAMP Type 21C of French origin. (US DoD)

CHEMICAL WEAPONS AND NEW BOMBS

With most of the available bombs proving of limited effectiveness early during the fighting in the Howeizeh marshes, the GHQ in Baghdad ordered the deployment of chemical weapons (CWs) instead. Although an issue around which all the surviving IrAF officers make a wide detour, the available evidence is rather obvious. Originally, the MIC launched the development of chemical weapons for deterrent purposes – foremost against Israel's 'nuclear option': however, the resulting agents were now to see continuously increasing use against Iran in a program subjected to tight security measures and controlled from a special HQ in Baghdad that planned and ran all the related operations on strategic, operational, and tactical levels.[36]

The first massive use of Iraqi CWs was reported by the Iranians during Operation *Khyber*. Certainly enough, the IrAF experienced numerous problems early on: foremost, bombs filled with chemical agents were released from much too high altitude to permit accurate, concentrated attacks. Nevertheless, because the IRGC's infantry lacked any means of protection, they regularly proved murderously effective. Within only 24 hours of their deployment, on 28 February 1984, the Iranians reported 400 casualties: this figure soon rose to 6,200, of whom 1,200 were killed in attacks that took place on 2, 3, 7, and 9 March 1984. The almost exclusive means of CW-deployment during this period were Spanish-made EXPAL BR.250 bombs filled with nerve agents like sarin and mustard.[37]

The BR.250s were soon followed by heavier BR.500s, Mk.84s (1,000kg) licence manufactured in Spain, and then by Portuguese-made bombs based on the US-made Mk.80-series. The first mission including the deployment of BR.500s was once again led by Major Nasser: flown in early March 1984 it resulted in the formation leader neatly placing three out of four of his bombs down the 20-kilometre long Iranian pontoon bridge to Majnoon Isle, cutting it at three points. During the following weeks, the Iraqis began using Mk.84s equipped with Jupiter fuses made in South Africa, which detonated them at between 10 and 12 metres above the ground or water surface, thus significantly increasing their lethality. In turn, relations with Pretoria resulted in the MIC acquiring the licence for production of the CB.470 CBU, under the local designation SCB.470.[38]

Wreck of one of many unexploded SAMP Type 21, deployed by Iraqi Mirages during the fighting in the Howeyzeh marshes: the soft soil tended to dampen the effects of their detonations, or cause fuses to fail, prompting the IrAF into searching for alternatives. (Farzin Nadimi Collection)

Wreckage of a Spanish-made, EXPAL BR.250WP chemical warfare bomb, as found by the Iranians during the fighting in the Howeyzeh marshes in April 1984. (Tom Cooper Collection)

Another type of weapon introduced by the IrAF around the same time were Cardoen CB.250 and CB.500 CBUs, made in Chile. However, according to Sadik, these weapons – essentially copies of US-made Mk.20 Rockeye CBUs – turned out to be poorly manufactured: they tended to open prematurely, shortly after release (thus resulting in their bomblets flying at the same altitude as the aircraft deploying them) and up to 50-60% failed to detonate.[39]

EXOCET RAIDERS

In addition to ordering the IrAF into action regardless of risks, Operation *Khyber* prompted Saddam into the realisation that the Oil Campaign run in the period 1980-1983 was an abysmal failure. It not only failed to diminish Iran's oil exports (by early 1984, these actually reached their highest levels since the revolution of 1978-1979), but also failed to prevent the flow of the Iranian reinforcements and supplies for BIK. Therefore, he ordered Sha'ban to press the newly-delivered Super Etendards into action – this time with the intention not to disrupt, but to cut off Iran's oil exports.[40]

AEROSPATIALE AM.39 EXOCET[16]

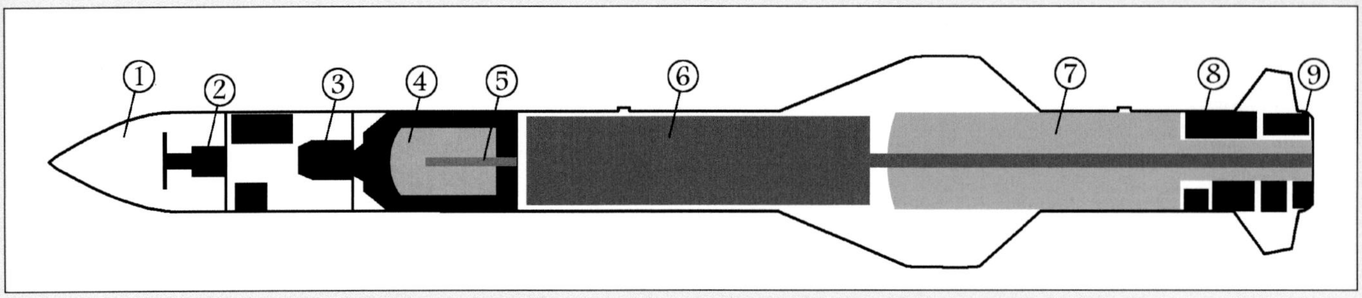

A simplified diagram of the internal arrangement of the 470cm (4.7m) long, 652kg (1,437lbs) AM.39 Exocet missile, including:

1) the radome made of dielectric material; 2) the Electronique Serge Dassault (ESD) ADAC radar seeker head and Sfena autopilot;

3) avionics compartment for the SAGEM inertial navigation system including a computer, vertical gyro, TRT RAM.01 radio altimeter, the guidance command processor, axial gyro, and radio altimeter antenna; 4) Société d'Etudes, de Réalisations et d'Applications Techniques (SERAT) cast steel case penetration and fragmentation 344mm warhead, weighting 160 kilograms, containing a 60/40 hexolite-type explosive;

5) fuse; 6) cruise (or sustainer) motor; 7) booster motor; 8) aft avionics compartment with 9) power-steering for fins.

This series of photographs is showing a Super Etendard of the Aeronavale while releasing an Exocet missile in the course of a test. Notable is how the booster motor was activated only once the missile was well bellow the aircraft. (Dassault/Aéronavale, via Hugues de Guillebon)

Manufactured by Aerospatiale's *Division Engins Tactiques*, the AM.39 Exocet was the air launched, active radar homing anti-ship variant of the original MM.38 Exocet sea-launched version. Its longer range and decreased weight became possible through the replacement of the light alloy motor envelopes of the original variant by thin steel ones, filled with more powerful solid fuel. The result was a shortened cruise motor that burned longer than in the MM.38, while providing the same thrust.

While the MM.38 entered service with the French Navy in July 1977, the AM.39 became available only in early 1980. The initial production rate was 18 units per month, and the 440th Exocet was delivered in early 1982, by when the company had secured orders from Argentina, France, Iraq, Pakistan, Qatar, and South Africa. After the contract for *Project Baz-3* was signed in February of the same year, the production rate was increased to 25 units a month.

Although usually claimed to have been first used in wartime operations in May 1982 – by Super Etendards of the Argentinean naval aviation against the Royal Navy during the Falklands/Malvinas War of the same year – actually, the AM.39 saw its first combat deployment in October 1980, when several were fired by Super Frelon helicopters of No.101 Squadron of the Iraqi Navy against merchant ships approaching BIK.

Functionality of the AM.39 Exocet missile was heavily dependent on following factors:

- The launcher aircraft had to be equipped with a suitable search radar and equipment necessary to program targeting data into the missile's seeker-head.
- The launcher aircraft had to be equipped with a source of power compatible with the missile's circuit, and necessary to power-up the missile before its release.
- The launcher aircraft had to be equipped with the necessary wiring – cabling for power supply and the communication between the cockpit and the missile, weighting about 40kg (81lbs) in total, and with a corresponding launcher, weighting another 75kg (165lbs). i.e. the full installation of an AM.39 Exocet was adding a total of 767kg (1683lbs) to the aircraft's or helicopter's weight.

Depending on the speed and altitude of the launch aircraft, the AM.39 Exocet had a range of up to 70 kilometres (or 44 miles) – if released from an altitude of more than 5,000 metres. In combat, it was most often released from ranges of less than 50 kilometres (32.3 miles), and altitudes of between 100 and 200 metres. Upon release, the missile free-fell 15-20 metres below the aircraft before the booster was ignited.

Two Iraqi Super Etendards thus launched their first combat sortie under circumstances described by one of the involved pilots in an interview to Brigadier-General Sadik:

> On 26 February 1984, we received an order to arm two of our aircraft with two AM.39 Exocet missiles. Later that day, me and a fellow pilot ferried to Jalibah forward operating base (FOB). Strict security was in place, and we were separated from several MiG-21 pilots from No. 11 Squadron, based there. At 2200hrs, we finally took off heading south before turning directly towards the Iranian port of Bushehr. At 2245hrs, we fired our first missiles in anger ever – against ships detected inside the port. We both saw flames rising from our targets. The next day, the Iraqi newspaper headlines read, "Iraq strikes using the Super Etendard". The

AEROSPATIALE AM.39 EXOCET (CONTINUED)

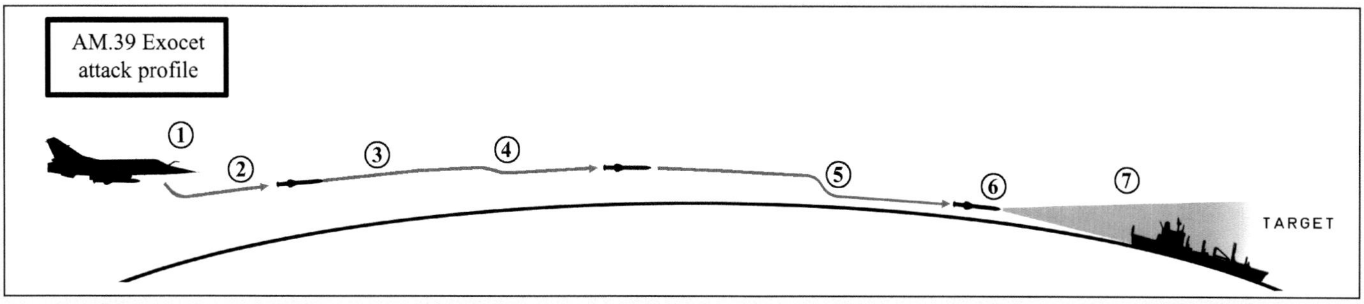

Diagram of the operational trajectory of the AM.39 Exocet anti-ship missile, including: 1) missile release; 2) & 3) the cruise phase during which the missile was steered along a pre-programmed route; 4) first descent to a lower altitude; 5) second descent to the flight altitude for terminal attack. At a pre-determined point, the ADAC seeker head would activate (6), guiding the missile on the target (7). (Diagram by Tom Cooper)

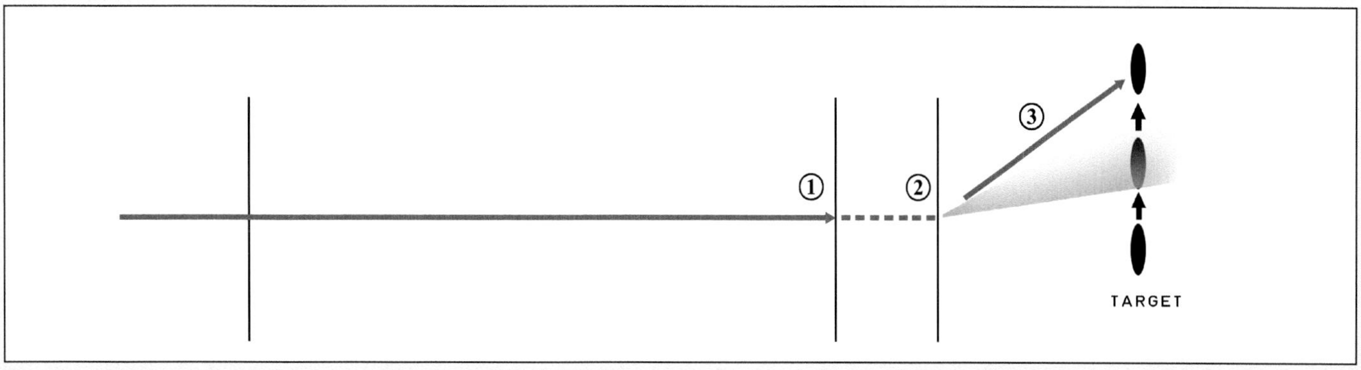

Top view of the operational trajectory and function of the AM.39 Exocet anti-ship missile. Upon release, the missile would cruise to a pre-determined point (1) before activating the ADAC seeker head; the seeker head would make one sweep starting from the left (2); and then adjust the trajectory of the missile to an intercept course (3). (Diagram by Tom Cooper)

During a high-altitude release, the missile could reach a supersonic initial speed, before decelerating to subsonic speed of Mach 0.93. During a low-altitude release, the missile always travelled at a speed of about Mach 0.90-0.93. About 1.5 seconds after release, and once stabilised and underway in the direction of its target, the missile's automatic guidance system would activate. This would steer the weapon along a pre-programmed route with the help of guidance from one axial and one vertical gyroscope, which worked in conjunction with three accelerometers. Coupled with the radio altimeter, the resulting 'inertial platform' allowed the missile to enter a gradual descent towards the sea surface: this was automatically selected so as to keep the missile high enough to acquire the target with its seeker head, if necessary, but low enough to avoid detection.

At the end of the cruise phase, the missile would activate its ADAC active radar seeker-head before descending to the sea skimming altitude for the terminal phase of its attack. Alternatively, the seeker-head could be pre-programmed to activate only later on, during the approach or terminal flight phase.

Like the Baz-AR, the AM.39 represented the peak of analogue technology. Once activated, the ADAC active radar seeker-head would sweep a predetermined zone, which had to be sufficient for any navigational and target designation errors (like those caused by the movement and manoeuvring of the target). The seeker-head was set to make one sweep starting from the left, to lock-on to the first target it acquired with a radar cross section (RCS) of 600 square metres or greater, and then guide the missile to the point with the highest radar-cross section on the target (usually the ship's bridge).[17]

Depending on the sea state, the flight altitude during the terminal phase could be programmed at between 2 and 6 metres. The general rule was for the missile to impact its target at the same altitude at which it was programmed to fly during the terminal phase. Because this was likely to result in the missile overflying a smaller target – or one sitting deep in the sea – the AM.39 was equipped with a proximity fuse, set to detonate the warhead when the missile was above the deck.

The Iranian decoys for Exocets were designed to exploit the relatively primitive technology of the ADAC seeker-head in the simplest possible fashion: because the latter began its scan from left towards right, every Exocet tended to go after the 'first target from the left', too; and, because the Iraqis were always attacking from the West, AM.39s always went for the northernmost target they would detect. Therefore, whenever alerted about an incoming Iraqi Exocet-strike, skippers of merchant ships involved in Operation *Caravan* were advised to seek a position to the south-east of the nearest decoy. Later on, supertankers involved in Operation *Tanker Shuttle* (see below for details) would be protected by smaller vessels towing decoys in front of them (i.e. 'to the left' as seen from the Iraqi point of view) while underway to Khark, or they would tow such decoys when underway towards the south.[18]

> Lloyds of London later confirmed that Iraq had attacked ships inside Bushehr harbour.

No reports that bear any relation to this attack were ever released by Iranian sources, and the list of ships attacked during that war subsequently published by the Lloyds of London, cites no vessel attacked on that date. On the contrary, merchants anchored in Bushehr or loading at Khark on 26 February 1984 denied that any attack had taken place.[41]

Iraq's campaign against tankers exporting Iranian crude thus began in earnest only a month later, on 27 March 1984, when two Super Etendards reached over 400 kilometres out of Jalibah FOB to attack south-west of Khark. Even then, their first victim was the Greek tanker *Filikon L*, carrying Kuwaiti crude for Italy: this was

The flight operating the Super Etendards was led by Major Haytham Khattab Omar: this photograph shows four of its five pilots at the end of their conversion course at Landvisau in October 1983. Notable is the 'censored' serial number applied underneath the cockpit, and the unusual inclination of the fin flash on the aircraft behind them. (Ahmad Sadik Collection)

lightly damaged by a missile that penetrated the hull two metres above the waterline on the starboard side, but its warhead failed to detonate. The ship was able to proceed and the missile was later defused by the US Navy. Less lucky was the South Korean supply ship *Heyang Ilho*, hit while underway in the Marjan offshore oilfield, 100 kilometres southwest of Khark, and sunk.[42]

The resulting irony escaped the public attention: in what is viewed by many as the 'beginning of the Tanker War', the Iraqi Super Etendard pilots hit a ship owned by an ally, carrying oil actually used to pay for their French-made aircraft, their training in France – and their French-made missiles – which then malfunctioned.

Superstructure of the Saudi supertanker *Al Ahood*, wrecked by an Exocet hit, on 7 May 1984. The ship was written off, though her load was saved – and delivered to France as a payment for the Iraqi Super Etendards and Exocets that caused the damage. (Tom Cooper Collection)

FIRE AND FORGET

The next attempt nearly ended in catastrophe: a pair of Super Etendards attempting to sneak upon a convoy including the Iranian tanker *Tabriz* some 150 kilometres south of Bushehr, on 30 March 1984, was intercepted by a pair of F-14As led by Colonel All-e-Agha. Trying to save precious AIM-54 missiles, the Iranian pilot descended and engaged with 20mm cannon instead: he missed and both Iraqis escaped into the Saudi airspace. Two days later, on 2 April 1984, one of two Super Etendards detected by the Iranians while passing the port of Umm Qassr at low altitude was narrowly missed by an AIM-7E-2 Sparrow fired by an F-4E from the TFB.6. Such experiences taught the IrAF that Super Etendards were in need of better support: henceforth, each mission over the Persian Gulf was covered by Syrel and Caiman equipped Mirage F.1EQ-2s, and MiG-23MFs that had the task of dragging IRIAF's F-14s away. With the necessary planning and organisation taking some time, it was only on 18 April 1984 that the Super Etendards finally served their purpose: on that day, one of two Exocets they had released hit the British-owned tanker *Rover Star,* underway under the flag of Panama, merely a mile from Khark. The missile failed to detonate and thus caused no damage: the ship completed her loading and then continued the voyage. On the contrary, the next 'successful' Super Etendard-strike once again resulted in rather ironic consequences: on 25 April 1984, the Saudi-owned *Safina al-Arab* was set ablaze by an

Kamal Hussein Kazem al-Ansari (standing in the centre) with a group of Iraqi technicians during the training at Landvisau in France. (via Ali Tobchi)

Exocet a few hours after leaving Khark with a load of 340,000 tonnes of crude bound for France. The fact that the Super Etendards thus had again hit a ship carrying a load that was, essentially, paying for them was of more than 'passing interest': while her Saudi owners had to declare their vessel as 'considered total loss' (CTL), this attack at least caused a loss of 1,000 tonnes of the load. Unsurprisingly, a week lapsed before an unapologetic Saddam admitted Iraq's responsibility.[43]

While there is no doubt that their pilots tried very hard, the results of the Iraqi Super Etendard operations remained poor over the following weeks. The Exocet that hit the Emirati-owned freighter *Sea Eagle* on 27 April failed to detonate, but the next tanker hit – by two missiles, on 7 May 1984 – was not only Saudi-owned, but also hauling crude directly to France: *al-Ahood* was declared CTL, though her load was saved by salvage ships.[44]

FAHD LINE AND MIRAGE ALLEY

In retaliation for Iraqi anti-ship attacks, on 7 May 1984 Iran launched its own campaign against vessels underway to Saudi and Kuwaiti ports. Already the first two such strikes had provoked the Saudi government into an unprecedented measure: the establishment of the 'Fahd Line' – a de-facto no-fly zone for Iranian aircraft encompassing all of the Saudi airspace, but also that around the Saudi offshore oilfields and thus positioned well to the east of, and outside of, the Saudi border. The zone was protected by recently delivered McDonnell Douglas F-15C Eagle interceptors of the Royal Saudi Air Force (RSAF), supported by E-3A Sentry AWACS of the ELF-1, based at Dahran AB. The IrAF exploited this opportunity to – supported by a Caiman-equipped Mirage, and two MiG-23MFs – sent two Super Etendards into the area south of Khark, on the afternoon of 21 May: after finding no targets within the designated area, the jets continued further east and fired their missiles from about 40 kilometres range at what their pilots considered would be ships anchored off Bushehr. Both aircraft returned to Wahda safely, and a MiG-25RB was launched to take post-strike photographs: the latter would have shown that the construction site of the nuclear reactor south of Bushehr was covered by smoke, and the Iraqis promptly misinterpreted this as that one of the tall constructions in this area had been hit by an Exocet.[45]

As the Iranians continued retaliating, tensions increased to a level where on 5 June 1984, the strong-willed Chief-of-Staff RSAF, Lieutenant-General Ahmad al-Buhairi, did something even his Minister of Defence – Prince Bandar Ibn Saud – attempted to avoid: he ordered the USAF AWACS to vector two F-15s to intercept two F-4Es from TFB.6 that crossed the Fahd Line. Reluctantly, the Saudi pilots followed the order and shot down one of the Phantoms, killing its crew. While the IRIAF pilots in Bushehr were eager to retaliate, realising it was ill-positioned to wage a war against Saudi Arabia at the same time it was fighting Iraq, Tehran refrained from seeking revenge: indeed the TFB.6 received a standing order not to cross the Fahd Line again. With a single blow, the IrAF was thus not only left free to roam up and down the western coast of the Persian Gulf at will, but could do so under protection of Saudi interceptors. Unsurprisingly, this area soon became known as the 'Mirage Alley' to the seamen underway in the area.[46]

Combined with the deception operations by the IrAF further north, and deployment of Caiman-equipped Mirage F.1EQ-2s, the availability of the Mirage Alley resulted in a gradual decrease of at least semi-successful intercepts of Super Etendards by the IRIAF. On 26 July 1984, one AIM-54A proximity fused next to a pair of Super Etendards passing Farsi Island without causing damage, while another missed on 7 August 1984. When, four days later, a pair of brand-new MiG-23MLs shot down and killed Colonel All-e-Agha while he was on a CAP protecting a caravan bound for BIK, the IRIAF was shocked to a degree where it stopped maintaining constant patrols over Khark. In attempt to lessen the strain upon its Tomcats – but also the supporting Boeing 707-2J9C tankers – it re-deployed a detachment of six from TFB.8 to TFB.6, from where these were scrambled only as necessary.[47]

This is what enabled the Iraqis to intensify and then move their anti-ship operations further south during the last four months of that year, and especially in December 1984. Nevertheless, the total efficiency of their operations remained poor. While comparing each and every resulting claim with actual results would go well beyond the scope of this project, it is sufficient to say that according to contemporary reports from Baghdad, more than 60 ships were destroyed in attacks by Super Etendards and Super Frelons between January and early May 1984. Actually, only 18 were hit: one supply vessel was sunk outright, while four merchants and tankers were written off – and at least two of these were tankers carrying crude used to pay for the entire Iraqi effort.[48]

The situation improved only slightly during the second half of

A post-strike reconnaissance photograph taken by a MiG-25RB showing the results of one of the strikes on the Iranian oil rigs in the Nowrouz oilfield, in the northern Persian Gulf, in 1984. While confirming damage through showing 'fire and smoke', most of these photographs were insufficient to let the Iraqis know exactly how much damage they had actually caused. (Ahmad Sadik Collection)

the year: while Baghdad claimed nearly 80 ships destroyed, 31 were actually hit (4 others were damaged in collisions due to Exocet attacks) by Super Etendards and by Super Frelons: three of these (none was a tanker) were sunk outright, while 19 were declared CTL. In turn, one Super Etendard (original serial number 67, IrAF serial 4667) was lost over the Persian Gulf: soon after releasing an Exocet in the direction of Khark during the night from 16 to 17 September 1984, Lieutenant Kamal Hussein Kazem al-Ansari disappeared without a trace. Overall, the Iranian oil exports continued to grow, the flow of the caravans to BIK experienced only periodic interruptions, and in Iran, Khark earned itself the reputation of invincibility.[49]

SADDAM'S PILOTS

By this time, one would expect either somebody at Saddam AB, or at least in Baghdad to develop second thoughts about the viability of the entire effort invested into the Oil Campaign. Nothing similar happened: Baghdad generally continued cheering Saddam's decision to persist with his expectation that wildly exaggerated claims would scare international shippers away from Khark and the Iranian ports. Although related media reports were successful in attracting an increasing amount of public attention in the West, and while the Saudis and Emiratis decided to stop sending their ships to Iran, others – better informed about the actual effectiveness of Iraqi anti-ship strikes than Baghdad ever was – refused to do so: in another paradox of this war, the ultimate casualty of Iraqi exaggerations was the credibility of the government in Baghdad.

Moreover, nobody in Iraq, and nobody in France was in a position to advise the Iraqi strongman. Before 1984, Exocets were deployed against relatively small merchant ships underway towards BIK. With the missile usually homing on the section of the ship with the highest radar cross section, the few that actually hit their targets tended to aim underneath the ship's bridge, and thus detonate inside the engine room. The combined effect of the impact, the detonation of the warhead, the unspent fuel of the missile and that in the ship often resulted in fatal damage. However, except for acquiring few photographs showing 'fire and smoke' caused by earlier attacks, and scant reports from surviving seamen, as of early 1984 neither the French nor the Iraqis had serious knowledge about what kind of damage an Exocet could – or could not – cause to a target the size of a very large crude carrier (VLCC), or the ultra-large cruder carrier (ULCC; colloquially 'supertanker'). Unsurprisingly, the imaginations on both sides of their partnership ran wild: only years later would they finally conclude that the AM.39 was simply not up to the task of sinking such huge ships, nor indeed of causing any significant damage to Khark.

Furthermore, although claiming that their radars positioned on the Faw Peninsula and the two offshore rigs further south were capable of detecting and tracking all the ships moving along the Iranian coast as far as 200 kilometres away, or that they operated a network of informers on Kuwaiti merchant ships and in the Port Authority of Abu Dhabi, neither the GMID, nor the IrAF had any serious idea about what was going on along the Iranian coast south of Khowr Mousa. At best, they were reliant on intercepting related radio communications of the IRIN. Therefore, Baghdad was completely unable to provide meaningful targeting intelligence to its Super Etendard pilots. Combined with the Iraqi predilection to close their ears to what one does not wish to hear, the result was precisely the mix of myths about the so-called Tanker War that's prevalent in related reporting to this day: always supported by Caiman-equipped Mirages, and MiG-23MF/ML-interceptors that were decoying Iranian F-14s away from them, well-trained pilots were flying what were actually very dangerous missions, but deploying their expensive weapons in highly inefficient way, and with unknown results. While there is little doubt that they were required to do their utmost in order to complete attacks on the selected targets, and that they did their best to follow their orders, the Exocet was a 'fire and forget' weapon: what happened upon its release was simply outside the powers of everybody involved and the Iraqi military intelligence had next to no reliable means of finding out if any had actually hit something – other than their being a related report released by the foreign media. Moreover, it appears the IrAF's internal security services became suspicious of pilots who had returned without firing their Exocets: unsurprisingly, these developed a strong tendency to fire at any target appearing on their radar screens, and declare another large naval target as destroyed. As so often, Saddam then added a cherry to the cake: always preferring to lavishly distribute medals, financial and other rewards to the pilots involved, he convinced them that they did well, one way or the other, and continued distributing decorations. Eventually, the Mirage and Super Etendard pilots involved soon became known as 'Saddam's pilots' within the IrAF.[50]

5
COMPLACENCY

The year 1984 ended, and the year 1985 began with a flurry of Iraqi claims for Exocet attacks in the area between 100 and 180 kilometres south and southeast of Khark: once again, the number of ships actually hit was less than 50% of those claimed as destroyed. Moreover, the Iranians subsequently emptied the sea: for a while at least, the Iraqi impression was that all the ships usually underway in this area had disappeared. Before their intelligence were able to find out what was going on, Iran launched its next big offensive in the Howeizeh Marshes, thus distracting Baghdad's attention away from the Persian Gulf.

IRAQI EXOCET

On 26 September 1984, the first two Mirage F.1EQ-5s were delivered to Saddam AB. The centrepiece of this new sub-variant's avionics was the SAGEM UNI 47 inertial navigation system (INS), coupled with the Cyrano-IVQ/C5 radar, which was capable of detecting surface targets out to a range of 120 kilometres. The nav/attack suite was also compatible with the Thomson-CSF TVT.601 IFF, which was interoperable with Soviet-made systems. Alternatively to carrying one AM.39 under the centreline for anti-ship attacks, the F.1EQ-5 could be equipped with the Thomson-CSF PDL.1EQ Patrick laser designator and Aerospatiale AS.30L laser-guided missiles, 20 and 569 of which were ordered, respectively. Before long, this sub-variant earned itself the reputation of a 'Rolls Royce' amongst Iraqi Mirage pilots, the first group of which – all drawn from already existing units – underwent a conversion course at Orange AB between May and August 1984, while their ground crews were trained at the Special Technical Instruction School in Reims, and at the Aeronavale's facility in Bourges. The F.1EQ-5s entered service with the newly-established No. 81 Squadron, based at Saddam AB and commanded by Major Haytham Khatab Ommar.[1]

As usual, French advisors first put No. 81 Squadron through intensive exercises before declaring it operational on 1 January 1985. However, pressure from above resulted in the unit flying its first combat mission over the Persian Gulf on 3 December 1984. Including two Super Etendards and two Mirage F.1EQ-5s (in addition to the usual Syriel-equipped example, a pair of Caiman-equipped aircraft, and at least two MiG-23s), this mission failed due to missile interface problems. Despite obligatory inspections and rehearsals, the second, launched on 2 January 1985, then also experienced additional failures. As so often, the devil was in the detail. The reason for the problems was that together with the F.1EQ-5s, the IrAF began deploying a new sub-variant of the AM.39, upgraded on the basis of earlier experiences: nick-named the 'Iraqi Exocet', this contained a seeker-head modified to make three radar sweeps before going for a target with more than 1,000 square metres RCS. If the target was smaller, the seeker head was to start a new search.[2]

Experiencing the typical set of 'teething problems' whenever a sophisticated weapon is rushed to operational service, the Iraqi Exocet was to continue malfunctioning even after the first batch was subjected to detailed inspections and several repairs by French

Table 5: Structure of IrAF's Mirage-Units, 1985-1988

Unit	Base	Commander	Notes
No. 79 Squadron	Abu Ubaida	Major Salah Ismail Nasser	Mirage F.1EQ-2/EQ-4; ground attack, reconnaissance with COR-2 and HAROLD, Baz-AR, Syrel and Caiman operations; detachment at Ali Ibn Abu Talib AB
No. 81 Squadron	Saddam	Major Haytham Khatab Ommar	Mirage F.1EQ-5; anti-ship operations; regular detachments at Wahda AB and diverse FOBs in southern Iraq
No. 89 Squadron	Saddam	Major Wallid	Mirage F.1EQ-2, Mirage F.1BQ; OCU, air defence & ground attack; detachment at H-2/Sa'ad AB and H-3/Wallid AB
No. 91 Squadron	Abu Ubaida	Lt.-Col. Munir Bashar Hassan	Mirage F.1EQ-4; ground attack

The first Mirage F.1EQ-5 – serial number 4560 – was initially retained in France and used for testing purposes. This photograph is showing it just before take-off, with an AM.39 Exocet test round. (Dassault)

Another pre-delivery photograph of the F.1EQ-5 serial number 4560, this time in what was probably the heaviest configuration on this type ever, including an AM.39 Exocet under the right wing, balanced by an RP.35 drop tank under the left; a pair each of dummy R.550 Magic missiles and Remora pods, and an Irakien drop tank under the centreline. Due to the limitations imposed by its internal power supply, this variant could still carry and deploy only one Exocet in combat. (Dassault)

advisors present in Iraq. For example, during an attack on a caravan underway for BIK on 7 January 1985, one failed to detonate after striking the bulk carrier *Topaz Express*, while another failed to detonate after holing the cargo ship *Hanlim Mariner*. With the French still busy searching for the cause of the problems, and the IrAF then busy fighting the next Iranian offensive, the Iraqis continued deploying Super Etendards and older Exocets instead. On 11 January 1985, two attempted to hit another caravan for BIK, and one of their missiles wrecked the bulk carrier *Iran Emdad*. Nevertheless, the rest of the convoy delivered its cargo and this was soon in action against Iraq. Indeed, technical issues with brand-new F.1EQ-5s and Iraqi Exocets continued to persist until at least November 1985, resulting in another year of rather meagre results for the Oil Campaign: only 34 ships were confirmed as hit by French anti-ship missiles, two of which (including just one tanker) were sunk, even if eleven others were declared CTL.[3]

TANKER SHUTTLE

If the appearance of Mirage F.1EQ-5s and new Exocets had any effects, then it was to prompt the IRIN into a major reorganization of all oil-exporting and caravan operations. Recognizing that the Iraqis were about to intensify their campaign, the Iranian seamen did their best to leave the enemy without suitable targets. Therefore, in February 1985, they decided to stop letting their customer's ships load directly at Khark, and shifted such operations to a 'temporary', floating terminal off the Sirri Island codenamed *Terminal-14* (or 'T-14'). Henceforth, the crude was picked up at Khark by a fleet of dedicated 'shuttle tankers' – vessels either purchased or leased within Operation *Val Fajr-1*. Equipped with upgraded fire-fighting equipment (sometimes also ESM-systems for detection of radar emissions from Cyrano-radars and Exocets), and operated by specially trained crews, shuttle tankers usually made way in convoys of four (seldom more) ships, escorted by warships of the IRIN. In turn, in attempt to decrease the strain upon worn-out IRIN warships involved in escorting operations, the size of caravans for BIK was decreased to between three and five merchants.[4]

While the number of shuttle tankers grew from the original 9 in 1985 to 34 in 1988, the actual centrepieces of this enterprise were so-called 'motherships': ULCCs filled from one side by shuttle tankers, and emptied from the other by customer tankers. By June 1986, additional motherships – including some of largest ships ever built – became available, all using the simple ship-to-ship technique. Two of these were positioned between Larak and Bandar Abbas (terminal codenamed T-18 run within frame of Operation *Val Fajr-2*), and the others near Hormuz Island. Finally, four ULCCs were chartered to serve for storage purposes at T-14.[5]

Another reason for numerous failures of the Iraqi Exocets in 1985 was that except for the seeker head, the rest of the missile remained the same – which meant that they continued experiencing problems after hitting targets the size of the VLCC or ULCC. Because the AM.39 was designed for use against lighter warship structures, many warheads malfunctioned when smashing through 31mm-thick hull plates of supertankers. Robust and extensive internal compartmentalisation, including a web of shell-plate longitudinals, usually limited the internal damage to one, perhaps two compartments adjacent to the point of impact. Moreover, the crude cargo frequently added to protection because – contrary to its distillates – it is hard to ignite. On their shuttle tankers, the Iranians introduced the use of the inert gas (carbon dioxide piped from the engine room), which further inhibited fire. Therefore, Exocets only had a chance of causing serious damage if impacting at high angle (where their detonation would then rupture the hull plates,

A view of a typical 'mothership' at the T-14 in 1985, while in the process of being loaded by a shuttle-tanker from one side, and unloaded by a customer's ship from the other. (Farzin Nadimi Collection)

subsequently leading to gaseous explosions), or if they penetrated five or more metres into the liquid cargo (where their detonation would cause a massive shockwave). However, with loaded supertankers having a freeboard of two or three metres, the majority of Exocets homed in on their sterns: there they often ruptured tanks for bunker oil, spilling this into the engine room. If the fire was not suppressed in time, the resulting conflagration regularly destroyed the highly automated and expensive control machinery, before resulting in the entire accommodation block ultimately collapsing into the hull. Even then this neither represented the loss of the hull nor – and this is particularly important – that of the load. On the contrary, in nearly all of the cases, the crude was re-loaded into another tanker.[6]

Moreover, replacement supertankers were easy to find: as of the mid-1980s, there was such a glut of these giant vessels on the market that damaged ships were cheaper to replace than repair. This reached proportions where it proved more cost-effective to scrap any ship hit by an Exocet that has suffered more than US$1 million worth in damage, and purchase a replacement in mint condition, than to pay for repairs. This was the only reason for the relatively high number of ULCCs and VLCCs declared CTL during this war. For similar reasons, claims that the Super Etendards and Mirage F.1EQ-5s represented something like a 'terror of the seamen' in the Persian Gulf during this war cannot but be considered a wild exaggeration: on the contrary: experiences of international shippers resulted in an outright rush of operators to send their older vessels staffed by some of their best crews to join the Iranian shuttle tanker fleet. In the words of one US observer:

> All were certainly able to deal with the disappointment of having to accelerate the upgrading of their fleets when one [supertanker] was hit. Even if the ship was never hit, the profits were so great that given the low probability of the ship being hit and the high rates that could be charged, the same operators not only never experienced problems with attracting competent crews through danger bonuses, but were also able to significantly upgrade their fleets.[7]

CROWN OF BATTLES

Replenished and reinforced with the help of a nearly uninterrupted flow of caravans for BIK, on 11 March 1985, the IRGC launched its next major offensive into Iraq. Like during Operation *Khyber* a year before, it used the Howeyzeh Marshes as a springboard for another attempt to cut off the Baghdad – Basra highway. Instead of ordering the IrAF to support the army, Saddam first declared the whole of Iranian airspace as a 'war zone', and then ordered the air force into an aerial onslaught on 30 major urban centres of Iran, thus initiating the so-called 'War of the Cities'. Within only three days between 12 and 14 March, 158 related combat sorties were flown, and additional ones followed over the next three weeks. Only when the situation on the ground became critical, would he correct his decision and order the IrAF to support Iraqi ground forces. Starting with 15 March, the Mirages from Abu Ubaida AB flew not only Syrel, Caiman and Baz-AR operations, but also repeatedly bombed Iranian positions using Spanish and Portuguese-made Mk.84s equipped with Jupiter fuses. Furthermore, they began deploying chemical weapons with the help of custom-made EXPAL BR.500MP bombs and R-400s (the latter was a locally-manufactured copy of the SAMP Type-21C).[8]

While his ground forces concluded the Crown of Battles successfully, Saddam was disappointed with the lack of results from the 'War of the Cities'. Furthermore, the GMID learned about the pending Iranian acquisition of Soviet-made S-75 (ASCC/NATO-code 'SA-2 Guideline') SAMs from Libya, and efforts to acquire additional anti-aircraft equipment from China and North Korea. Correspondingly, and on advice from Sha'ban, the strongman in Baghdad re-directed the next effort of the IrAF towards cutting off Iran's oil lifeline.[9]

By early 1985, the Iraqi Mirages were a regular sight over the southern battlefields of the Iran-Iraq War: as well as supporting every large operation through Syrel and Caiman operations, they foremost flew battlefield interdiction strikes, in the form of bombing installations used to distribute Iranian troops and supplies to the frontlines. Notable is the complete absence of the national insignia on this example: deleted before their delivery flights, these were sometimes not re-applied once the aircraft was in Iraq. (Ahmad Sadik Collection)

In addition to flying CAS, BAI, and anti-ship operations, on 24 March 1985 the Iraqi Mirages also hit several Iranian oil rigs in the northern Persian Gulf. This post-strike photograph was taken by a COR-2-equipped Mirage F.1EQ-2 on 26 March 1985. (Ahmad Sadik Collection)

COR-2-equiped Mirage F.1EQ-2 serial number 4032 returning from a sortie in early 1985. (Ahmad Sadik Collection)

A TOUGH NUT TO CRACK

Related preparations began as soon as the fighting in the Howeyzeh marshes died away, in May 1985. Over the following weeks, about a dozen reconnaissance sorties were flown by MiG-25RBs, one of which brought back photographs showing the installation of the Swiss-made Skyguard air defence system on Khark. Still overcautious about the prospect of exposing Mirages to such opposition, and knowing that MiG-23s usually managed to drag the F-14 CAP away towards the north without too many problems, Basu devised a plan according to which the superior navigation and electronic warfare systems of the Mirages were to be used to bring more-survivable Su-22s over the island. Correspondingly, in July 1985, a group of Mirage-pilots from No. 81 Squadron was ordered into a series of joint exercises with Su-22M-3-pilots from No. 69 Squadron against a 1:1,000 replica of Khark constructed on the Lake Thartar.[10]

Launched on 15 August 1985, the resulting mission saw two Mirage F.1EQ-5s 'guiding' six Sukhois through the Kuwaiti airspace and well to the south before turning north to attack: in this fashion, they approached their target at an altitude of only 15 metres while exploiting the 'blind spot' of the SAM-site at Kharko, created by the elevation of Khark and installations constructed atop of it. To further improve their protection and that of the entire formation, each Mirage was equipped with two Remora ECM-pods: integrated with the aircraft's navigation system, these were detecting, identifying, and countering both pulse and continuous wave radars thus providing self-protection against air and ground threats.[11]

In addition to two FAB-500ShN parachute-retarded bombs, each of the Sukhois was equipped with a single SPS-141 jamming pod: operating in three interchangeable sub-bands (within an overall RF range of 4.7 to 10.8GHz), these were providing self-protection in the forward hemisphere only, by the means of range and velocity gate

The Mirage F.1EQ-5 serial number 4565 as seen at the start of its delivery trip to Iraq: this was one of two Mirages involved in the strike on Khark on 15 August 1985. (Jacques Guilleme Collection)

pull-off, and cooperative blinking jamming. This combination of Remoras and SPS-141s promised to protect the involved aircraft from Iranian HAWK SAMs, F-4Es, and to disrupt even the work of F-14s.[12]

As the formation approached within sight of Khark, the two Mirages turned west, leaving the Sukhois on their own: four Su-22M-3s then targeted the T-Jetty, and two the Azarpod Terminal. Led by Major Abdul Salam Sayed ad-Dulayimi, the Sukhois attacking the T-Jetty delivered their bombs from level flight at only 30m altitude, causing massive damage to the point where the jetty joined with the pier connecting it to the island. However, the two that went for the Azarpod Terminal found their target obscured by a tanker loading there, and hit the empty ship instead. A post-strike reconnaissance sortie by a MiG-25RB brought back photographs showing huge pillars of smoke emanating from the T-Jetty. Actually, this 'devastating blow to the Iranian war effort' – which, as Baghdad boasted, 'reduced Khark to rubbles' – was anything but: it did cause a 48-hours disruption in exports, and a 12-day disruption in the flow from one of the mainland pipelines. However, with the terminal being built for significantly higher export levels than run in 1985 and the Iranians meanwhile applying repairs at an amazing speed, enough pipelines and berths remained operational to continue loading the crude, no matter how much fire and smoke the Iraqis caused.[13]

A post-strike reconnaissance photograph taken by a MiG-25RB after the air strike of 15 August 1985. Amongst others, it shows a massive fire at the joint of the T-jetty with the pier connecting it to the island, caused by bombs deployed by Su-22s. (Ahmad Sadik Collection)

The IrAF re-attacked Khark with SPS-141-protected Su-22s on 18 and 25 August, then by MiG-25RBs on 1 and 2 September, and then targeted the Sea Island Terminal with the same pair of Mirages that escorted the Sukhois during the first attack, on 15 September 1985. However, once again, the target was obstructed by a berthed tanker: the North Korean VLCC *Son Bong* was sunk as a consequence. Thus, it was only in the course of another attempt, four days later, that the Sea Island/Azarpod Terminal was finally knocked out. While denying exaggerated Iraqi claims, Tehran this time reacted by chartering smaller tankers to continue loading from the T-Jetty – and thus managed to continue exporting.[14]

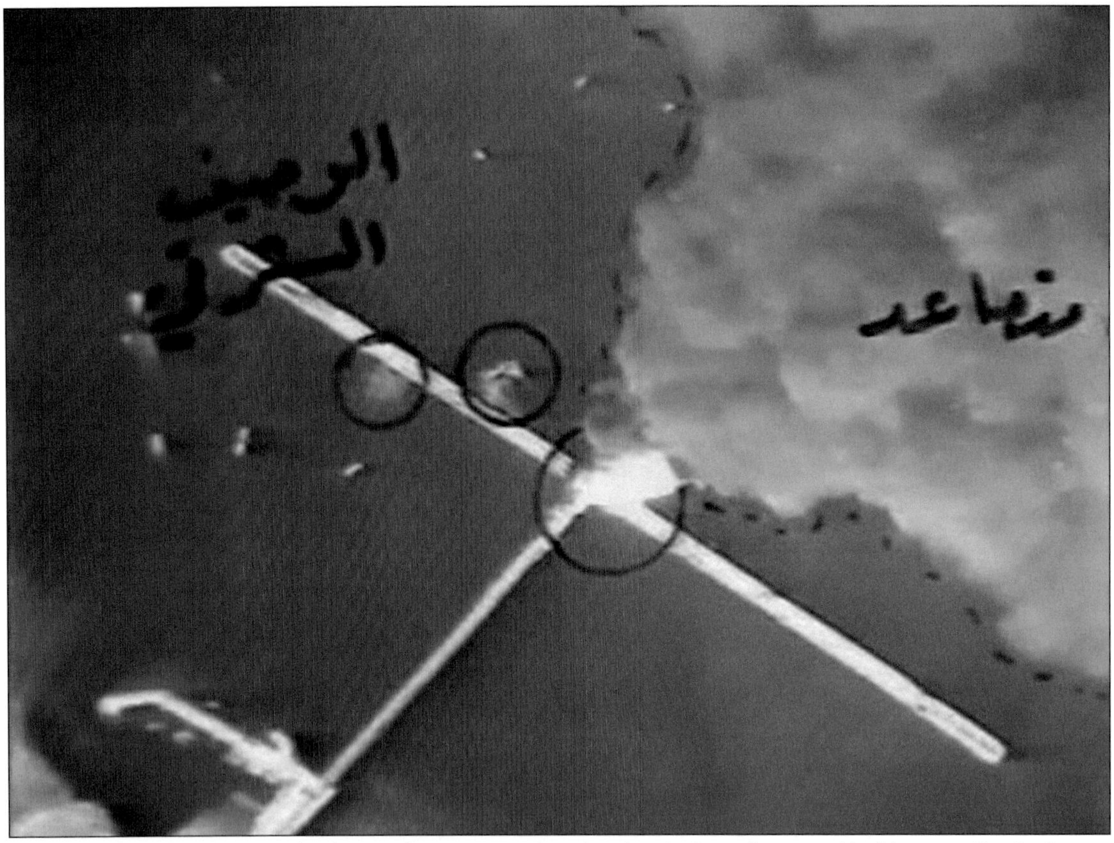

A crop from another photograph taken on the same occasion, showing the huge fire caused by hits scored by the Su-22M-3 section led by Major Abdul Salam Salyed ad-Dulayimi. (Ahmad Sadik Collection)

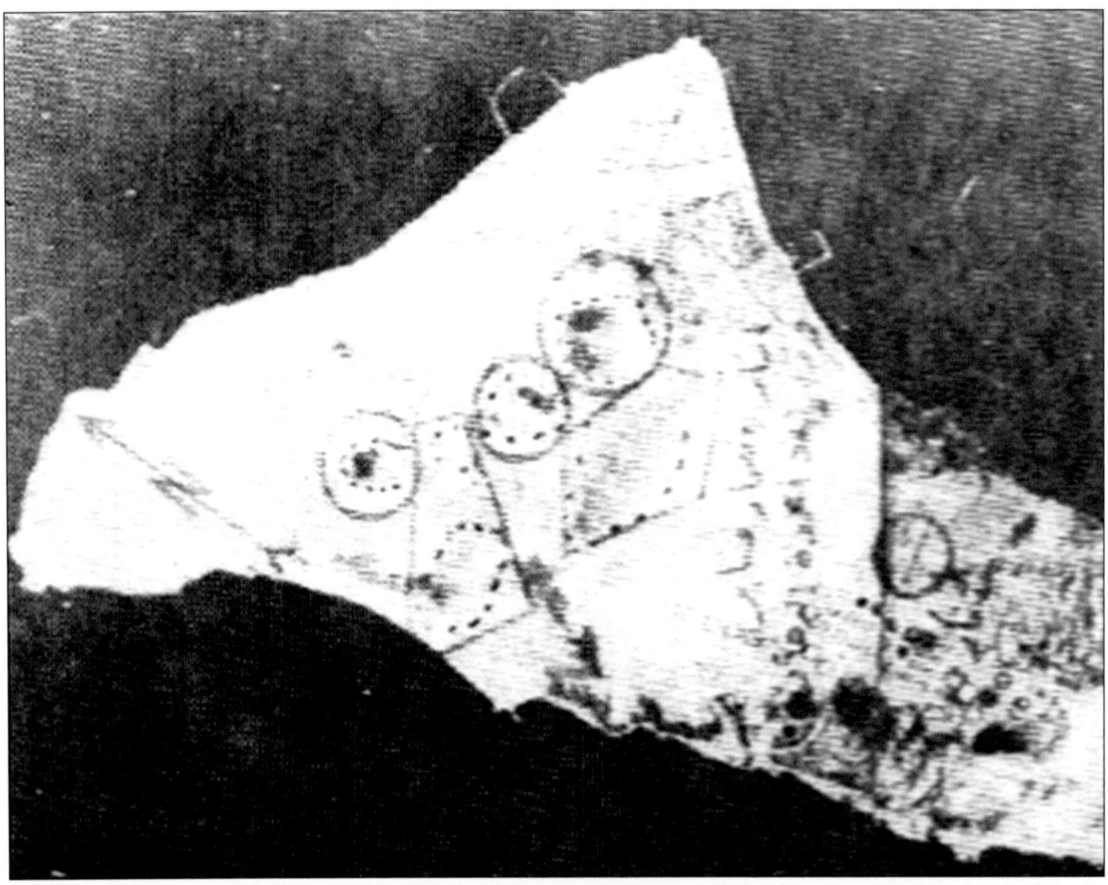

Showing traces of several impacts that actually missed their targets, this is another reconnaissance photograph of Khark taken by an IrAF MiG-25RB on 2 September 1985: two weeks later, the same was used to 'demonstrate the precision of attacks with AS.30Ls' by Baghdad's propaganda machinery – although the weapon was not yet deployed by the IrAF at that point in time. (Ahmad Sadik Collection)

PROJECT BAZ-4

Ultimately, in what was the most effective period of the Oil Campaign run by the IrAF by the time, 30 air raids on Khark were undertaken between 15 August and 30 November. Although this caused Iran a loss of US$1 billion in oil revenues, and clearly demonstrating the IrAF's potential to bring Tehran to the bargaining table, this effort was discontinued: the strongman in Baghdad remained unwilling to commit his air force fully. Thus, as spectacular as it was, with one exception, this campaign was neither pressed home, nor sustained enough and – ultimately – it failed to lastingly reduce Tehran's ability to wage war. Indeed, Iran made a quick recovery and continued exporting: already by October 1985, the rate of exports was even slightly higher than before the attacks. Whether Baghdad then concluded that a physical destruction of Khark and other oil exporting facilities was essentially impossible, or because Saddam and his confidantes seriously convinced themselves that they had curbed Iranian exports, they decreased the intensity of attacks on the crucial island: for nearly a year after, Khark was only, 'kept under pressure through area bombing raids by MiG-25RBs'.[15]

On the contrary, the GHQ was soon back to business as usual – which was to run a tit-for-tat Oil Campaign, while the MIC was back to negotiating with Paris in order to keep the Mirage 2000 deal alive, and planning for after the war. Thus, on 23 September 1985, the French and the Iraqis signed the contract for

Table 6: Overview of *Project Baz-4*, September 1985

Contract designation	Date of Order	Number of Aircraft	Version	Serial Numbers	Roll-Out Dates	Acceptance Dates
BAZ-421x	23 Sep 1985	9	Mirage F.1EQ-6	4600-4608	18 Dec 1987 – 14 Feb 1988	13 Jan 1988 – Feb 1990
BAZ-421x	23 Sep 1985	6	Mirage F.1BQ	4609-4614	18 Oct 1987 – 17 Jan 1990	
BAZ-421x	23 Sep 1985	9	Mirage F.1EQ-6	4615-4623	14 Feb 1988 – 14 Feb 1989	

The Mirage F.1EQ-5 serial number 4562 served as a test-bed for diverse new weapons and a prototype for the F.1EQ-6 variant (including the installation of the Sherloc RWR). This photograph is showing it equipped with a Raphael TH reconnaissance pod under the centreline, a Remora pod, and the conformal Alkan Corail chaff and flare dispenser on P0 hardpoints (wing underside, between the main pylon and fuselage). The latter were to replace Sycomors, thus saving precious underwing hardpoints. (Thomson-CSF/Collection Raffiant, via Michel Benichou)

Project Baz-4, which stipulated the delivery of 18 Mirage F.1EQ-6s (the first version capable of carrying two AM.39s at once), starting in early 1988. Moreover, while the Iraqis claim that the BF RWRs installed on earlier variants was 'perfectly good enough against the Iranians', the F.1EQ-6s were to receive an entirely new, Thomson-CSF Sherloc digital RWR. Finally, the contract for *Project Baz-4* included an order for six Mirage F.1BQ two-seaters, necessary to convert additional pilots to the type.[16]

Overall, the period 1984-1985 was one during which a complacent Baghdad – meanwhile surviving only thanks to additional loans from Kuwait and Saudi Arabia – continued increasing the capacities of the IrAF Mirage-fleet at the cost of real capabilities. The whole of Iraq was to pay a dear price for Saddam's ignorance.

6

BITTER YEAR

By early 1986, the Iraqi capabilities with regards to COMINT/ELINT/SIGINT were fully developed, and included the Japanese-made RM-858 HF/DF systems deployed to monitor Iranian communications at strategic level. However, the GMID remained unable to intercept and decrypt the high frequency troposcatter and microwave communications used by the Iranians to pass their high-level decisions. Thus, on the evening of 9 February 1986, the Iranians took the Iraqis by surprise through launching an amphibious assault on the Faw peninsula, capturing the town with the same name, and then almost reaching the port of Umm-ol Qassr in the west and southern outskirts of Basra in the north. Thus began a battle that was to provide the crucial impulse for the ultimate outcome of the entire war.[1]

Undertaken under the cover of bad weather, the Iranian offensive on Faw caught the Iraqis wrong-footed. The clouds and rain hampered not only the IrAF, but also the movement of Iraqi ground forces, and deployment of chemical weapons: as a result, the first series of Iraqi counterattacks was easily repulsed. When the Iraqis brought in their reserve forces to stage massive counterattacks, they only managed to bleed both sides white: the Faw Peninsula remained in Iranian hands. The resulting panic – in Baghdad but also within the GCC – was a particularly sobering experience for Saddam; indeed, the 'bitter pill' necessary for him to *finally* place the conduct of the war into the hands of professional military officers. The result was a series of deep reforms that was to have profound effect upon the subsequent flow of the war. No other branch of the Iraqi military was to benefit from these as much as the IrAF: Sha'ban and his staff were now given a free hand with regards to planning and conducting operations that were to cause serious – and lasting – economic problems for Tehran and, indeed, to demonstrate not only to the Iraqis and to the international community, but even to the 'hawks' in Tehran, that the IrAF was capable of winning a war.

IrAF UNLEASHED

As of 1986, the deployment of Mirages for electronic warfare was a matter of life or death for the IrAF. Syrel-equipped Mirages were usually underway along a 200-400km long race-track pattern at an altitude of 5,000-10,000 metres, always at least 40-50km, sometimes deeper inside Iraq, from where they would monitor the activity of the Iranian air defences. The information obtained by them was then fused into the KARI, so that commanding officers could manage the battle in the real time. Much more than any ARMs, Caiman-equipped F.1EQ-2s played a crucial role in suppressing the work of the Iranian MIM-23Bs. When the weather over Iraq cleared sufficiently for the IrAF to take-off, and Major-General Sha'ban deployed nearly all of his fighter-bombers into the counteroffensive, Syrel and Caiman-equipped Mirages were to play a crucial role once again. Recognizing that the essence of the battle for Faw was the ability of both sides to bring in reinforcements and supplies to the front lines, his first target was Railway Station 7, in Khorramshahr, used to bring the mass of the Iranian infantry to the combat zone. For this operation, Sha'ban ordered all the available Mirages of No. 79 and No. 91 Squadrons from Abu Ubaida AB to lead a strike that was to include at last 12 MiG-23BNs from No. 49 Squadron (Abu Ubaida AB), 16 MiG-23BNs from No. 29 Squadron and 12 Su-22M-2/3s from No. 5 Squadron (Ali Ibn Abu Talib AB), and 16 Su-22M-4Ks from the Wahda-based No. 109 Squadron. Due to the proximity of the target to their bases, all the aircraft were able to carry their full bomb-loads. The strikers were supported by one MiG-25RB that flew pre-strike reconnaissance, two pairs of MiG-23MLs that flew a CAP, four Su-22M-2s armed with Kh-28 ARMs, four Caiman and two Syrel-equipped Mirage F.1EQ-2s. However, while the weather over Iraq was excellent on that morning, that over Iran remained bad: the first MiGs that reached their CAP-station reported massive cumulus clouds over the target zone. With the mass of more than 80 Iraqi aircraft meanwhile less than 10 minutes away, the ADOC reacted by ordering the MiG-23 pilots into a supersonic dash over the target zone to check the weather more closely: their pilots again reported clouds. It was thus on Major Nasser – the leader of the first formation from No. 79 Squadron and meanwhile a seasoned veteran – to save the entire enterprise by providing a more detailed report. Supported by Caimain-equipped Mirages that successfully suppressed the nearby Iranian HAWK SAM-site, the Iraqi formations then saturated the target area though dive-bombing attacks from 6,000 metres. Although releasing their bombs from as high as 4,000 metres, they completely wrecked Railway Station 7 – including a large marshalling yard with a train carrying a load of MIM-23 missiles. This was to become the prototype for nearly all of the subsequent interdiction operations undertaken by the IrAF for the rest of the war.[2]

EXOCETS GOING BALLISTIC

With the weather hampering operations over south-western Iran on 15 February 1986, Sha'ban re-directed squadrons equipped with F.1EQ-4s and F.1EQ-5s to the Oil Campaign. However, all through January 1986, No. 81 Squadron continued suffering from problems related to Iraqi Exocets, as recalled by Sadik:

> In early 1986, a number of Exocets went out of control upon launch: instead of dropping down they "went ballistic", began to climb. Already after the first incident, we summoned the French representative. Confronted with the report of our pilots and asked for an explanation, he denied the French were to blame, instead accusing the IrAF of bad maintenance. We formed a committee headed by General Amer Rasheed (the head of the MIC and a scientific adviser to the Minister of Defence) to rectify the problem. A thorough investigation proved that all the measures taken by the ground crews and pilots were according to prescribed procedures. We summoned the representative to the GHQ again and confronted him with our findings. Finally, he called France and had a long discussion on the matter. The next day, he came back to say that Aerospatiale and Dassault didn't think that the problem was caused by them. Concluding that the matter was not taken seriously enough by the French companies, the MIC decided to exert political pressure. A letter was delivered to the French president, explaining the importance of the matter. Later the same day – and it was Friday – both technicians from Aerospatiale and Dassault were working on solving the mysterious problem. A simulator in France was activated, too. By Monday, the results were on the desk of President Mitterrand. It showed at least five possible reasons for the missiles to initiate a climb upon launch. A batch of seven Exocets previously delivered to Iraq was returned to France for inspection and, for more than a month, we had none on hand.[3]

Lacking anti-ship missiles, Sha'ban ordered a strike on the Genaveh manifold instead: on 23 January, nearly half of the particularly sensitive and irreplaceable turbines were wrecked. However, even this attack failed to stop the throughput for more than a day: the Iranians quickly constructed a bypass supported by a number of small booster pumps.[4]

After necessary repairs, the French rushed a batch of Iraqi Exocets back to Baghdad in mid-February 1986, and No. 81 Squadron – supported by Caiman-carrying F.1EQ-2s of No. 79 Squadron and a CAP of MiG-23MLs – returned to the waters of the Persian Gulf later the same month. This time, the missiles functioned flawlessly and five confirmed hits were scored between 23 and 28 February 1986. Furthermore, as soon as the fighting on the Faw Peninsula died away, No. 81 Squadron launched its first long-range/low altitude raid against the oil refinery of Esfahan. Flown on 18 March 1986 by four F.1EQ-5s armed with four SAMP Type 25 bombs each, along a route based on the report about gaps in the Iranian radar coverage mentioned earlier, this devastated the main control room: the sensitive facility was hit by three out of four bombs released by Major Nasser, the leader of the Iraqi formation. While most of the installations were quickly repaired, the control room was not: for the rest of the war the Iranians were forced to run the massive refinery manually. During the following days, the F.1EQ-5s further wrecked four Iranian shuttle tankers using Exocets. However, because the raid against the Esfahan refinery was the only such operation undertaken during this period, its overall effects remained limited: Sha'ban, Basu and the rest of the IrAF's planning cell were still a year away from learning the crucial lesson.[5]

Indeed, leaving the Iranians enough time to repair the refinery in Esfahan, the IrAF flew the next raid against a similar target only on 7 May 1986, when four F.1EQ-5s from No. 81 Squadron, supported by five other Mirages that acted as tankers (see below for details), launched their most daring raid by that point in time to bomb the Rey refinery outside Tehran. Once again using intelligence about the gaps in the Iranian radar coverage, Major Omar led his formation from Hurrya AB, outside Mosul, into a successful attack that knocked out one of the processing units and left a large part of the refinery afire.[6]

LASER-HOMING WEAPONS

In March 1986, No. 81 Squadron was bolstered through the return of the first group of pilots to complete a training course in France for the deployment of laser-homing weapons. Together with the unit's commander, all were promptly put through additional exercises and then rushed into combat. The first AS.30L sortie was flown by Major Omar and his wingman on 4 July 1986 against what the Iraqis understood was a 'ship laying a flexible underwater pipeline near Genaveh', supposedly, 'in support of a new loading point on the coast about 40 kilometres north of Khark'. Executing a text-book, low-altitude attack, Omar established a lock-on from 12 kilometres and fired from 9 kilometres to score a direct hit. Unknown to the Iraqis, his target was neither a merchant, nor a tanker, or a pipeline-lying ship, but one of the Exocet-decoy and ZU-23-equipped vessels designed to attract their attention: *Iran Sedaghat*, an IRGC-operated anti-aircraft ship. The crew extinguished the fire and managed to return to Bushehr where the vessel was repaired.[7]

The Mirage F.1EQ-5 serial number 4560, as seen while armed with two AS.30Ls and the Thomson-CSF PDL.1EQ Patrick laser designator under the centreline, during pre-delivery testing in France. (Dassault, via Michel Benichou)

Major Haytham Khattab Omar climbing into the cockpit of the Mirage F.1EQ-5 serial number 4570, equipped with the Patrick under the centreline: this jet was used for the first combat deployment of the AS.30L, on 4 July 1986. (Ahmad Sadik Collection)

BLACK THURSDAY

Realising the IRIAF was once again exhausted and weakened by losses it suffered during the fighting for Faw, on 20 July 1986, Major-General Sha'ban felt free to publicly threaten Iran with, 'severe blows', 'newly acquired equipment…[with] decisive effects', and his intention to 'bring Iran to its knees'. After diverting the IRIAF's attention towards north through an unsuccessful AS.30L attack on the Qatoor Bridge, in northern Iran, on the border to Turkey, on 31 July, he ordered another all-out attack on Khark.[8]

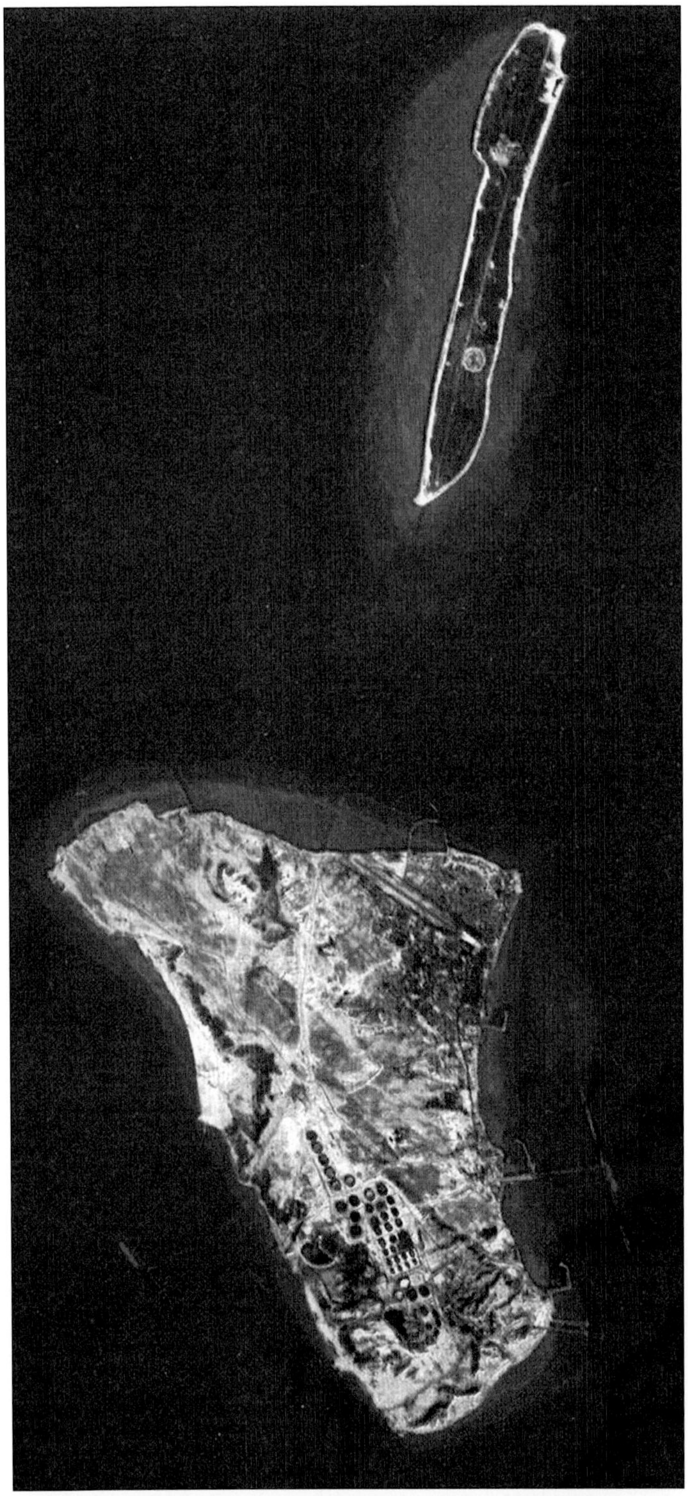

While most of the Iraqi reconnaissance photographs of Khark taken during the war show only this island, this US satellite photograph is showing the northern of the two rocks – Kharko – too, together with one crucial detail: the position of the MIM-23B I-HAWK SAM-site installed there. Also notable is the massive damage caused by Iraqi raids against the T-Jetty, and multiple oil slicks. (Tom Cooper Collection)

The first sign of trouble for the Iranian defenders was the – now usual – appearance of two high-flying, Caiman-equipped F.1EQ-2s, at 0930. An air raid alert was sounded, but this proved too late: at 0934, a pair of low-flying Mirages delivered a tremendously precise strike on the MIM-23B I-HAWK SAM-site at Kharko: both of its HPARs were bombed out by a total of eight SAMP 21Cs. The second pair of Mirages then destroyed the command post of this site with eight additional bombs, at 0939. Khark was without its principal means of defence. Indeed, free from the 'Death Valley', the second Iraqi wave hit home at 1053hrs: two F.1EQ-5s from No. 81 Squadron (escorted by a pair of F.1EQ-4s from No. 89 Squadron equipped with Super 530Fs and Remoras) hit two berths on the T-Jetty with AS.30Ls. They were followed by two F.1EQ-4s of No. 79 Squadron and four Su-22M-3s from No. 69 Squadron which simultaneously bombed the Sea Island and the T-Jetty, and set the two tankers berthed there – *Mistra* and *Magnum* – on fire. The third Iraqi wave appeared at 1351 and consisted of Su-22s that hit and cut off the main pipeline bringing the crude from the mainland, and several storage tanks. Finally, the T-Jetty was hit at 2032hrs again, and cut off from the island.[9]

For all practical purposes, this was the most devastating attack ever delivered upon Khark: by targeting air defences, loading installations, storage tanks, pipelines and berthed tankers in quick succession, the Iraqis not only caused massive material damage, but also disabled all but two loading berths, *finally* causing significant postponements in exports. Unsurprisingly, the day became known as the 'Black Thursday' to the oilmen at Khark. Ironically, and like so many times before and after, it was the Iraqis who came to their aid: instead of continuing this offensive, Sha'ban and Basu stopped it and decided to try something else – in turn buying time for the Iranians to apply repairs.[10]

IN-FLIGHT REFUELLING

The new idea in Baghdad was to combine the freedom of operations IrAF's pilots enjoyed down the western side of the Persian Gulf with another new capability – in-flight refuelling (IFR). Always fascinated by the Iranian IFR-capabilities, and obsessed with the idea of bombing Tehran, the Iraqis were quick in ordering their F.1EQ-4s to be equipped correspondingly. When deliveries of that variant began, in 1983, the issue was that of finding a suitable tanker. The IrAF first attempted to improvise: a fuel truck was parked and secured inside the cargo hold of an Il-76MD transport, and connected to a Douglas/Intertechnique D-704 refuelling pod installed underneath the rear cargo door. However, the solution was soon discarded: the relatively short range of the Mirage meant that in order to reach targets as far as Tehran the in-flight refuelling part of the mission would have to be undertaken inside Iranian airspace. As of 1983, this was not feasible and thus the IrAF decided to use F.1EQ-4s as tankers. Pilots that used to fly Super Etendards had received related training already in France, and subsequently they acted as instructors in Iraq. By mid-1986, preparations reached the point at which the Iraqi Mirages were ready to fly their first long-range strike supported by in-flight refuelling.[11]

OIL SHOCK

On 12 August 1986, four Mirage F.1EQ-4s from No. 81 Squadron launched from Wahda AB, each carrying a single Irakien fuel tank and four SAMP Type 21 250kg bombs. Supported by the usual set of Syrel and Caiman-carrying Mirages, and MiG-23s that distracted the attention of the Iranian air defences towards the north, and by no less than 12 F.1EQ-4s and F.1EQ-5s that acted as tankers, and after

The reason for the Iraqis always approaching Khark from the southern side during their raids in the 1985-1988 period: the relatively high elevation of the island and installations constructed above – especially in comparison with the nearly flat Kharko – created a 'radar shadow' for the SAM-site installed on the latter island, and thus hid their approach. (Tom Cooper Collection)

Damage caused by the Iraqi air raid on the T-Jetty on 'Black Thursday': notable is the massive destruction of the network of steel pylons used to support the construction of the jetty and the pipelines. (Farzin Nadimi Collection)

three IFR-operations run at an altitude of only 60 metres above the sea surface, they ranged over 650 kilometres deep over the Persian Gulf before turning north – and attacking the T-14 Terminal at Sirri. Their appearance was not entirely unexpected: the IRIN became aware of a possible raid already in June, when a high-flying aircraft was detected while passing by (see below). Alerted, the Iranians promptly fired two Frenchmen working at the local terminal and began moving various elements of the T-14 to Larak. However, bad weather had forced the return of motherships back to Sirri. Thus, when the Iraqi Mirages jinked upwards prior to their bomb runs, their pilots sighted no fewer than six crude-laden motherships and 12 other tankers around, all waiting to load before the 1 September deadline for production cut-backs ordered by the Organisation of Petroleum-Exporting Countries (OPEC).[12]

Ignoring the feeble anti-aircraft fire, the Iraqi pilots – exhausted by the long trip at low altitude – did their best: one set the tanker *Azarpod* on fire, killing 16 crewmembers and causing a fire that enveloped the storage tanker *Kleila*, where 3 were killed. Eventually, *Azarpod's* skipper was forced to beach his ship to prevent her from sinking. Two other vessels came away with relatively light damage.[13]

Only two days later, the IrAF recorded its next success, when a formation of four Mirages bombing Iranian troops on the central frontlines sighted a single IRIAF F-5E passing by. Lieutenant Mohammad Nazar broke the formation and started a chase until reaching the range for R.550 Magic: his missile scored a direct hit, forcing the Iranian pilot – Captain Abbas-Ramezani – to eject.[14]

The next Iraqi raid was even more spectacular: exploiting the defection attempt of an Iranian F-14A pilot to Iraq – which prompted the IRIAF to ground its Tomcat-units for nearly two weeks – on 5 September 1986, the IrAF deployed four F.1EQ-5s (supported by six tankers) to raid Lavan Island, 880 kilometres away from Iraq. Led by Major Omar, this attack wrecked the tanker *Mokran* while she was loading.[15]

SHOT IN THE FOOT

Although militarily insignificant – because the Iraqis failed to cause any damage to the local on-shore facilities, the Iranians quickly replaced the lost shuttle tankers, and saved most of their cargoes – the raids of Sirri and Lavan are widely misunderstood as major propaganda coups, only demonstrating that the much appreciated strategic depth of Iran was compromised by the increasingly overwhelming Iraqi airpower. Actually, in combination with attacks on refineries, they temporarily phased out half of Iran's refining capacity, forcing Tehran to ration fuel during the following winter. The only problem was that the Iraqi intelligence failed to find out about this, and thus never informed the IrAF's planning cell. Similar operations were once again discontinued and through the rest of September 1986 the IrAF flew anti-ship attacks with Exocets only.[16]

Indeed, the next IrAF attempt against Khark was outright feeble. On 6 October 1986, a pair of AS.30L-armed F.1EQ-5s – escorted by two F.1EQ-4s – was sent to hit the loading berths. By this time, even the most ignorant clerics in Tehran had become aware of the importance of F-14s for the defence of this crucial facility, and thus steps were undertaken to increase the number of FMC aircraft through the procurement of spare parts on the black market.

Two F.1EQ-4s in the process of in-flight-refuelling training from an Il-76MD transport modified to serve as a tanker, in 1983. This solution was concluded as impracticable. (via Ali Tobchi)

The solution with F.1EQ-4s equipped with Douglas/Intertechnique D-704 in-flight refuelling pods acting as tankers for other F.1EQ-4s and for F.1EQ-5s was found much more satisfactory by the Iraqis, because it enabled them to extend the range of their fighter-bombers through refuelling operations undertaken inside Iranian airspace and at low altitude. This photograph was taken in late 1985, during one of many related training sorties. (via Ali Tobchi)

The Iranian tanker *Azarpod* was the first victim of an Iraqi long-range raid: she was hit by bombs released by Major Omar on 12 August 1986 while anchored at Sirri, and her skipper was forced to beach her in order to prevent her sinking. (Ahmad Sadik Collection)

Moreover, the IRIN and the IRGC had bolstered the defences through the deployment of several of their warships in the area, and the deployment of fast patrol boats. Their radars and observers enabled the Iranians to detect incoming Iraqi raids so that Tomcats from TFB.6 could be scrambled on time. The Iraqi formation was thus detected while still approaching Khark, around 1630hrs, and attacked by the F-14A flown by Major Jamshid Afshar (RIO Hassan Afghan-Toloee). In a rush to prevent the Iraqis from reaching their

Drawn by Major Omar, this map shows the route and composition of the formation that raided the tanker *Mokran* while this was loading on south-western berth of the Lavan Island on 5 September 1986. (Ahmad Sadik Collection)

targets, the Iranian pilot fired his AIM-7E too early. Shortly before entering the range for attack with his AS.30L, the lead Mirage-pilot was warned that his aircraft was tracked by an enemy fighter. Seconds later, an air-to-air missile detonated nearby: decoyed by the Remora pod it failed to cause damage. The Iraqis continued their attack: one AS.30L hit the centre of the T-Jetty, but the other caused only minor damage to the tanker *Faroship L*. Once again, Khark remained operational.[17]

TIT-FOR-TAT PERIOD

Still in the process of 'learning by doing', Sha'ban's planning cell switched targets once again. After the Mirages once again exploited the known gaps in the Iranian radar coverage to bomb a defence industry complex outside Esfahan, on 12 October, a day later the IRIN warships were early in picking-up a pair of Exocet-carrying F.1EQ-5s – flown by 1st Lieutenant Manhal Kazem Jassem al-Bayati, and 1st Lieutenant Karim Zaidan – and alarming the F-14s. As the Iraqi pair passed low over Faylaka Island in Kuwait, al-Bayati's aircraft was blown away by a direct hit from an AIM-54A. The IrAF attempted to exact revenge by dispatching four F.1EQ-5s to hit TFB.7 and Shiraz International, on 15 October: for a year longer, the Iraqis were not to find out that all the Tomcats had been withdrawn from there. Moreover, this highly promising low-level-raid ended in a flop due to poor planning: although taking the Iranians completely by surprise, and claiming the destruction of 'three Boeing 747 tankers and C-130 Hercules transports' on the ground (subsequently increased to '23' by the Iraqi propaganda machinery), the involved pilots dropped their bombs and then hit an IranAir Boeing 737 with gunfire, killing at least five civilians in the process. Moreover, No. 81 Squadron suffered another loss on 17 October 1986, when the F.1EQ-5 flown by 1st Lieutenant Hussayn Hasson Muhammad Ahmad was shot down by gun-fire from IRIN warships while attacking a salvage vessel underway with a caravan for BIK.[18]

Sha'ban then ordered a major air strike on Bandar-e Imam Khomeini: on 11 November 1986, the port and the nearby petrochemical complex (the construction of which was abandoned in 1980) were ravaged by a 130-aircraft raid, proceeded by a Baz-AR strike of Mirage F.1EQ-2s from No. 79 Squadron against the local HAWK SAM-site. With a repeat of this exercise being pointless, three days later, the F.1EQ-5s of No. 81 Squadron successfully targeted Sassan, Reshadat (former Rostam), and Resalat (former Raksh) rigs. The same unit also reinforced its anti-ship campaign: in October, November and December 1986, it fired more than 30 AM.39s, scoring at least 15 hits on 12 different shuttle tankers and one supply ship. However, the results were sobering: only one vessel was sunk and three tankers declared CTL, while at least one of the Exocets failed to detonate after hitting a target that was already written off. Therefore, Saddam personally issued the order for No. 81 Squadron to fly its longest-ranged raid ever and hit the Val Fajr-2 Terminal at Larak. Run in accordance to a plan devised by the French instructor Jean Michel Cantin (which subsequently served as a prototype for this kind of operation), this mission was launched on 25 November 1985: it included two Mirage F.1EQ-5s – led by

1st Lieutenant Manhal Kazem Jassem al-Bayati was shot down and killed by an IRIAF F-14A, while underway during an anti-shipping mission, on 13 October 1986. (via Ali Tobchi)

Lieutenant-Colonel Haytham Khattab Omar, and loaded with two RP.35 and one Irakien drop tanks, and two SAMP Type 21 bombs each – supported by three tankers. After flying down the entire 'Mirage Alley' to Abu Dhabi, the jets cut over Dibba in northern Oman before turning north to attack from an entirely unexpected, southern direction. The highly experienced Iraqi flight leader and his wingman then delivered a particularly precise attack, indeed the most successful Iraqi anti-ship strike by that date: Omar's bombs caused fires that wrecked the *Antarctica*, while *Dynasty*, *Shining Star*, *Tabriz*, and *Tenacity* all suffered varying amounts of damage but were subsequently repaired.[19]

Tehran quickly compensated for the losses through an acquisition of 18 smaller vessels – the sheer number of which was decentralizing the risk while increasing the export flexibility – and continued the steady increase of its crude oil exports. Obviously, what Baghdad was still unaware of was that such tit-for-tat attacks only served the purpose of lessening the pressure upon Khark and – even more importantly – the remaining Iranian oil refineries. In the words of *The Economist*:

> The effect of Iraq's assaults has been less than it might have been on the Iranians because practice has made them expert at quick repair and improvisation…Iran's nimble-footedness, combined with the original capacity of the Khark and Genaveh facilities, has kept the Iraqis from cutting Iran's oil lifeline…[20]

Switching targets once again, Sha'ban then dispatched the Mirages into two spectacular raids. On 6 December 1986 two F.1EQ-5s supported by two tankers, exploited the – now well-known – gaps in Iranian radar coverage to cause heavy damage to the Neka powerplant, on the coast of the Caspian Sea. On 12 December, a similar formation bombed an explosives factory constructed into

The Boeing 737 of IranAir that was hit on apron of Shiraz International in the Iraqi raid of 15 October 1986. (Farzin Nadimi Collection)

the side of Elbrus Mountain, in the Lavizal district of northern Tehran, though with less success.[21]

However, much worse than any of air raids by the Iraqi Mirage in 1986 was the dramatic drop of oil prices on the international markets, known as the 'Oil Shock of 1986' amongst oil-exporting nations of the Persian Gulf. From the Iraqi point of view, the effects upon Iran were comparable to a major battlefield victory. Remarkably, while even the intelligence assessments in Baghdad of late 1986 noted a reduction of Iranian oil revenues by 40%, industrial production by 65%, and an increasing unemployment, the IrAF failed to exploit this opportunity.[22]

BLUNDERED 'FINAL' OFFENSIVES

Ignoring the worsening condition of the entire country, the IRGC remained determined to capture Basra at any cost, and in December 1986 initiated its biggest offensive by the time, Operation *Karbala-4*. Although this four-week-long slugging match ended in a bloody disaster, the 'hawks' in Tehran quickly brought in additional forces and launched an even bigger enterprise with the same aim, Operation *Karbala-5*, at 0100 of 9 January 1987. The IrAF reacted in its – now – standard fashion: with massive interdiction strikes. However, a combination of technical snags and bad weather delayed the take-off of the Caiman-carrying Mirage F.1EQ-2s early that morning: as a result, the ADOC left the first pair of Tu-16 bombers underway to strike the Abadan area to enter the combat zone in full view of Iranian radars at an altitude of 12,200 metres. One was promptly shot down by a HAWK SAM despite deploying on-board jammers and a kilometres-long cloud of chaff. Of course, the IrAF continued its operations and flew 662 attack sorties by 12 January, and another 1,600 by 17 January. The Iranians countered through a deployment of three MIM-23B I-HAWK SAM-sites and there is little doubt that these did cause some problems: during the month, and amongst others, they scored at least three confirmed kills against Mirages, in turn forcing the IrAF to devote much of its efforts to large-scale strikes on Iranian air defence positions.[23]

Operation *Karbala-5* strained the Iraqi Army to near breaking point – but: it failed to punch through. After seven weeks of bitter fighting and immense losses on both sides, the Iranians were not only still outside Basra: an Iraqi counterattack on 1 March 1987 made it clear that they had also finally lost the strategic initiative.

BLACK FEBRUARY

Although the massive deployment of electronic countermeasures kept the IrAF losses during Iranian offensives within tolerable limits, mid-way through *Karbala-5* – which the Iraqis sardonically named 'The Great Harvest' – Saddam lost nerve and on 17 January ordered the IrAF into a new round of the War of the Cities. In the following 42 days, his fighter-bombers indiscriminately targeted 66 urban centres in a total of 860 sorties. This effort was not only pointless, or tragic for massacring between 3,000 and 5,000 civilians, but cost the entire IrAF – and its Mirage-units in particular – a number of pilots and aircraft: because fuel was at a premium for operations deep within Iran, they usually carried no Remora or Sycomor pods, and were thus poorly protected while operating within areas defended by IRIAF interceptors.[24]

On the afternoon of 2 February 1987, a quartet of F.1EQ-4s from

Wreckage of the Mirage F.1 shot down on 14 February 1987 by what the Iraqi pilots called the 'Death Valley' – an Iranian MIM-23B I-HAWK SAM. Its pilot, 1st Lieutenant Hamid Khalil Zakher was captured. (Farzin Nadimi Collection)

No. 91 Squadron was intercepted by the F-14A flown by Captain Mohammed Esmaeli Peyrovan (RIO 1st Lieutenant Habib Hakimi Kazerooni) shortly after bombing the aluminium factory in Arak and killing at least 30 of the workers. Taken by surprise, the Mirage flown by 1st Lieutenant Jamal Najah Fakhri ash-Shaikhli was shot down by one AIM-54A while still over the city: the pilot ejected safely, but parachuted directly into Arak where he was lynched by an outraged mob. On 16 February 1987, one of at least four Mirages attempting to raid Gachsaran was shot down by the F-14A piloted by Major Amir Aslani (RIO Parviz Moradi). A pair of F.1EQ-4s from No. 79 Squadron, escorting a formation of fighter-bombers, managed to extract at least some revenge only a day later, when they shot down the F-5E flown by Captain Hamid-Barzegari Nasr-Abadi over Lake Urumia. However, when the IrAF attempted to suppress the IRIAF through a Baz-AR attack on its major early warning radar station near Karaj, on 22 February 1987, it flew straight into a well-set trap: about a week before, the Iranians had re-deployed one of their MIM-23B I-HAWK SAM-sites high atop a nearby hill, thus increasing its engagement range. The result was that the Mirage F.1EQ-5 flown by 1st Lieutenant Yahya Kasim Ahmad from No. 81 Squadron was shot down and the pilot captured. Overall, it was one of the worst months of the entire war for the IrAF, becoming known as 'Black February': the consternation was sufficient for Baghdad to order the development of an extended-range version of the SS-1c Scud-B missile, thus launching the project al-Hussein.[25]

TANKER PLINKING

Through early 1987, No. 81 Squadron ran a three-month long campaign of Exocet attacks against the Iranian tanker shuttle. Eventually including over 100 anti-ship sorties alone (in addition to a similar number of sorties flown by Syrel and Caiman-carrying Mirages, and operations by MiG-23s), this was the most intense such operation of the war. Once again, the results were mediocre: 13 ships had been hit (three of them twice), three of which were declared CTL. After a temporary break in early April, anti-ship attacks were resumed mid-month, but resulted in only four further hits. A US intelligence support summarized this period as follows:

> Most anti-tanker strikes have occurred within the Iraqi declared war zone, which lies east and north of a line connecting the following points: 2930N/03830E, 2925N/04909E, 2900N/04930E, 2830N/04930E, and 3820N/05100E. All tankers within the closure area are considered targets. More specifically... all Iraqi anti-shipping attacks since January 1985 have occurred in an undeclared area consisting of a triangle bounded by 2943N/05010E, 2710N/05010E, and 2710N/05152E, with 85% of the attacks taking place within a 60nm radius of Bushehr. Attacks south of 2730N have been traditionally directed at shore facilities or sea-based oil terminals...102 ship attack profiles were flown during the first half of 1987, with the percentage of success roughly equivalent to previous years. At least a third of all Iraqi anti-shipping attacks conducted in 1986 occurred at night (1600Z-0200Z). Ship attacks thus far in 1987 have followed the same pattern.[26]

Much more successful was another strike of Mirage F.1EQ-5s from No.81 Squadron against the Sirri terminal. Instead of targeting easily replaceable ships, this time the Iraqi bombs hit the main loading terminal, destroying or badly damaging the jetty, manifold, and loading arms. The Iranian repair crews worked feverishly, but the loading of tankers could be resumed only a month later, and even then: the Iranians had to use a 3,000 metre-long flexible hose with a much reduced throughput.[27]

In the meantime, the IRGC had intensified its operations in the Persian Gulf, and launched a series of attacks on merchant ships underway to various GCC states, especially Kuwait. When Kuwait City requested help not only from the USA and Great Britain, but from the Soviet Union too, Washington announced the decision to put the country's tanker-fleet under the US flag on 7 March 1987. The vessels in question were to be escorted by warships of the US Navy, a continuously increasing number of which were not only deployed inside the Persian Gulf, but some of which began operating close to the Baghdad-declared exclusion zones along the Iranian coast. Indeed, as soon as the Iraqi Mirages re-launched their attacks they found themselves on a collision course with the US military. On 14 May, a pair of Mirage F.1EQ-5s from No. 81 Squadron approached the USS *Coontz* (DDG-40) 'in an aggressive manner': the crew of the guided missile destroyer reacted swiftly, powered up its radars and weapons and issued a radio warning that prompted Iraqi pilots to turn north – where they hit the shuttle tankers *Rodosea* and *Stilikon* with one AM.39 each (both vessels continued their voyage). Three days later, the Mirages attacked a caravan returning from BIK, and hit the ore/oil carrier *Aquamarine* and the tanker *Zeus*: both ships were left dead in the water, but then towed to Bushehr for repairs. Uncertain about results of these strikes, Baghdad ordered another attack for the same evening.[28]

CODE-NAME SUZANNA[29]

All through 1985 and early 1986, director of the IrAF Intelligence Department, Brigadier-General Mudher al-Farhan, was busy collecting intelligence about the work of the Iranian tanker-shuttle. Every day at 1800hrs, he would brief Major-General Sha'ban about related developments. At one point in time, Sha'ban realized that the IrAF was in possession of no reconnaissance photographs of any of the new loading terminals in the lower Persian Gulf. About a week after a related report was submitted to the GHQ, two officers of the GMID arrived in Sha'ban's office, making him an interesting offer: the intelligence service was ready to provide one of the Dassault Falcon 50 business jets operated on its behalf for a clandestine operation the purpose of which would be to 'visually inspect' some of the future targets. Masquerading as a biz-jet carrying 'three wealthy Iraqi businessmen', on 24 June 1986, the Falcon 50 made a trip from Amman in Jordan, via Iraq and Kuwait down the commercial corridor in the Persian Gulf, to Mumbai, in India, while carrying three experienced Mirage-pilots and a professional photographer. Underway, it made an 'unintended navigational error' and thus passed as close to Sirri as possible – enabling the photographer to take a series of photographs. As mentioned above, the Iranians noticed this overflight and this prompted them into moving the T-14 Terminal further south: before this could be done, the Iraqis attacked Sirri, on 12 August 1986.

While studying the resulting report, Sha'ban then came to the decision to deploy the same aircraft for anti-shipping operations in the lower Persian Gulf. On his request, the IrAF Technical Directorate (then commanded by Brigadier-General Attya) prepared a study that proposed the installation of the same Cyrano IVQ-C5 radar and the fire-control system of the Mirage F.1EQ-5 into a Falcon 50. With such work being beyond the IrAF's capabilities, decision was taken to request help from the DIA in Paris. As result of related negotiations, the Falcon 50 with the registration YI-ALE was sent to France. During its rebuild at Villaroche, it retained its usual controls on the left side of the cockpit but received a complete

The Falcon 50 with registration YI-ALE, before her conversion in France undertaken in late 1986. (Ahmad Sadik Collection)

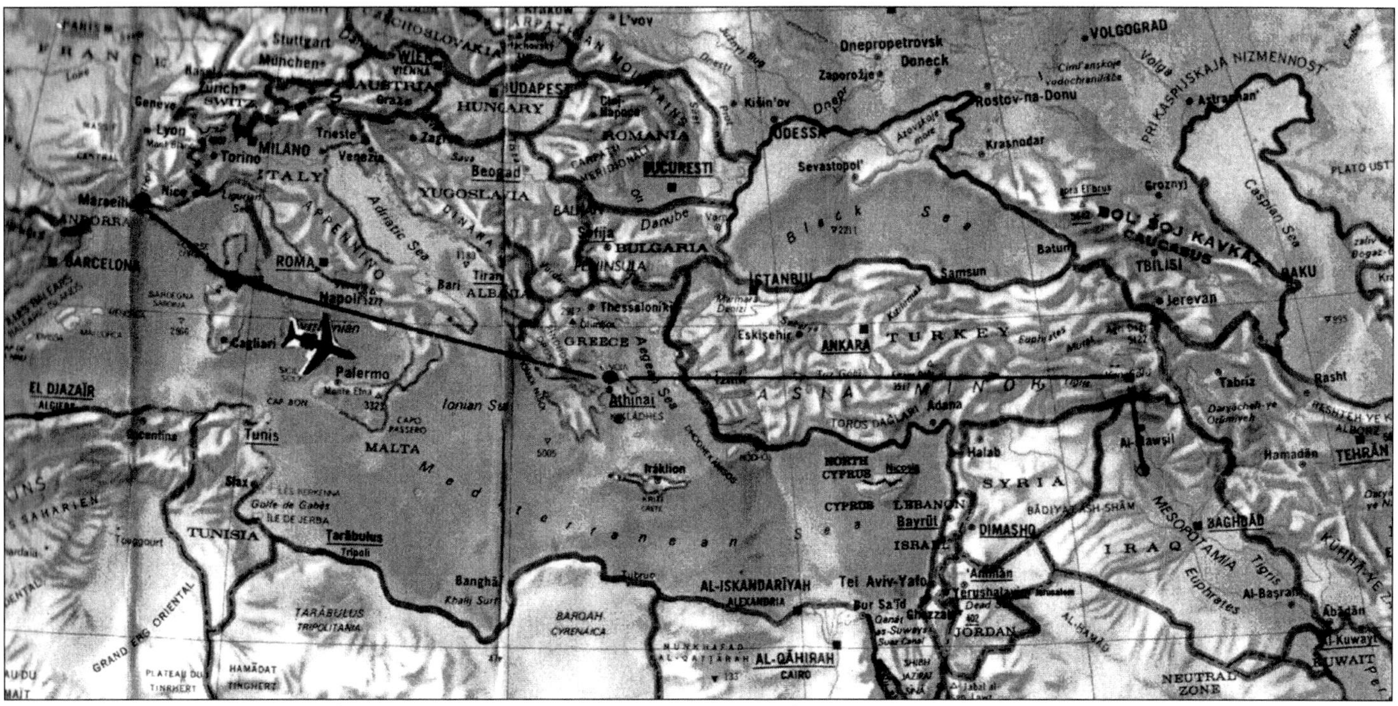

A map depicting Suzanna's delivery flight to Iraq on 9 February 1987. (Ahmad Sadik Collection)

cockpit of the F.1EQ-5 on the right side. External changes were even more dramatic: its registration was deleted and it received the typical pointed nose of the Mirage F.1 containing the Cyrano radar – and one launcher for AM.39 Exocet missiles under each wing. Following extensive testing in France, it was flown to Iraq on 9 February 1987 and commissioned into the IrAF service – reportedly under the designation 'Yarmouk' – six days later. Within the GHQ in Baghdad, the aircraft became known by her code-name, *Suzanna*.[30]

Following a series of training flights, on the morning of 17 May 1987 *Suzanna*'s crew received the order to load two Exocets and then transfer to Wahda AB for an operation over the Persian Gulf. Launched early in the evening under protection of a pair each of MiG-23s and MiG-25s, this brought the aircraft to the usual position north of Bahrain, at which the pilot turned left and then handed the commands over to his co-pilot, the one handling the Mirage-controls. After acquiring a suitable target, at 2108-2109 two Exocets were released from ranges of 35 and 24 kilometres. This time, both missiles hit their target – the US Navy's frigate USS *Stark* (FFG-37), the senior officers of which failed to realise she was under threat. While the first missile failed to detonate, the second went off, killing 37 sailors. The luke-warm attempt by two RSAF F-15C to intercept the Iraqi aircraft as this was returning towards the north, ordered

USS *Stark* as seen on the morning after the attack, still on fire and heavily listing to the port. (US Navy)

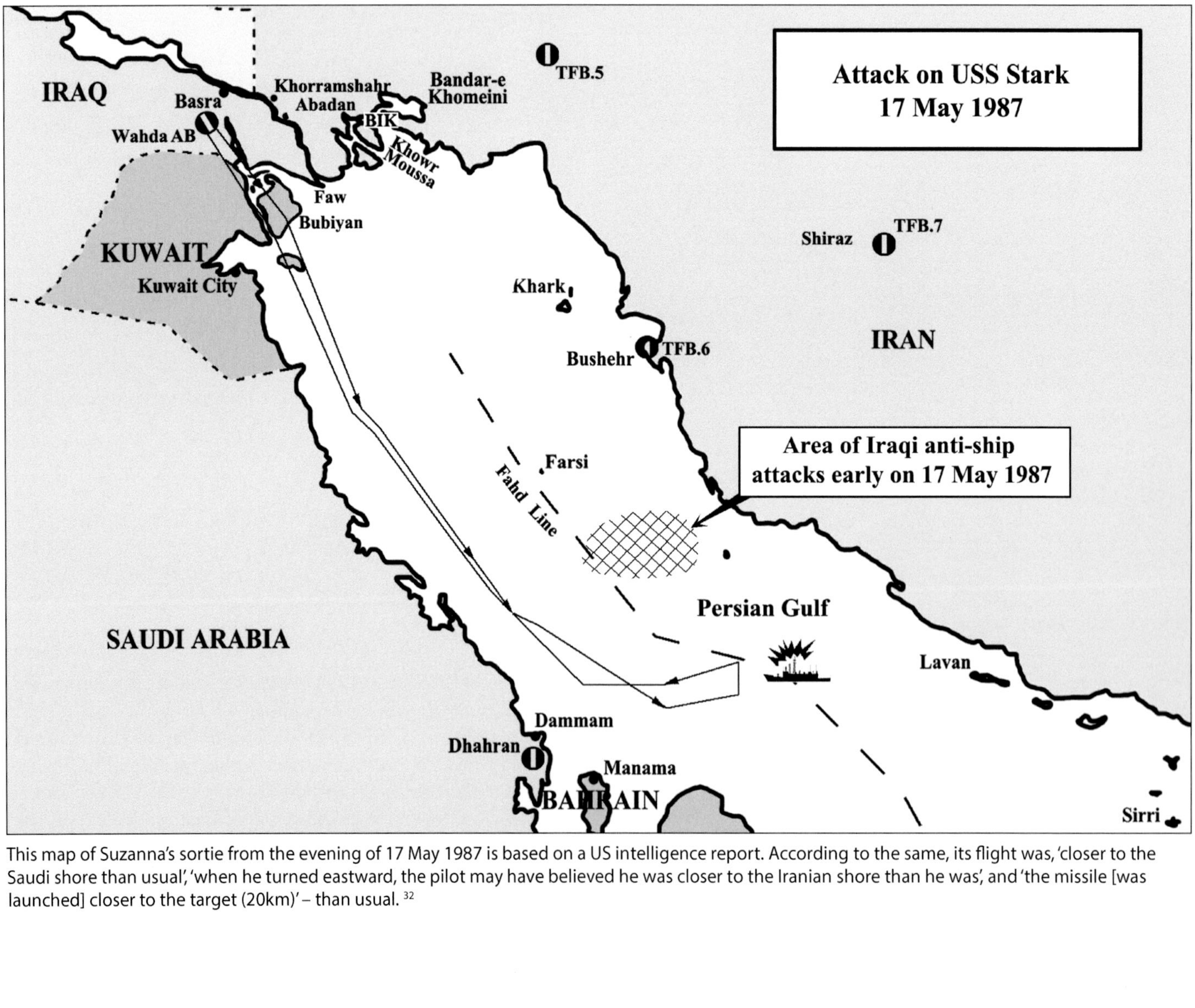

This map of Suzanna's sortie from the evening of 17 May 1987 is based on a US intelligence report. According to the same, its flight was, 'closer to the Saudi shore than usual', 'when he turned eastward, the pilot may have believed he was closer to the Iranian shore than he was', and 'the missile [was launched] closer to the target (20km)' – than usual. [32]

by the crew of one of the ELF-1's E-3A AWACS, remained unsuccessful. Shaken, but understanding the seriousness of this affair, Baghdad subsequently apologised for this unintentional attack, and compensated the Pentagon and the families of the sailors killed for all the damage caused. In turn, the USA entered an uneasy strategic alliance with Baghdad, and – under excuse of 'better coordination' with the Iraqi military in order to avoid further incidents of this kind – began providing Iraq with, amongst other items, intelligence about the movement of Iranian shuttle tankers in the lower Persian Gulf.[31]

Happy allies: Captain Abdul Karim Mohammed (left) shaking hands with Captain James M Drager (skipper of USS *Guadalcanal*), after being picked out of the Persian Gulf, on 31 August 1987. (US DoD)

COMPETITION WITH SADDAM

Politically-motivated restraint and the need to replenish the stock of Exocets kept the Iraqi Mirages away from the Persian Gulf for nearly a month after attack on the USS *Stark*. However, when realising that the Iranians had exploited this opportunity to expand their shuttle fleet and stock additional crude in motherships anchored near Larak and Hormuz, No. 81 Squadron was ordered to resume the campaign on 1 July 1987. By then, the links between Washington and Baghdad were as close as that the US Navy's warships began providing verbal radio warnings of IRIAF interceptors to the Iraqi aircraft. Unsurprisingly, Mirage F.1EQ-5 pilots became extremely bold and began targeting ships as far south as Farsi. By the end of September, up to 25 shuttle tankers were hit, mostly by Exocets. Not entirely satisfied, Saddam additionally ordered the 224th Missile Brigade into action again. Between 18 September 1987 and 14 May 1988, this unit launched a series of attacks with the brand new al-Hussein missiles at Lavan. Out of 15 strikes documented by the Iranians, 11 hit barren land or surrounding sea, or overflew the island and hit the overlooking mainland mountains, while four caused some damage to several storage tanks.[33]

Thanks to the US warnings, the Iraqi pilots became reckless. Soon after passing over the Bubiyan Island in Kuwait while underway to strike the port of Farsi Island on 29 August 1987, a formation of four of F.1EQ-4s lost one aircraft to a technical malfunction: the Mirage returned safely to Wahda AB, but had to be replaced by a spare that lacked the Remora and Sycomor pods. The formation continued the mission, but then made a navigational mistake which caused it to remain much too long in the target zone. This delay was perfectly sufficient for Major Va'ali Oveisi (RIO 1st Lieutenant Aziz Nasir-Zadeh) to scramble in an F-14A from TFB.6 and catch-up with the Iraqis: as the Mirages pulled up after their bombing runs, the spare aircraft – piloted by Captain Abdul Karim Mohammed – received a hit from an AIM-54A. Mohammed ejected safely after distancing from the target zone, and was picked up by the US Navy's amphibious warfare ship USS *Guadalcanal* (LPH-7), two days later. Ironically, convinced the IRIAF was 'no more', and its F-14s 'not operational', the IrAF subsequently concluded that his Mirage was shot down by a US-made FIM-92A Stinger MANPADs, which the GMID heard the Iranians have obtained a few months earlier from the Mujahidden in Afghanistan.[34]

Therefore, the IrAF remained undeterred. On 2 October 1987 it deployed a single MiG-25RB to photograph the entire length of the Iranian coast. The aircraft eventually ran out of fuel and was forced to land at Abu Dhabi International, causing quite some excitement amongst the local authorities before it was permitted to return to Iraq via Saudi Arabia, two days later. In turn, based on intelligence collected in this fashion, on 5 October 1987 No. 81 Squadron launched its longest-ranged and most complex raid ever. Supported by no fewer than 16 F.1EQ-4s and F.1EQ-5s that acted as tankers, eight fighter-bombers loaded with two Type 25 each delivered simultaneous attacks on Farsi, Lavan, Larak, and Hormuz. While four easily replaceable motherships and tankers were damaged at Larak and Hormuz, the attack on Lavan caused damage that was to prove far more decisive in the long run.[35]

Less successful was an attempt by No. 89 Squadron to strike the oil facilities in the Gachsaran area, on 14 November 1987: this was intercepted by a pair of F-4Es from TFB.6 while transiting BIK area: one of several air-to-air missiles fired by the Iranians hit the aircraft flown by 1st Lieutenant Karim Abdul-Rahman al-Bayati, forcing him to eject into captivity.[36]

POINTLESS TARGET[37]

In November 1987, the GHQ in Baghdad had ordered the IrAF into one of the most pointless missions of the war: an attack on the construction site of two nuclear reactors south of Bushehr. Launched in cooperation between Tehran and Germany in 1975, the construction of this project was stopped in January 1979, when Reactor 1 was 75-85% complete and Reactor 2 45-70% complete. The construction site was subsequently abandoned and no further work was undertaken for the next 15 years.[38]

Nevertheless, in 1982, the Iraqi intelligence received – obviously bogus – reports about 'renewed contracts' between Germany and Iran, and thus a high-level committee was formed including officers of the GMID and the IrAF Operations Directorate, which became responsible for, 'monitoring the further progress'. For entirely unexplainable reasons, in early 1984, this committee convinced itself that the work on the construction site had resumed and that the Iranians requested the Germans to construct a 50cm thick concrete dome over both reactors. Sadik explained:

The Arcole penetrating bomb was an 'enhanced penetrator' version of the Matra BGL-250/400 series, originally developed for *Project-Baz.* It entered service with in Iraq in 1986. (Matra)

A pair of BGL-400s as installed on the F.1EQ-5 serial number 4561, together with Patrick designator pod. The weapon was used several times in the configurations depicted in this photograph before the IrAF abandoned its further application due to disappointing performance. Ironically, a completely reworked variant was to see its first combat deployment by the French air force against Iraq during the war over Kuwait, in 1991. (Matra)

This piece of information turned into a source of headache for the Iraqi committee because the IrAF had no weapon that could penetrate such an obstacle. Sha'ban then ordered the Director of the Armament Directorate to search for possible suppliers. It turned out that the only country ready to provide help was France, where the Arcole penetrating bomb was under development. The MIC proposed to cooperate in this project, hoping the resulting weapon would be capable of penetrating the dome of the Iranian reactors at Bushehr.[39]

The situation changed in 1987 when the GMID obtained the original plan for the reactor – only to find out that the actual thickness of the dome was much less than originally reported. With the IrAF meanwhile roaming the skies over the Persian Gulf at will, the decision was taken to attack. Assessing the site as 'defended by numerous anti-aircraft artillery pieces and SA-7-teams', F-4Es and F-14As', Basu and his team planned a mission following now-standardised patterns: supported by a Syrel-carrying F.1EQ-2, a quartet of MiG-23MLs that would drag the IRIAF interceptors away from the target zone, and a MiG-25 that would cover the withdrawal of the attacking aircraft. As soon as Iranian interceptors would react, the actual strike package would attack from the south-east; eight F.1EQ-4s (supported by ten tankers) would then target the domes with Mk.84s; the second wave would consist of two F.1EQ-5s attacking with AS.30Ls while escorted by a pair of F.1EQ-4s; while a single MiG-25PDS would cover the withdrawing formation. Contrary to earlier practices, the selection of pilots was left to the CO of Saddam AB and his staff: what remained similar to earlier times was a series of intensive exercises, including the construction of a mock target, in the desert west of Saddam AB.

The operation was launched on the morning of 17 November 1987. Eight F.1EQ-4s (supported by ten tankers) delivered their bombs at 0945. They were followed by two F.1EQ-5s (escorted by a pair of F.1EQ-4s) that attacked with AS.30Ls at 1600. On the next day, four F.1EQ-4s armed with Mk.84 – supported by five tankers and five other aircraft – repeated the exercise under similar circumstances. The operation was declared as a complete success: nobody involved thought to ask why the RWRs of the attacking Mirages registered no threats at all, or that the Iranians never opened fire at them. Nevertheless, the IrAF was to strike the same – still abandoned – construction site at least once again, on 19 June 1988.

SHEEP FOR BRITONS

Following the unnecessary intermezzo in Bushehr, No. 81 Squadron reinforced its anti-ship campaign: between mid-November and end of December 1987 at least 18 of its Exocets scored hits. Although the unit thus achieved its best monthly result of the entire war, overall

The second Mirage F.1EQ-6 manufactured for Iraq was one of only six aircraft of this sub-variant to reach Iraq before the end of the war with Iran. Like 11 examples of the earlier F.1EQ-5 variant it was painted in camouflage suited for operations over the sea (see colour section for details). (Photo by Jean-Francois Lipka)

effectiveness remained minimal for the same set of problems as usual: finding the Iranian shuttle tankers alone was anything but easy, not to mention at least rendering them CTL. Indeed, while not one tanker was written off, two successful strikes repeatedly hit the same ships; three hit IRGC-operated anti-aircraft defence ships towing decoys, while at least three of the vessels damaged by Exocets were actually salvage ships operated either by the Singaporean company Semco, or by the National Iranian Oil Company. Nevertheless, the Iraqis were celebrating – as were their French advisors: upon hearing rumours that the attack on *Salvital* (hit off Pars on 13 November) had killed four British crewmembers, the chief representative of Dassault in Iraq donated four slaughtered sheep to the CO of No. 81 Squadron. When *Salvenus* was hit, six days later, and the rumour had it that another four Britons were killed, the French donated another four slaughtered sheep to the unit.[40]

Far more effective was the next raid on Larak: flown by three Mirage F.1EQ-5s on 22 December 1987, it resulted in bomb hits on one mothership (*Seawise Giant*, then the largest ship in the World), one storage vessel, and three customer-tankers.[41]

Table 7: Known IrAF Strategic Air Strikes on the Iranian Economy, 1987

Date	Target Area	Target	Involved Aircraft and Notes
2 Feb	Arak	aluminium factory	Mirage F.1EQ-4 (bombs)
16 Feb	Gachsaran	oil installations	Mirage F.1EQ-4 (bombs)
17 Feb	Tabriz	oil refinery	Mirage F.1EQ-4 (bombs)
7 Apr	Sirri	loading terminal	Mirage F.1EQ-5 (bombs)
7 May	Tehran	oil refinery	Mirage F.1EQ-5 (bombs)
13 May	Esfahan	oil refinery	Mirage F.1EQ-5 (AS.30L)
29 Aug	Farsi	loading terminal	Mirage F.1EQ-4 (bombs)
29 Sep	Nekka	powerplant	Mirage F.1EQ-5 (bombs)
29 Sep	Qatour	bridge	Mirage F.1EQ-5 & Su-22M-4K
5 Oct	Hormuz	loading terminal	Mirage F.1EQ-5 (bombs)
5 Oct	Larak	loading terminal	Mirage F.1EQ-5 (bombs)
5 Oct	Lavan	powerplant	Mirage F.1EQ-5 (bombs)
10 Oct	Ahwaz	Tang-e Fani	Mirage F.1EQ-4 (bombs)
10 Oct	Ahwaz	Bid Boland	Mirage F.1EQ-4 (bombs)
14 Nov	Gachsaran	oil installations	Mirage F.1EQ-4 (bombs)
22 Dec	Larak	loading terminal	Mirage F.1EQ-4/5 (bombs)

PROJECT BAZ-5

Combat attrition during 1987 had forced the MIC into placing another order for Mirage F.1EQs. General Audran was assassinated in 1985, and with him the Iraqis had lost their most influential friend in Paris, while Dassault was keen to close the assembly line for F.1s and manufacture Mirage 2000s instead. Heavily indebted and already unable to pay even for what the French had delivered by that time (by 1987, Iraq owed France more than US$6 billion alone for aircraft and armament provided since 1981), Baghdad could not afford a new type, and the Mirage 2000IQ-deal had to be postponed again. Related negotiations thus went on for months, until the MIC offered the French a contract for the construction of an overhaul and maintenance centre for the F.1 in Iraq, and the Saudis and Kuwaitis agreed to finance the new deal. Eventually, Dassault decided to assemble a final batch and the contract for *Project Baz-5* was signed on 9 December 1987, stipulating deliveries of 12 additional Mirage F.1EQ-6s and 4 two-seaters.[42]

Indeed, thanks to Kuwaiti financing, France rushed to deliver the first Mirage F.1EQ-6 from *Project Baz-4* to Iraq in February 1988. This variant was equipped with the Cyrano IV-SP1 radar – the first including digital processors and other technology from Mirage 2000 – and internal underwing hardpoints for installation of Alkan chaff and flare dispensers. While five additional examples followed by June of the same year, they saw only very limited action during the war with Iran. The same was valid for eight Raphael TH reconnaissance pods that arrived in Iraq around the same time: each was equipped with a radar theoretically capable of tracking ground targets with a resolution of between three and six metres from 100 kilometres away, and feeding the resulting image to the ground station in real time. However, the system experienced numerous technical malfunctions early on, and saw only very limited service.[43]

Table 8: Overview of Project Baz-5, December 1987						
Contract designation	Date of Order	Number of Aircraft	Version	Serial Numbers	Roll-Out Dates	Acceptance Dates
BAZ-521x	9 Dec 1987	6	Mirage F.1EQ-6	4650-4655	18 Dec 1989 – 16 May 1990	last delivered on 30 May 1990
BAZ-521x	9 Dec 1987	4	Mirage F.1BQ	4656-4659		never delivered
BAZ-521x	9 Dec 1987	6	Mirage F.1EQ-6	4660-4665		never delivered

7
BEST TIMES

After a year of high-intensity combat operations, Baghdad's inability to continue paying for expensive French weapons caused a shortage of Exocets and even spares for Mirages. This crisis was once again resolved with the help of Kuwaiti loans, only for Baghdad to become concerned about a possible Iranian spring offensive. While – at least initially – still running the Oil Campaign as before, Sha'ban and Basu began replacing Mirages with a new anti-ship weapon; instead, the F.1EQs were ordered to make more use of bombs and to strike different targets. Almost by accident, the combination of a growing number of Iraqi air raids against crucial targets deep in Iran, major strategic mistakes by the IRGC, and the massive Iraqi deployment of chemical weapons then resulted in the collapse of the Iranian capability to continue waging the war. With the battered IRIAF offering only sporadic resistance the IrAF was largely free to operate deep over western Iran: this is why the final phase of the war is recalled as the best times of the Iraqi Mirages.

BADGER ALLY

The necessity for Baghdad to secure another multi-billion dollar loan from Kuwait in order to finance *Project Baz-5*, and acquire a fresh batch of Exocets, resulted in the IrAF re-launching the Oil Campaign only in mid-January 1988. Seven shuttle tankers were confirmed as hit by Exocets by the end of the month, but none was written off. Finally concluding the Mirage-Exocet combination as insufficient, the GHQ then pressed its new weapon into action. It was already by 1986 that continuous problems with AM.39s had prompted the MIC into placing an order for four Xian H-6D bombers in China. Representing a slight upgrade of the Tu-16 bomber, these aircraft were equipped with the Type 245 surveillance radar, capable of detecting large surface targets from a range of 150 kilometres. The first three arrived in Iraq in the same year, together with 100 CHETA YJ-6L (exported under the designation 'C.601' or 'CAS-1 Kraken') anti-ship missiles that had a range of 120 kilometres. The unit operating them – No. 10 Squadron – was declared operational in December 1987. Although theoretically far more vulnerable to the Iranian interceptors than F.1EQs, thanks to the Fahd Line and the related availability of the Mirage Alley – soon 're-named' to the 'Badger Alley' by the seamen underway in the Persian Gulf – and US Navy's warnings, the H-6Ds and C.601s were to prove far more successful: by mid-March, their missiles scored seven confirmed hits.[1]

Whenever they returned over the Persian Gulf the effectiveness of the Mirage operations remained minimal. On 7 February 1988, two F.1EQ-5s found their way to the berths on Khark blocked by the Iranian supertanker *Khark-5*, and bombed the ULCC instead. Two days later, No. 81 Squadron attempted its last large-scale anti-ship raid of the war. The first formation of three aircraft barely passed Farsi Island when it was intercepted by the F-14A flown by Captain Hossein Khalili (RIO 1st Lieutenant Mustafa Qiyassi), scrambled from TFB.6. Instead of engaging the lonesome Tomcat in an air combat, all three Iraqis jettisoned their drop tanks and anti-ship missiles and attempted to beat a hasty retreat. Khalili cut their turn and shot down the F.1EQ-5 flown by 1st Lieutenant Harith Ahmed, who was killed. Only three hours later, the same Iranian crew was scrambled again to intercept another Mirage formation and this time claimed two kills: though the Iraqis deny having suffered any further losses.[2]

FATAL BLOWS

Other Iraqi units were much more successful. In January 1988, a squadron-sized Su-22 raid wrecked the oil refinery of Tabriz. On

A pre-strike reconnaissance photograph of the Rey oil refinery, showing aiming points for the mission on 22 February 1988. (Nabeel N Sideeq, via Ahmad Sadik)

22 February four of No. 79 Squadron's F.1EQ-4s (supported by five tankers) led by Major Nabeel N Sideeq then wrecked the Rey oil refinery outside Tehran. Combined with No. 81 Squadron's raid on Lavan, on 20 January 1988, it was precisely this series of strikes that maimed the Iranian war-fighting capability: it caused a massive shortage of fuel all over Iran. Worse yet – at least from the Iranian point of view – was the fact that these strikes caught the IRGC with the majority of its forces deployed for a new offensive into northern Iraq: combined with the critical shortage of fuel, the poor state of the Iranian road and railway networks meant that the majority of the Pasdaran would remain in north-western Iran – and thus well away from crucial battlefields in the south – for the rest of this conflict.[3]

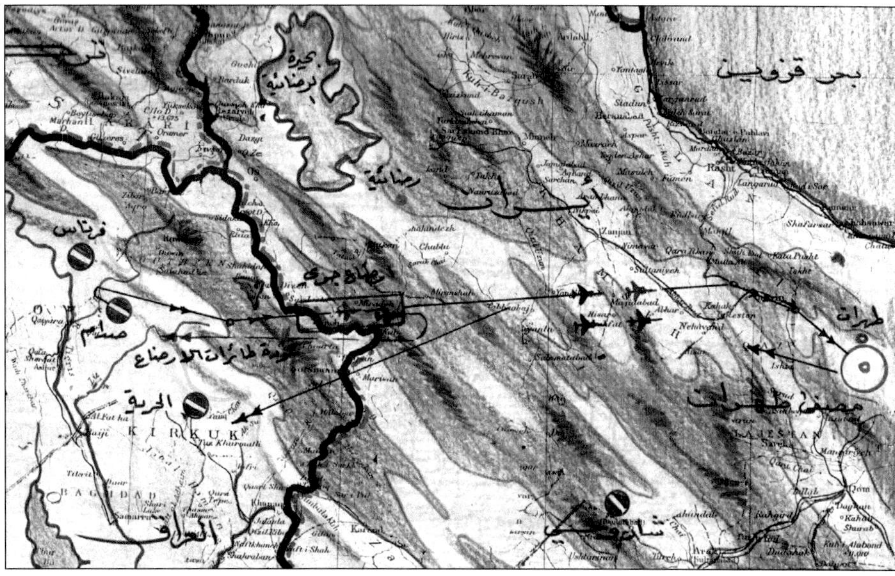

A map of No. 79 Squadron's raid on Tehran's Rey oil refinery of 22 February 1988, as drawn by the leader of that mission. (Ahmad Sadik Collection)

When the Iranians then did launch their much-expected big offensive – Operation *Val Fajr-10* – during the night to 14 March 1988, they destroyed the 43rd Division of the Iraqi Army and threatened Suleimaniyah and Kirkuk. However, as all the reinforcements rushed to the battlefield and up to 200 sorties flown by the IrAF failed to show effects, Saddam ordered the air force into a massive deployment of chemical weapons. In the course of a 45 minute raid by more than 50 MiG-21s, Mirage F.1EQs and Su-22s flown during the afternoon of 16 March 1988, the town of Halabja was saturated with hundreds of bombs filled with nerve agents. While this attack hit next to no Iranian troops, but massacred between 3,200 and 6,800 civilians instead, it demoralized the majority of IRGC's combatants to a point where they became unwilling to continue the war.[4]

Post-strike reconnaissance photograph (probably taken by a Harold-equipped Mirage F.1EQ), showing the huge column of smoke caused by the raid of 22 February 1988. (Ahmad Sadik Collection)

THE ENDGAME

Unaware of what they had already caused, Sha'ban and Basu continued ordering their units into additional strikes. After not venturing anywhere near Khark for five weeks, on the evening of 19 March 1988, a pair of F.1EQ-5s armed with Spanish-made Mk.84s took the Iranians by surprise and delivered a low-altitude slash attack on supertankers *Avaj* and *Sanandaj* as these were loading crude. The two pairs of 1,000kg heavy bombs they dropped caused far more damage than any Exocets could: *Avaj* lost 22 of her crew and was gutted by fire, while *Sanandaj* lost 26 and broke into two. Both ships were written off. However, on the way out, either the two fighter-bombers, or one of escorting Mirages, then came under attack by an F-14A and was shot down.[5]

Although causing the greatest loss of life during the Oil Campaign, even this attack failed to achieve its purpose. On the contrary, statistics available in the official Iranian documentation clearly show that despite 189 successful Iraqi strikes on shuttle tankers there was not only no reduction in the tonnage of the crude oil exported, but also none in the amount of oil products imported. Indeed, the amounts constantly rose, until reaching at least 100% of those from 1984. Thus – and contrary to the strikes on Iranian oil refineries – the overall effectiveness of the Iraqi effort against the tanker shuttle remained minimal.[6]

It is almost certain that the analysts by Iraqi intelligence drew similar conclusions, because the attack of 19 March 1988 was followed by the longest lull (six weeks) before the anti-shipping offensive was resumed, and then by H-6Ds. In the meantime, the IrAF flew far more effective air strikes on the oilfields in Khuzestan and the refineries in Tabriz and Esfahan, further magnifying Tehran's problem with fuel supply. While these remained unopposed, operations over the Persian Gulf did not: a pair of Mirage F.1EQ-5s underway to attack the radar station on Farsi Island using AS.30Ls, on 21 April 1988 was intercepted by the F-14A flown by Colonel Arsalan Khademi (RIO Captain Abbad Sanat'kar) scrambled from TFB.6. Shortly after the Iraqi Captain Amer Abdullah fired one AS.30L from a range of four kilometres and made the usual turn away from the target, an AIM-7E-2 Sparrow proximity fused a few metres behind it. Abdullah managed to nurse his badly damaged Mirage for an emergency landing at Dhahran AB, in Saudi Arabia, where this was stopped by the arrestor net at the end of the runway. At least officially, this incident did not upset the IrAF. Unofficially,

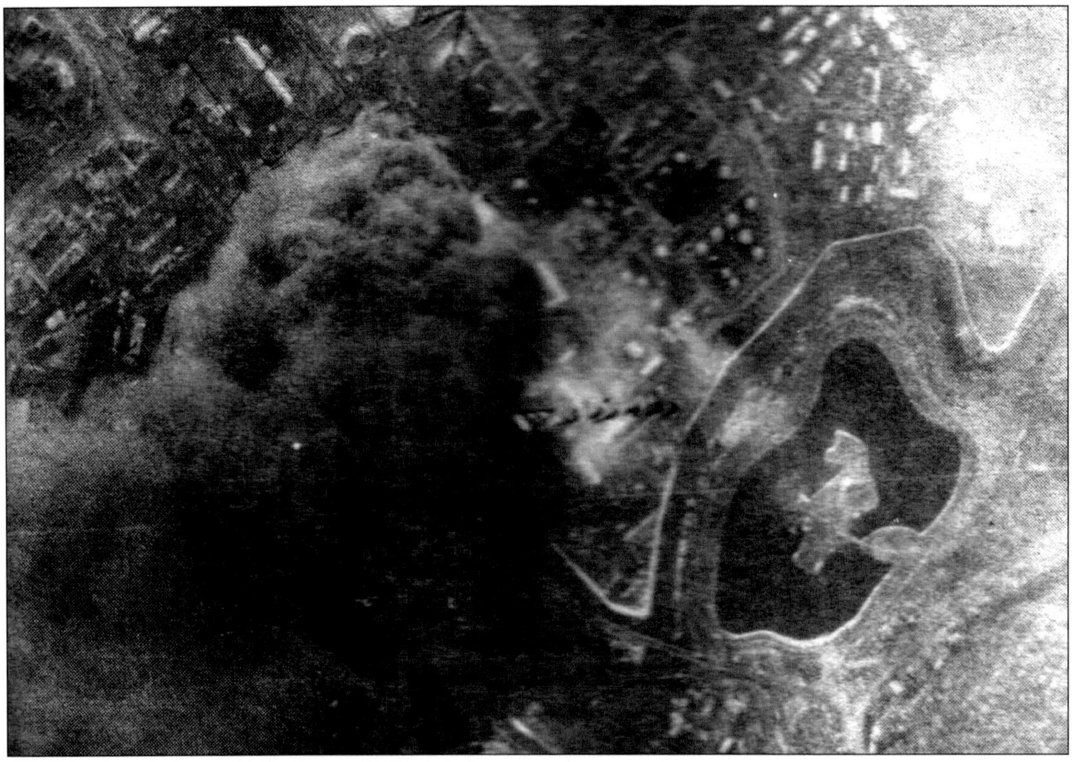

On 5 March 1988, other IrAF units demolished the Kermanshah oil refinery, as visible on this post-strike photograph. The destruction of key Iranian oil refineries in early 1988 was one of major reasons for Tehran's decision to accept a UN-mediated cease-fire. (Ahmad Sadik Collection)

The Mirage F.1EQ-4 serial number 4510, a veteran of at least a dozen long-range raids, was shot down during a repeated strike on Esfahan's oil refinery on 3 April 1988. (Dassault, via Michel Benichou)

The Mirage F.1EQ-5 serial number 4569, as seen at the end of the runway at Dhahran AB, after Captain Abdullah made an emergency landing on 21 April 1988. The Remora pod – visible under the right wing – prevented the Sparrow fired by an Iranian F-14 from causing much more damage. (via Ali Tobchi)

its Mirage-community drew different conclusions and decided to avenge the near-loss at earliest opportunity.[7]

LIBERATION OF FAW

As of spring 1988, the Mirage F.1EQ-4s and F.1EQ-5s were still the only fighters in service with the IrAF equipped with guided weapons. Certainly enough, Su-22M-2Ks could deploy Kh-28 anti-radar missiles, and the Su-22M-3/4Ks could – in theory – use Kh-29L (ASCC/NATO codename 'AS-14 Kedge'). However, while considered even more powerful and cheaper than the AS.30L, this combination suffered from a major drawback: once the Su-22 launched a Kh-29L, its pilot had to continue moving in the direction of the target until the missile impact. The reason was that the laser-marker was installed in the nose cone and fixed in all axes, thus forcing the pilot to continue flying the aircraft straight towards the target upon weapons release. The Mirages equipped with the Patrick pod had no such limitations. Therefore, the decision was taken to mate the two systems: the F.1EQ-5s would designate targets, while the Su-22M-3Ks would launch their Kh-29Ls and pull out. The Mirage could then continue guiding the missile, but was free to perform whatever manoeuvre was required. Related work was undertaken in Iraq, and resulted in the combination of the Patrick designator with the Kh-29L. This underwent a successful test on 20 September 1987 and was prepared for combat: indeed, a decision was taken to assign it the crucial role during the coming offensive for the liberation of the Faw: the attack on the 'cylinder-type' pontoon bridge over the Shatt al-Arab – the primary communication route for the Iranian troops on the peninsula, positioned so far

A reconnaissance photograph of the Iranian 'pipe' (or 'roller') bridge over the Shatt al-Arab, before this was destroyed by Mirage-guided Su-22s and their Kh-29 missiles on 17 April 1988. (Ahmad Sadik Collection)

south that it was outside the range of the Iraqi long-range artillery.

While all earlier attempts to knock out this crucial facility had failed, on the morning of 17 April 1988, four Mirage F.1EQ-5s and F.1EQ-6s – protected by the usual combination of MiG-25PDS', MiG-29s, Syrel and Caiman-carrying Mirage F.1EQ-2s, and Kh-28-armed Su-22M-2Ks – designated the targets for about a dozen attacks flown by an entire squadron of Su-22M-4Ks. They not only cut the pipe-bridge in at least six points, but also demolished the Iranian headquarters and artillery positions. The rest of the IrAF supported the following onslaught of the Republican Guards and the Army by plastering positions of the sole Iranian brigade defending the peninsula with chemical weapons. The Iranian defences quickly collapsed, and Faw was declared completely liberated on the evening of 18 April 1998.

GIRAFFE OVER THE SEA

After Captain Abdullah's F.1EQ-5 was nearly shot down by an F-14A over the Farsi Island, pilots of No. 89 Squadron developed a plan to return the favour and ambush one of the IRIAF's F-14As. A suitable opportunity offered itself as soon as a new early warning radar station was set up at the liberated Faw peninsula: on 24 April 1988, a pair of Mirage F.1EQ-4s and F.1EQ-5s was each scrambled into action. Using a combination of offensive split and the Giraffe tactics, the F.1EQ-5s then acted as bait for a single Tomcat underway on a CAP about 50 kilometres south of Khark, dragging the Iranian fighter in front of the two F.1EQ-4s until Captain Ahmed Hussein Khalaf established a lock-on and fired one Super 530F from a range of 10 kilometres. According to Iraqi sources, Hussein's missile either scored a direct hit, or detonated right underneath target's cockpit, and the pilot was subsequently credited with a confirmed kill. However, whatever the Iraqis saw or concluded after reviewing the gun-camera film, Major Jalal Zandi managed to land the badly damaged Tomcat back in Bushehr: the IRIAF did not lose a single F-14A in all of 1988.[8]

SPRINGTIME OVER THE KAROUN RIVER[9]

For the rest of the war, the IrAF operated under the condition of not only aerial supremacy over Iran: it actually enjoyed total aerial superiority at least over the Khuzestan province and the central frontlines. Sadik described one of the typical multi-squadron operations from Abu Ubaida AB launched in May 1988:

> Following the breakfast all pilots were summoned to the briefing room. The commander of the base, Brigadier-General Fahad, presented the plan for attacks on the Iranian army camps and several roads in the southwest of Iran in support of Operation *Tawalkalna All-a-Allah*. To facilitate the movement of their troops, the Iranian engineers erected two pontoon brides over the Karoun River, and our General Staff requested the destruction of both of these. The strike was to be led by a Mirage F.1EQ-5 that would designate targets for multiple Su-22Ms equipped with Kh-29L missiles. These would be followed by all the F.1EQ-2/4s of No. 79 Squadron and all the F.1EQ-5s of No. 91 Squadron, mostly equipped with general purpose bombs. The stand-off jamming element consisted of two Mirage F.1EQ-2s equipped with Caiman pods, the anti-radar section consisted of two Su-22M-2Ks from No. 109 Squadron equipped with Kh-28s, while top cover was provided by a pair of MiG-29s. Well to the rear, a lonesome Mirage F.1EQ-2 monitored the work of the Iranian air defences with help of its Syrel pod.
>
> After taking off at 0800hrs, the lead F.1EQ-4 – call-sign "Noor-1", flown by Major Kifah – took a position southwest of Ahwaz. From there, Kifah acquired his target and put his marker at the right end of the pontoon bridge. Shortly after, he heard a call from "Barke-1" – the lead Su-22M-3K from No. 69 Squadron – confirming he was tracking the marked target. Barke-1 then launched the missile. A few seconds later Kifah was stunned to see his display turning white. It took additional seconds before the heat, smoke and debris cleared enough for him to realize that the Patrick suffered no failure, but that the massive detonation of the Kh-29L blotted out the FLIR-picture. Next he saw that the targeted bridge was cut off from the river bank, and thus Kifah switched his attention to the left end of the bridge, repeating the procedure. This time, the Kh-29L was released by "Barke-2'. The second missile scored a direct hit, once again turning the display in the Mirage's cockpit white. What was left of the bridge was floating down the brownish water of the Karoun River. With their job over, the three pilots distanced from the combat zone, leaving it free for incoming formations of MiG-23BNs, Mirage F.1EQs and Su-22s: they bombed and rocketed Iranian camps and troop concentrations to great extents and without any disturbance. Once the entire ballet was over, a MiG-25RB passed high above to take post-strike reconnaissance photographs, and finally a Mirach-100 unmanned aerial vehicle was deployed to find out if there would be any Iranian troop movements in reaction. Coming of age, the IrAF was displaying a perfect example of a well-organized, large-scale operation, saturating a relatively small area with a combined air strike of dozens of fighter-bombers.

Table 9: Known IrAF Strategic Air Strikes on the Iranian Economy, 1988[11]			
Date	Target Area	Aiming Points	Involved Aircraft and Notes
8 Jan	Tabriz	oil refinery	Su-22
20 Jan	Lavan	oil refinery	Mirage F.1EQ-5
7 Feb	Khark	T-Jetty & Sea Island Terminal	Mirage F.1EQ-5
11 Feb	Genaveh	tank farm	Mirage F.1EQ
11 Feb	Genaveh	Manifold	Mirage F.1EQ
14 Feb	Baghi Malak	booster-pumping station	MiG-23BN
22 Feb	Rey/Tehran	oil refinery, distillation towers	Mirage F.1EQ-4
5 Mar	Kermanshah	sugar factory	MiG-23BN, Su-22
5 Mar	Kermanshah	oil refinery	MiG-23BN, Su-22, Su-25
10 Mar	Razan	booster-pumping station	MiG-23BN
10 Mar	Azneh	booster-pumping station	Su-22
11 Mar	Mahshahr	liquid gas refinery	MiG-23BN, Mirage F.1, Su-22
15 Mar	Genaveh	Manifold	Mirage F.1EQ
16 Mar	Mahshahr	tank farm	MiG-23BN, Mirage F.1, Su-22, Su-25
17 Mar	Shiraz	oil refinery	Mirage F.1EQ
19 Mar	Khark	ULCCs	Mirage F.1EQ
29 Mar	Lavan	oil refinery	Mirage F.1EQ
3 Apr	Tabriz	oil refinery	Mirage F.1EQ
3 Apr	Esfahan	oil refinery	Mirage F.1EQ-4
4 Apr	Mahshahr	tank farm	MiG-23BN, Mirage F.1EQ, Su-22, Su-25
4 May	Shiraz	oil refinery	Mirage F.1EQ-4
14 May	Larak	oil terminal	Mirage F.1EQ-4
21 Apr	Farsi Island	radar station	Mirage F.1EQ
23 Jun	Ahwaz	production wells, Oilfield No. 1	Su-22
23 Jun	Ahwaz	production wells, Oilfield No. 2	Mirage F.1EQ
23 Jun	Kaj Saran	production wells, Oilfield No. 2	Su-22
23 Jun	Kaj Saran	production wells, Oilfield No. 3	Su-22
23 Jun	Bibi Hakima	production wells, Oilfield No. 1	MiG-23BN
23 Jun	Bibi Hakima	production wells, Oilfield No. 2	MiG-23BN
30 Jun	Kinjan	gas separation plant	Mirage F.1EQ
6 Jul	Genaveh	Manifold	Mirage F.1EQ
6 Jul	Gorreh	booster-pumping station	Mirage F.1EQ
7 Jul	Genaveh	tank farm	Mirage F.1EQ
16 Jul	Sadab	booster-pumping station	Su-22
17 Jul	Ahwaz	booster-pumping station	Su-22
19 Jul	Bezrawiah	booster-pumping station	Su-22
19 Jul	Gorreh	booster-pumping station	Mirage F.1EQ
20 Jul	Gorreh	booster-pumping station	Mirage F.1EQ
3 Aug	Kinjan	gas-separation plant	MiG-23BN
3 Aug	Bezrawiah	booster-pumping station	Su-22
4 Aug	Tabge Fani	booster-pumping station	MiG-23BN

FINAL ACT

Through June 1988, the IrAF returned to raid targets deeper inside Iran, especially the oil fields in the Ahwaz, Kaj Saran, and Bibi Hakima areas. On 23 June, four Mirage F.1s from Nos.79 and No.89 Squadrons led by Lieutenant-Colonel Omar attacked the oilfields in the Ahwaz area using AS.30Ls to cause several massive oil-well fires. Genaveh was once again on the receiving end of the Iraqi attacks through July, when also a number of pumping stations all around south-western Iran were hit: slowly but certainly, the IrAF was running out of targets. Perhaps in the light of the latter fact,

Although the IrAF veterans still stress that the Mirages were ranging freely deep within the Iranian airspace as of 1988, their long-range raids remained costly. This is the fin of the Mirage F.1EQ-4 flown by Captain Khazal Ismail Majid al-Qattan, shot down near Esfahan on 4 May 1988. (Farzin Nadimi Collection)

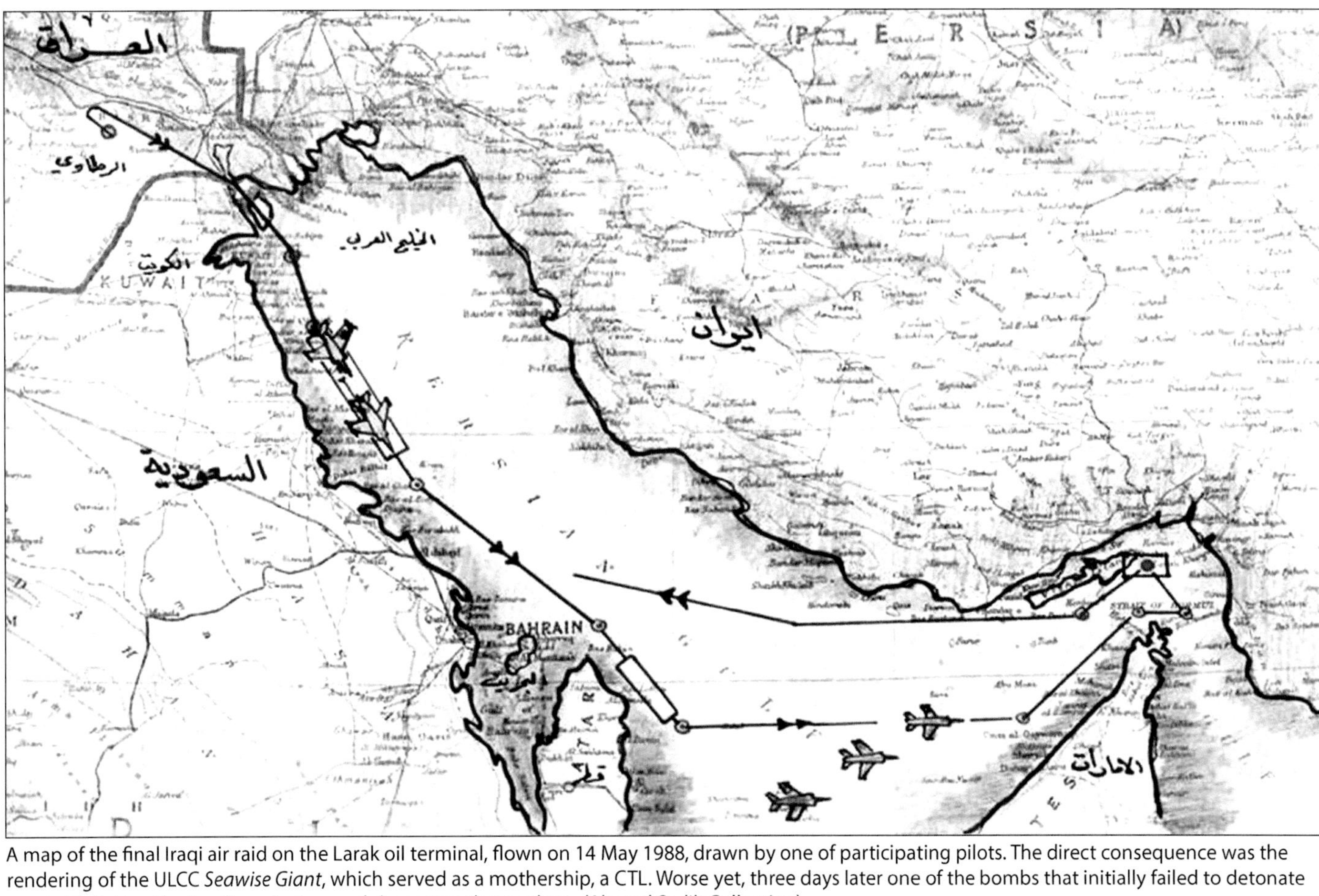

A map of the final Iraqi air raid on the Larak oil terminal, flown on 14 May 1988, drawn by one of participating pilots. The direct consequence was the rendering of the ULCC *Seawise Giant*, which served as a mothership, a CTL. Worse yet, three days later one of the bombs that initially failed to detonate went off, sinking the tug *Scan Partner* and damaging three others. (Ahmad Sadik Collection)

on the morning of 19 July 1988 No. 81 Squadron flew its final air strike on the abandoned construction site of nuclear reactors south of Bushehr. Self-conscious as never before, the Iraqis executed this operation in a particularly interesting style: four Mirage F.1EQ-5s from No. 81 Squadron supported by five tankers flew west of Kuwait and through the Saudi airspace before turning east and crossing the Persian Gulf. Expecting to take the Iranians by surprise, the planners made a mistake by routing the formation much too close to Farsi Island: a warning was issued on time and the F-14A flown by Captain Mohammed Esmaeli Peyrovan (RIO Captain Haiderzadeh) scrambled to intercept. Still underway at low altitude, the Iraqi formation reached the Iranian coast nearly 80 kilometres south of Bushehr before turning north: by flying over the ground and then attacking the Iranians in Bushehr from the rear, it managed to evade an interception. However, as the Mirages jinked upwards before dropping all their bombs on the target, Peyrovan was able to catch-up with them and open fire. His AIM-9 Sidewinder then smashed the F.1EQ-5 serial number 4573 into the sea: the pilot, Captain Mahmoud Hamid al-Anni, was killed on the spot. While the media in Baghdad subsequently claimed a victorious air battle and downing of two Tomcats into the sea off Khark, there was little doubt about the outcome of the final air battle of this war – and the tragic futility of the Iraqi loss.[10]

Almost unsurprisingly after this flop, instead of Mirages, the last strike deep inside Iran was flown by MiG-23BNs on 4 August 1988, and resulted in the Tabge Fani oil pumping station being wrecked by multiple Iraqi bombs. The air war between Iran and Iraq was thus ended by the fighter-bomber type that began it in September 1980.

CONCLUSION

Between April 1981 and June 1988, France delivered a total of 86 single-seat Mirage F.1EQs of four different variants, and 15 Mirage F.1BQ two-seat conversion trainers. During this period the type became the workhorse of the IrAF: the four units operating them had flown a lower number of combat sorties against Iran than those operating MiG-21s or Su-22s, but their mounts proved far more versatile, while offering excellent flight performance (especially at low altitudes), superior precision in navigation and weapons delivery, and load-carrying and self-defence capabilities. In the words of a post-war study of the IrAF Intelligence Department:

> The Mirage F.1 was employed for day-time CAS, interdiction, tactical bombing, strategic bombing, for attacks on naval targets, and for air defence. One of the reasons for this wide use was the availability of advanced targeting and weapons-control-systems on this aircraft.[12]

Their excellently trained pilots performed most of their tasks superbly, and there is little doubt that the type eventually outperformed all the other combat aircraft in the Iraqi arsenal – and then by a wide margin. Iraqi Mirages might not have scored many aerial victories, but those they did achieve were some of the most important aerial victories of the war. Operated in hit-and-run fashion they scored four crucial kills against Iranian F-14s, thus destroying the aura of invincibility of this type, and providing an example for other interceptor units of the IrAF. Later during the war, they did suffer numerous losses to the Iranian interceptors, but by then these no longer mattered within the overall context because by then the IrAF was in possession of aerial dominance. In turn, and at least according to whatever is left of the official IrAF documentation, exactly 25 Mirage F.1EQs were written off due to combat reasons

Captain Mahmoud Hamid al-Ani was the last Iraqi Mirage-pilot shot down and killed during the war with Iran: his Mirage F.1EQ-5 serial number 4573 was felled by an F-14A on 19 July 1988. (via Ali Tobchi)

during the war (representing 29% of the total IrAF loss), mostly while involved in ground-attack or anti-ship operations.[13]

Much less is known about other related statistics. For example, Baghdad is known to have received between 734 and 770 AM.39 Exocets by 1988, out of which over 550 were fired in combat. While 70 or 72 may have been released by Super Etendards, it remains unknown how many of these were fired by Super Frelons and how many by the Mirages. What is certain is that AM.39s hit at least 257 diverse vessels, outright sinking between 4 and 6, while resulting in between 65 and 80 others being subsequently written off. Out of 569 AS.30Ls ordered under *Project Baz-3*, about 240 were delivered to Iraq before Aerospatiale cancelled further shipments due to the Iraqi inability to pay for them: 75 of these were deployed in combat in 1987 alone.[14]

That said, it is foremost thanks to their electronic warfare capabilities that the Iraqi Mirages became the spearhead of the IrAF: the availability of the Syrel pod enabled the ADOC to run all major aerial operations in real time with high degree of confidence, while Caiman pods not only virtually opened the skies over the battlefields, but also opened the way deep into Iranian airspace. Moreover, the French decision to deliver such advanced equipment to Iraq resulted in a number of other governments following in fashion, thus enabling Baghdad to obtain very advanced electronic warfare capabilities by 1988.

The Iraqi Mirages were not the only type to deliver the blows that forced Ayatollah Khomeini to 'swallow the bitter pill' and end the war by accepting a UN-negotiated cease-fire with Iraq, effective from 8 August 1988; however, there is no doubt that they did play a crucial role in that drama. Major-General Ra'ad Hamdani, one of the most accomplished Iraqi military commanders of the 1970s-1990s period, summarized the effects upon Iran as follows:

> The losses and the amount of destruction inflicted on the Iranian economy by the war...were a factor...So, the charm of the revolution, as each revolution and each new movement has its power, the power and the holiness of Khomeini significantly declined. Moreover, the willingness of Iranian soldiers to sacrifice themselves weakened considerably.[15]

That all said, the deployment of the Iraqi Mirages during the war with Iran is going to be remembered – in Iraq, in France, and in Iran – as a symbol for a period when the IrAF was the pride of nearly all of the Arab World, in full swing and possession of aerial dominance: indeed, as the first example ever of an Arab air force establishing itself in such a position over its opponent.

Table 10: Total Deliveries of Mirage F.1s to Iraq, April 1981-August 1988

Variant	Number of Aircraft
F.1BQ	15
F.1EQ-2	32[16]
F.1EQ-4	28
F.1EQ-5	20
F.1EQ-6	6
Total single-seaters	86[17]
Total two-seaters	15

A still from a Patrick video showing the AS.30L strike on the Ahwaz Production Unit 2, flown by Lieutenant-Colonel Omar on 23 June 1988. Notable is that the missile was released from 2,500 metres range, while the Mirage was underway at a speed of 948km/h and an altitude of 458 metres. (Haytham Khattab Omar, via Ahmad Sadik)

PRIMARY DOCUMENTS

Written excerpts and photographs from private documentation of the following veteran IrAF pilots were provided by Brigadier-General Ahmad Sadik:

Mohammad Ahmad

Fayez Baqir

Rabee' Dulaymi

Jameel Salwan

Mohammad Sa'aydon ('Pilot Memoir', privately published document from 2005)

Mohammad Salman

Major-General Haytham Khattab Omar ('Memoirs of the Commander of the Iraqi Air Force')

BRITISH DEFENCE ATTACHÉ IN BAGHDAD, *Annual Report: IrAF through British Eyes* (FCO 8/4379, British National Archives)

CIA, Iraq's Air Force: *Improving Capabilities, Ineffective Strategy; An Intelligence Assessment*, October 1987, CIA/FOIA/ERR

DIA, *Electronic Warfare Forces Study – Iraq*, 9 August 1990, National Archives

IRAQI MINISTRY OF DEFENCE, *History of the Iraqi Armed Forces, Part 17; The Establishment of the Iraqi Air Force and its Development* (in Arabic), (Baghdad, Iraqi Ministry of Defence, 1988)

IRAQI AIR FORCE & AIR DEFENCE COMMAND, *An Analytical Study on the Causes of Iraqi Aircraft Attrition during the Iran-Iraq War* (in Arabic), (self-published for internal use, May 1991; English transcription provided by Sadik)

IRAQI AIR FORCE & AIR DEFENCE COMMAND, *The Role of the Air Force and Air Defence in the Mother of All Battles: After Action Report* (in Arabic), (self-published for internal use, 5 November 1991, captured in 2003 and translated as 'A 1991 Dossier on the Role of the Iraqi Air Force in the Gulf War', by the US Department of Defence-sponsored Conflict Records Research Center (CRRC Record Number SH-AADF-D-000-396) in the course of the 'Project Harmony')

IRIAF, *204 KIA and 58 POW pilots of the Sacred Defence* (in Farsi), (self-published for internal use, listing 204 IRIAF pilots and crewmembers that were killed and 58 that were captured during the war with Iraq by their full rank and name, aircraft they flew, date of their death or captivity; date and place of issue unknown; copy provided by Farzin Nadimi)

Iraqi Air Force Martyrs Website, 1931-2003, *iraqiairforcememorial.com*

ONI, *SPEARTIP 009-88; Persian Gulf Fighter Developments*, 18 April 1988 (released in response to FOIA enquiry, October 2000)

ONI, *SPEARTIP 014-90; Iraq Fighter-Interceptor Capabilities* (date of publishing blotted out; released in response to FOIA enquiry, October 2000)

ONI, *Request for Persian Gulf Related Info*, June 1987 (released in response to FOIA enquiry, October 2000)

BIBLIOGRAPHY

Alnasrawi, A., *The Economy of Iraq: Oil, Wars, Destruction of Development and Prospects, 1950-2010* (Westport: Greenwood Press, 1994; ISBN 0-313-29186-1)

Atrill, M. & Rolfe, M., *Dassault Mirage F1: A comprehensive study of the aircraft, its history and operators* (Oxon: The Aviation Workshop, 2006; ISBN: 1-904643-10-8)

Bergquist, Maj R. E., *The Role of Airpower in the Iran-Iraq War* (Maxwell AFB: Air University Press, 1988)

Biziewski, J., *Irak-Iran 80-88* (Wydawnictwo Altair: Warsaw, 1993)

Cooper, T. & Bishop, F., *Iran-Iraq War in the Air, 1980-1988* (Atglen: Schiffer Military Publishing, 2002; ISBN: 0-7643-1669-9)

Cooper, T. & Bishop, F., *Iranian F-14 Tomcat Units in Combat* (Oxford: Osprey Publishing Ltd, 2004; ISBN 1-84176-787-5)

Cooper, T., Sadik, *Général de Brigade* A., Bishop, F., *La guerre Iran-Irak: Les combat aériens, Hors-Serie Avions No. 22 & No. 23* (Outreau: Éditions LELA PRESSE, 2007)

Cooper, T., Nicolle, D., with Nordeen, L., Salti, P., and Smisek, M., Arab MiGs, Volume 4: Attrition War, 1967-1973 (Houston: Harpia Publishing, 2013, ISBN 978-09854554-1-5)

Cooper, T., Nicolle, D., with Müller, H., Nordeen, L., and Smisek, M., Arab MiGs, Volume 5: October 1973 War, Part 1 (Houston: Harpia Publishing, 2014, ISBN978-0-9854554-4-6)

Cooper, T., Nicolle, D., with Grandolini, A., Nordeen, L., and Smisek, M., Arab MiGs, Volume 6: October 1973 War, Part 2 (Houston: Harpia Publishing, 2015, ISBN 978-0-9854554-6-0)

Cooper, T. & Salti, P., *Hawker Hunters at War: Iraq and Jordan, 1958-1967* (Solihull: Helion & Co., 2016; ISBN: 978-1-911096-25-2)

Cooper, T., *MiG-23 Flogger in the Middle East: Mikoyan I Gurevich MiG-23 in Service in Algeria, Egypt, Iraq, Libya and Syria, 1973-2018* (Warwick: Helion & Co., 2018; ISBN: 978-1-912390-32-8)

Dildy, Douglas C., Cooper, T., *F-15C Eagle vs MiG-23/25, Iraq 1991* (Oxford: Osprey Publishing, 2016, ISBN: 978-1-4728-1270-4)

Flintham, V., *Air Wars and Aircraft: A Detailed Record of Air Combat 1945 to the Present* (London: Arms and Armour Press, 1989; ISBN 0-85368-779-X)

Francona, R., *Ally to Adversary: an eyewitness account of Iraq's fall from Grace* (Annapolis: Naval Institute Press, 1999; ISBN 1-55750-281-1)

Guillebon, H. de, 'base secrète en Irak, les Mirage F1 de Saddam Hussein', *Fana de l'Aviation No. 546* (2015)

Guillebon, H. de, 'L 'affaire des "Super Étendard" irakiens' Première partie', *Fana de l'Aviation No. 555*/2016; 'Deuxième partie', *Fana de l'Aviation No.* 556/2016; 'Troisième partie', *Fana de l'Aviation No.* 557/2016

Guillebon, H. de, 'Le "Bazar" de Bagdad: Les programmes secrets avec l'Irak, 1977-1984', Première partie', *Fana de l'Aviation No.* 567/2017; 'Deuxième partie', *Fana de l'Aviation No.* 568/2017; 'Troisième partie', *Fana de l'Aviation No.* 569/2107

Guillebon, H. de, 'Les "Mirage" traquent les pétroliers, Golfe persique, 1985-1988, Première partie', *Fana de l'Aviation,* No. 578/2018; 'Deuxième partie', *Fana de l'Aviation,* No. 579/2018; 'Troisième partie', *Fana de l'Aviation,* No. 580/2018; 'Quatrième partie', *Fana de l'Aviation,* No. 581/2018

Gunston, B. & Spick, M., *Modern Air Combat: the aircraft, tactics and weapons employed in aerial warfare today* (London: Salamander Books Ltd., 1983; ISBN: 0-86101-1627)

Gunston, B., *Modern Airborne Missiles* (London: Salamander Books Ltd., 1983; ISBN: 0-86101-160-0)

Gunston, B., *The Illustrated Encyclopedia of the World Rockets & Missiles* (London: Salamander Books Ltd., 1979; ISBN: 0-817-26870-1)

Gunston, B., *The Illustrated Encyclopedia of Aircraft Armament* (London: Salamander Books Ltd., 1988; ISBN: 0-517-56607-9)

Hiro, D., *The Longest War: The Iran-Iraq Military Conflict* (Routledge, Chapman and Hall Inc., 1991; ISBN 0-415-90406-4)

Hooton, E. R., Cooper, T., Nadimi, F., *The Iran-Iraq War, Volume 1: The Battle for Khuzestan, September 1980-May 1982* (Solihull: Helion & Co Ltd, 2016; ISBN: 978-1-911096-56-6)

Hooton, E. R., Cooper, T., Nadimi, F., *The Iran-Iraq War, Volume 2: Iran Strikes back, June 1982-December 1986* (Solihull: Helion & Co Ltd, 2016; ISBN: 978-1-911096-57-3)

Hooton, E. R., Cooper, T., Nadimi, F., *The Iran-Iraq War, Volume 3: Iraq's Triumph* (Solihull: Helion & Co Ltd, 2017; ISBN 978-1-911412-44-8)

Hooton, E. R., Cooper, T., Nadimi, F., *The Iran-Iraq War, Volume 4: The Forgotten Fronts* (Solihull: Helion & Co Ltd, 2017; ISBN: 978-1-911512-45-5)

Hooton, E. R. & Cooper, T., *Desert Storm, Volume 1* (to be published by Helion & Co in 2019)

Hoyt, T. D., *Military Industry and Regional Defense Policy; India, Iraq and Israel* (Oxon: Routledge, 2007; ISBN: 0-714-65714)

Huertas, S. M., *Mirage: The Combat Log* (Atglen: Schiffer Publishing Ltd., 1996; ISBN: 0-7643-0168-3)

Interavia (monthly magazine, various volumes from the late 1980s), (Interavia SA, Geneva: ISSN 0020-5168)

Jackson, P., 'Dassault Mirage 2000', *World Air Power Journal, Volume10/ Autumn/Fall 1992* (ISBN: 1-874023-17-4)

Jackson, P., 'Dassault Mirage F1: Gallic Guardian', *World Air Power Journal, Volume 17/Summer 1994* (ISBN: 1-874023-43-3)

Khalil, S. al-, *Republic of Fear: the inside story of Saddam's Iraq* (London: Hutchinson Radius, 1989)

Lake, J. (editor), *Grumman F-14 Tomcat: Shipborne Superfighter* (London: Aerospace Publishing Ltd., 1998; ISBN: 1-874023-41-7)

Lennox, D. (editor), *Jane's Air-Launched Weapons* (Surrey: Jane's Information Group Ltd., 2001; ISBN: 0-7106-0866-7)

Liébert, M. & Buyck, S., *Le Mirage F1 et les Mirage de seconde generation à voilure en flèche, Vol.1* (Outreau: Éditions LELA PRESSE, 2007; ISBN: 2-914017-40-5)

Levinson, J. L. & Edwards, R. L., *Missile Inbound: The Attack on the Stark in the Persian Gulf* (Annapolis: Naval Institute Press, 1997; ISBN: 1-55750-517-9)

Manoucherians, L., 'RF-4E: The incredible Story of Iranian Photo Phantoms and the Pilots who flew the most daring Reconnaissance Missions during the Iran-Iraq War', *Iranian Aviation No. 12* (TOP KIT Publishing)

Metz, H. C., *Iraq: A Country Study* (Washington: GPO for the Library of Congress, 1988)

Miller, D & Miller, C., *Modern Naval Combat* (London: Salamander Books Ltd., 1986; ISBN: 0-86101-231-3)

Murray, W & Woods, K. M., *The Iran-Iraq War: A Military and Strategic History* (Cambridge: Cambridge University Press, 2014)

Nadimi, F., *The Iranian Oil Industry and The Iran-Iraq War of 1980-88* (PhD thesis, The University of Manchester, 2011)

Namaki, A. R., Afghar, Q., Nowroozi, M., Arevan, M.-R., Monadi, V., Yaghoubi, S., Badi'ee, M.-S., Eshghi-Fakour, A. R., *In the Sky of Babylon, Volume 1: History of Iran-Iraq War in the Air* (in Farsi), (IRIAF Strategic Research and Studies Office, 2005)

Navias, S. & Hooton, E. R., *Tanker Wars: The assault on merchant shipping during the Iran-Iraq conflict, 1980-1988* (New York: I. B. Tauris & Co Ltd., 1996; ISBN 1-86064-032-X)

O'Ballance, E., *The Kurdish Revolt 1961-1970* (London: Faber and Faber Ltd., 1973; ISBN: 0-571-09905-X)

O'Ballance, E., *The Gulf War* (London: Brassey's Defence Publishers, 1988; ISBN 0-08-034747-9)

Razoux, P., *Operation 'Sugar'* (unpublished article)

Riad, M., *The Struggle for Peace in the Middle East* (Consett: Quartet Books, 1981)

ISBN: 978-0704322974

Richardson, D., *Techniques and Equipment of Electronic Warfare* (London: Salamander Books Ltd., 1985; ISBN: 0-86101-265-8)

Sadik, Brig Gen A. & Cooper, T., 'Les "Mirage" de Baghdad: les Dassault "Mirage" F1 dans la force aérienne irakienne', *Fana de l'Aviation No.* 434/2006; 'Deuxième partie', *Fana de l'Aviation No.* 435/2006

Sadik, Brig Gen A. & Cooper, T., 'Un Falcon 50 lance-missiles: Avion d'affaires contre navire de guerre', *Fana de l'Aviation No. 470* (2007)

Sadik, Brig Gen A., and Cooper, T. *Iraqi Fighters, 1953–2003: Camouflage & Markings* (Houston: Harpia Publishing, 2008; ISBN 978-0-615-21414-6)

Sampson, A., *Die Waffenhändler: Von Krupp bis Lockheed, Die Geschichte eines tödlichen Geschäfts* (Reinbek bei Hamburg: Rowohl Verlag GmbH, 1977; ISBN: 3-498-06118-6)

Shakibania, M. & Bibak, S., *Tomcat Fights* (TV documentary, Iran, 2012)

Shaw, I., and Santana, S., *Beyond the Horizon: The History of AEW&C Aircraft* (Houston: Harpia Publishing LLC, 2014; ISBN: 978-0-9854554-3-9)

Spick, M., *Modern Fighting Aircraft: F-14 Tomcat* (London: Salamander Books Ltd., 1985; ISBN 0-86101-194-5)

Styan, D., *France and Iraq: Oil, Arms and French Policy-Making in the Middle East* (New York: I. B. Tauris & Co Ltd., 2006; ISBN 1-84511-045-5)

Timmerman, K. R., 'Mirage sur l'île Kharg', *Defense & Armament* (magazine, in French), October 1985

Thomson-CSF, *Cyrano IV plus MTI: Airborne Fire Control Radar* (Manual)

Tripp, C., *A History of Iraq* (Cambridge: Cambridge University Press, 2000; ISBN: 0-521-55404-7)

Williams A. G. & Gustin, Dr. E., *Flying Guns: The Modern Era* (Ramsbury: Crowood Press Ltd., 2004; ISBN: 1-86126-655-3)

Wise, H. L., *Inside Danger Zone: The U. S. Military in the Persian Gulf, 1987-1988* (Annapolis: Naval Institute Press, 2007; ISBN: 978-1-59114-970-5)

Wolfe-Hunnicut, B., *The End of the Concessionary Regime: Oil and American Power in Iraq, 1958-1972* (PhD thesis, Stanford University, 2011)

Woods, K. M., Murray, W., Nathan, E. A., Sabara, L., Venegas, A. M., *Saddam's Generals: Perspectives of the Iran-Iraq War* (Alexandria: Institute for Defense Analyses, 2010)

Woods, K. M., Murray, W., Holaday, T., with Elkhamri, M., *Saddam's War: An Iraqi Military Perspective of the Iran-Iraq War* (Washington D.C.: National Defense University, 2009)

Zatarain, L. A., *Tanker War: America's First Conflict with Iran, 1987-1988* (Drexel Hill: Casemate, 2008; ISBN: 978-1-932033-84-7)

NOTES

Foreword and Acknowledgments

1 Project al-Hussein was related to stretching the range of the Soviet-made R-17E ballistic missile, better known in the West under the designation given to it by the Air Standardisation Coordinating Committee (ASCC) of the North Atlantic Treaty Organisation (NATO) – as 'SS-1c Scud-B'.

2 The IRGC is running an assassination campaign against the IrAF officers that served during the war with Iran, 1980-1988. For details see, 'Wikileaks Exposes Iran's Secret Revenge on Iraqi Pilots for 1980s War', *ABC News*, 6 December 2010 & 'Iraq War Logs: Iranians "organized assassinations"', *The Guardian*, 22 October 2010. According to such and similar reports, 182 former Iraqi pilots were assassinated between 2003 and 2009, while another 800 felt forced to flee the country. For an excerpt from one of the interviews provided by Sadik to Seymour M. Hersh, see Michael Ignatieff, 'Chain of Command: What Geneva Conventions?' *New York Times* (henceforth NYT), 17 October 2004.

3 The name of the negotiator and all details about his family are withheld for reasons related to the security of the latter. The French company in question is mentioned in this book but not explicitly cited within the context of this affair in order to avoid possible legal issues.

4 For the usual reports about Iraq placing an order for 50 Mirage 2000s – but only years later – see such as Gilbert Sedbon 'Iraq Negotiating Mirage 2000 Purchase', *Flight International*, 11 May 1989.

Chapter 1

1 The following sub-chapter is based on Cooper *et al*, *La guerre Iran-Irak, No.22*; Cooper *et al*, *Arab MiGs, Volumes 2, 3 and 4*; Cooper *et al*, *Hawker Hunters at War*; Sadik *et al*, *Iraqi Fighters*; Iraqi MOD, *History of the Iraqi Armed Forces, Part 17*; O'Ballance, *The Kurdish Uprising* & Tripp, *History of Iraq*.

2 The following sub-chapter is based on Sadik, 03/2005 (henceforth 'Sadik, 03/2005'); O'Ballance, *The Kurdish Revolt*, pp.144-147; Styan, pp.88-89; Trip, pp.188-189 & Cooper *et al*, *Arab MiGs, Volume 4*, pp.204-205.

3 Unless stated otherwise, the following sub-chapter is based on Sadik *et al*, *'Les "Mirage" de Baghdad'* & Sadik *et al*, *Iraqi Fighters*, p.123.

4 Sadik *et al*, *'Les "Mirage" de Baghdad'*; Sadik *et al*, *Iraqi Fighters*, p.123 & Cooper *et al*, *Arab MiGs, Volume 6*, pp.122-123.

5 SEPECAT stood for *Société Européene de Production de l'avion Ecole de Combat et d'Appui Tactique* (European Company for Production of Training, Combat, and Tactical Support Aircraft). Originally, it was a joint venture of Breguet and the British Aircraft Corporation (BAC), until Breguet was assimilated into Dassault, while BAC became British Aerospace (BAe) Warton.

6 Sadik, 10/2007.

7 Hoyt, (page number not declared) & CIA, *Iraq's Intelligence Services: Regime Strategic Intent – Annex B*, 23 April 2007, CIA, FOIA Electronic Reading Room (henceforth 'CIA/FOIA/ERR').

8 Sadik, 03/2006 & Hoyt. Because of his military expertise, Amer Rasheed was often referred to as 'Missile Man'.

9 Sampson, pp.290-292; Jackson, Mirage F.1, pp.48-50 & Liébert *et al*, *Vol.1*.

10 Sadik, 03/2006.

11 For details on the clashes in question – better known as the 'Sameta Affair' – see Hooton *et al*, *Desert Storm, Volume 1* (to be released by Helion in the Middle East@War series in 2019).

12 Hoyt & Sadik, 03/2005.

13 Sadik *et al*, *'Les "Mirage" de Baghdad'*.

14 Jakowitsch, various interviews, 2009-2013. Each of the contracts in question actually consisted of an entire group of contracts, regulating major aspects of the related agreements, ranging from the training of Iraqi personnel in France and at home, deployment of French advisors to Iraq, research and development of engines, avionics, armament, ejection seats, to the delivery dates, terms of payment, guarantee periods and other. In order to keep the resulting myriad of agreements and regulations easy to oversee, each contract was assigned its own, successive number. In the case of *Project Baz*, this always starting with the designation BAZ-121.

15 Sadik *et al*, *'Les "Mirage" de Baghdad'*; Sadik *et al*, *Iraqi Fighters*, pp.123-125 & Jakowitsch, various interviews, 2009-2013. The only difference between the F.1EQ and F.1EQ-2 was the upgraded software for the nav/attack system of the latter variant.

16 *Project Baz(-1)* included an order for 100 Super 530F-1s, with deliveries to commence in 1982. According to Euromissile's website, through that year and in 1983, a total of 352 Super 530F-1s were exported to Iraq before production ceased in 1985 (in total, 1,486 Super 530Fs were produced). As subsequent developments were to show, the first Super 530Fs had already reached Iraq in 1981.

17 Sadik, 03/2005 & 03/2006; de Guillebon, *'Le Bazar de Bagdad'*. Notable is that as in the case of many other items of equipment for electronic warfare, the French systems were all made to counter Soviet-made systems, while the Iraqis needed systems that could counter US, British and Israeli-made equipment.

18 Liébert *et al*, pp.241-251, 265-280 & 343-349; Gunston, *Missiles*, pp.90-91 & Gunston, *Aircraft Armament*, pp.97-101. The BLG.66 was manufactured in three variants: 66AC (with anti-tank ammunition), 66EG (anti-personnel ammunition), and 66IZ (anti-runway ammunition). SAMP stands for *Societe des Ateliers Mécaniques de Pont-sur-Sambre* (Company of the Mechanical Workshops of Pont-sur-Sambre): the primary French designer of a wide range of general-purpose bombs. Notable is that most of the armament in question was either still undergoing development or had only recently entered service in France. For example: while the R.550 Magic entered service in the AdA only in 1975, Iraq was the launching customer for the Super 530F (first contract for the AdA was signed in the second half of 1977). On the contrary, the acquisition of CC.420 was necessary because this pod was designed for the two-seat Mirage F.1B that, unlike single-seaters, was equipped with no internal 30mm cannon.

19 Sadik, 03/2006 & DIA, *Electronic Warfare Forces Study – Iraq*, (henceforth *EWFS-Iraq*), p.iii.

20 *Ibid.*

21 *Ibid.*

22 *Ibid.*

23 Guillebon, 'Le Bazar de Bagdad, Troisième partie'.

24 Sadik, 03/2006 & Guillebon, 'Le Bazar de Bagdad'.

25 Guillebon, 'Le Bazar de Bagdad'.

26 *Ibid.*

27 J. H., retired missile warfare analyst of the DIA, interview, 10/2002.

28 *Ibid* & Guillebon, 'Le Bazar de Bagdad'. While diverse French sources emphasise the sensitiveness of this project because the Baz-AR was a state-of-the-art French weapons system, and the original missile included US-made technology and parts made in Great Britain, J. H. commented as follows: 'Sure, it was a somewhat elderly system, but still deadly by the time it reached Iraq. Nevertheless, it appeared no one in the NATO gave a damn about its transfer to Iraq. Indeed, even once reports surfaced that the Soviets got their hands on at least one of these missiles – and there is no doubt that the British got wind about this affair – this only prompted one round of "serious talks" over this issue between Great Britain and France'.

29 Woods *et al*, *Saddam's War*, pp.25-32; Sadik, 03/2005 & 03/2006; Jakowitsch, 09/2009 & Liébert *et al*, p.243. The 'missing' Mirage F.1EQ-3 was an intermediate version that was never realised: the Iraqis opted to go for the F.1EQ-4 because they considered it as 'closer to their ultimate objective': the Dassault Mirage 2000 (for details, see below).

30 All contracts for Iraqi Mirages were given alpha-numeric designations. Those for *Project Baz* (later *Baz-1*, due to additional orders), were all designated in the sequence from BAZ-121 upwards; those for *Project Baz-2* in the sequence starting with BAZ-221 etc.

Chapter 2

1 Sadik, 03/2005 & CIA, *Iran-Iraq: Determining Who Started the Iran-Iraq War*, 25 November 1987, CIA/FOIA/ERR. One of the paradoxes of Iraq under Saddam is that while Tehran did manage to establish underground political networks and a few expatriate groups that opposed the Ba'ath regime in Iraq, the Iranians were never able to gain any popular support among the Iraqi Shi'a. Nevertheless, the related Iranian activity did make not only Saddam, but also many top Iraqi military commanders – the majority of whom were Sunni – generally suspicious of the Shi'a, regardless how loyal to Baghdad these proved to be.

2 For a detailed description of the operations in question, see Hooton *et al*, *Iran-Iraq War, Volume 4* (details in Bibliography).

3 For details on related Iraqi preparations, see Hooton *et al*, *Iran-Iraq War, Volume 1*.

4 Woods *et al*, *Saddam's War*, p.32. Precise details of what exactly happened on 4 September 1980 on the border between Iran and Iraq remain elusive. The Iraqi media (for example: *Baghdad Observer*, on 7 September 1980) originally reported a 'severe artillery attack' on – literally – two villages. However, subsequently, this affair was stylized into 'the first day of the Iranian aggression', and the Iranians were accused of 'bombing and shelling Iraqi cities and towns', including Baghdad, and 'killing women and children'. Sufficient to say that there is no evidence that anything of this kind has ever happened. Nevertheless, most of Iraqi sources interviewed over time consider this day – 4 September 1980 – as 'the day the Iran-Iraq War began'.

5 Hooton *et al*, *Iran-Iraq War, Volume 1*, pp.17-19. The pilot of the Mi-25 apparently managed an emergency landing before dying; the subsequent fate of his mount and that of the other crewmembers remains unknown. The pilots of the MiG-21R and the Su-22 were both killed in action.

6 IrAF, *Analytical Study*, p.3; Sadik, 03/2005; Woods, *Saddam's Generals*, pp.207-210. There is little doubt that some of such standpoints are based on general sloppiness of Iraqi preparations, but also the overwhelming secrecy. Not only Sadik, but also multiple generals interviewed by Woods *et al* have stressed that the IrAF received the plans for the attack on 22 September 1980 only one or two days earlier, and then in the form of a plan for a 'training exercise'. Unsurprisingly, the Iraqi military went into that war without a strategic concept, without ideas about strategic and operational aims and implications, and without an operational and tactical focus: indeed, many of its top commanders seem to have shared Saddam's hopes that their invasion would collapse Iran on its own, 'one way or the other'.

7 CIA, *The Iraq-Iran War: Military Performance and Prospects*, December 1980, CIA/FOIA/ERR.

8 According to Sadik (03/2006), even the first IrAF CO of Saddam AB was appointed only in February 1981.

9 Guillebon, 'Le Bazar de Bagdad, Deuxieme partie'.

10 Jackson, 'Mirage 2000', p.77.

11 Sadik, 03/2006.

12 Williams *et al*, p.131-135.

13 Sadik, 03/2005 & 03/2006. French IFF-transponders were removed and Soviet-made systems installed shortly after delivery.

14 Sadik, 03/2005, 03/2006, 03/2007, 10/2007. Notable is that the Iraqi misapprehension with regards to the IRIAF installing AIM-7s on its F-14s was only reinforced by the defection of an Iranian Tomcat-pilot to Iraq,

in September 1986 (for details, see Cooper, *MiG-23 Floggers in the Middle East*): according to Sadik, the manuals the pilot in question brought with him cited the Iranian F-14As as 'incompatible' with the AIM-7 Sparrow, thus 'confirming' earlier Iraqi intelligence. Moreover, the lack of insight and understanding of the AWG-9 weapons system within the IrAF is obvious from claims that when deployed from the Tomcat, AIM-7s had a shorter range than when deployed from the Phantom – despite availability of contemporary Western publications pointing out that the AWG-9 enabled the deployment of Sparrows (and Sidewinders) from longer ranges than possible from the F-4E Phantom II and the F-15A Eagle (for an example see Spick, *F-14*, pp.49-52).

15 According to Sadik, the Intelligence Directorate of the IrAF was closely following Iranian F-14 operations since their start in 1976. During the war, multiple COMINT, ELINT, and SIGINT units were established, and these had the standing order that prioritised reporting of any appearance by IRIAF Tomcats. Furthermore, several MiG-21 units may have attempted to engage F-14s in air combats, and two pilots claimed aerial victories against them: cross-examination of available Iranian accounts provided no confirmation for such reports and there is no evidence that the IrAF found any solution for fighting the F-14 before November 1981.

16 Sadik, 03/2005, 03/2006, 10/2007. Heavy losses by the IrAF in the first period of war are also confirmed by the IrAF *Analytical Study*, which pointed out that during the 'first period of the war' – between 4 September 1980 and 1 May 1981 – Iraq suffered a loss of 48 aircraft ('25% of which were MiG-21s') in a total of 14,290 sorties.

17 Sadik, 03/2006; Cooper *et al*, *La guerre Iran-Irak, No.23* & Guillebon, 'Le Bazar de Bagdad, Deuxieme partie'.

18 Sadik, 03/2005 & 03/2006; Cooper *et al*, *La guerre Iran-Irak, No.23* & Manoucherians, 'RF-4E'. Notably, the Iranians misidentified the Mirages engaged on 1 September as 'MiG-23s', and claimed one of them as shot down.

19 Shaw *et al*, pp.89 & *SPEARTIP 014-90*, p.25.

20 Sadik, 03/2005 & 03/2006; Hooton *et al*, *Iran-Iraq War Vol.1*; Hoyt.

21 Hoyt.

22 Sadik, 03/2005.

23 Sadik, 03/2005 & 03/2006 & *IAF through British Eyes*. Notably, the IrAF's *Analytical Study* (p.3) cited the IRIAF as in possession of '10 HAWK SAM-regiments each consisting of 3 batteries, and each battery with six launchers' at the start of the war. The discrepancy between 30 sites cited in that document, and 50 reportedly detected by MiG-25RBs in the 1981-1983 period is caused by the Iranians deploying a large portion of their MIM-23Bs in the so-called 'assault mode', where only half the site would be concentrated around one location.

24 Sadik, 03/2006 & IrAF *Analytical Study*, p.4-7. According to Sadik, the Kh-28C was custom-tailored for targeting early warning radars operating in the C-band; the Kh-28E was the variant specifically equipped to target HPARs of the MIM-23-system.

25 DIA, *EWFS-Iraq*, p.14.

26 Sadik, 03/2005 & 03/2006. Sadik's information on the capability of the Khoofash to read the Iraqi military communications in real time was independently confirmed in the course of Project Harmony: a series of interviews run by the US team that extensively de-briefed top Iraqi military officers and worked itself through whatever was left of the official Iraqi military documentation after 2003, see Murray *et al*, pp.70-71.

27 Sadik, 03/2005 & Namaki *et al*, pp.115. The total of 28 claims cited here includes all those known as claimed by the IRIAF interceptors and ground based air defences. Only about a third of these could be cross-confirmed on the basis of information from Iraqi sources.

28 Sadik, 03/2006. While the Iraqis fired two Super 530F-1s at this opportunity, it seems that both had targeted the same Tomcat. The IrAF credited Major Mukhalad with the kill.

29 Javad A. (IIAF/IRIAF researcher), interview, January 2017 & Keyvan V (IIAF/IRIAF researcher), interview, September 2015.

30 Namaki *et al*, pp.125 & Javad A., interview, January 2017. While Sadik confirmed one MiG-23 as shot down on 25 November, he credited it to an IRIAF F-4E. On the contrary, the IRIAF credited an F-14-pilot, Captain Gholam-Reza Khorshidi with a 'Mirage'kill scored by one AIM-54A fired from a range of 35 kilometres.

31 *Ibid* & Sadik, 03/2006. While many of the IRIAF claims in question remain unconfirmed, the Iranians are not known to have lost any F-4Es over Khuzestan on this day.

32 Sadik (03/2006) 'confirmed' the loss of only one Mirage, citing its pilot as Abdul Ghani as-Saoti – but stressed that he was shot down by an AIM-7 Sparrow fired from an F-4E. On the contrary, the Iranian media reported the downed Mirage-pilot as Abdul Ghani Sayed ad-Dulaymi, while the IRIAF officially credited Captain Khorshidi with his 'second Mirage-kill' – once again scored by an AIM-54A, this time from a range of 16 kilometres (Shakibania *et al*, *Tomcat Fights*). According to Namaki *et al*, p.127, the captured pilot, 'proved a valuable source on Iraqi Mirage operations'.

33 Sadik, 03/2005 & 05/2007.

34 Sadik, 03/2006; O'Ballance, p.102 & Murray *et al*, p.199 (the latter quoted the correspondence between the IrAF, the Air Defence Command, and the GMID regarding IRIAF capabilities, dated with 25 December 1981).

35 Sadik, 03/2005, 08/2005, 03/2006, 10/2007 & Shakibania *et al*, *Tomcat Fights*. While Sadik confirmed this loss, he credited it to an F-4E of the IRIAF. As in the case of all the air combats from the September-November 1981 period, only one Iraqi account of all the action (the one for 4 December 1981) has been published by Iraqi sources so far: thus, and like in most of cases of this kind, a reconstruction is possible only with the help of Iranian sources.

36 *Ibid*; IRIAF, *204 KIA & 58 POWs*; Manoucherians, 'RF-4E'.

Chapter 3

1 Metz, Iraq: *A Country Study*; O'Ballance, pp.74-76 & pp.108-109. In another paradox of the Iran-Iraq War, while nearly all of the interviewed Iraqi officers described the IRIAF's offensive on the Iraqi oil-exporting industry from the fall of 1980 as 'completely ineffective', and the Iranian aerial operations in general as 'incompetent' (indeed, Sadik once stressed that throughout eight years of war not one Iranian bomb had hit its target), in a press conference held in Baghdad on 4 March 1982, the Iraqi Deputy Oil Minister admitted publicly that, '...the Iranian military activity had caused considerable damage to Iraqi oil facilities, especially at Basra, but also at Kirkuk'. Sufficient to say that over 95% of related 'Iranian military activity' was undertaken by the IRIAF.

2 Sadik, 03/ 2005; Jakowitsch, 09/2012 & *IAF through British Eyes*.

3 Sadik, 03/2006; Jakowitsch, multiple interviews, 2000-2013; Liébert *et al*, pp.242-244. Notable is that at the same time, the MIC placed an order worth US$1.7 billion for arms made by the Egyptian branch of the AOI: this was also financed by the Saudis and Kuwaitis.

4 Jackson, 'Mirage 2000', pp.80-81.

5 Sadik, 01/2007 & Jakowitsch, 01/2013.

6 Sadik, 01/2005.

7 Metz, *Iraq: A Country Study* & Jakowitsch, multiple interviews, 2009-2013.

8 CIA, *Iraq's Air Force* & DIA, *EWFS-Iraq*; Sadik, 03/2005 & 03/2006; Jakowitsch, multiple interviews, 2000-2013 & O'Ballance, pp.112-113. While the CIA's report confirmed Saddam's standing order to avoid losses, the DIA (p.7) stated, 'Iraq adopted a total threat avoidance policy after unacceptable losses in aircraft at the beginning of the war'. Sadik confirmed the existence of the 'Sukhoi clique' within the top ranks of IrAF, and – repeatedly – described it as 'Soviet-trained and influenced officers that preferred the cheaper and simpler Su-22s on account of their better combat survivability'. However, he would not name any of the generals in question. Independently, Jakowitsch confirmed the existence of the 'Sukhoi clique' within the top ranks of the IrAF, and that this began plotting a coup against Saddam. However, his knowledge about the generals in question and related affairs was insufficient to identify specific names.

9 Sadik, 01/2007; Jakowitsch, multiple interviews, 2009-2013; Liébert *et al*, pp.242-244 & Jackson, Mirage 2000, p.80-81 & 86. Notable in relation to this contract is that Egypt bought 16 Mirage 2000EM interceptors and four 2000BM trainers in December 1981, and that the contract for 15 Alpha Jet MS1 and 15 Alpha Jet MS2 was signed by Cairo during the same month as the Iraqi order for Mirage F.1EQ-5s and Mirage 2000s. Also of interest is the date and similarity of the AdA's order for 70 Mirage 2000Ds – aircraft with almost the same equipment, capabilities, and purpose as the Mirage 2000s ordered by Baghdad in February 1982: this is offering the possibility that the AdA eventually did the same as in the case of supposedly embargoed Mirage 5s manufactured for Israel in the 1968-1969 period; i.e. that it inherited aircraft originally produced for export. Meanwhile, the Saudis continued their negotiations with London instead and in 1985 placed a huge order for Tornados and Hawks within the frame of *Project al-Yammamah*.

10 Sadik, 03/2006 & 10/2007 & *IAF through British Eyes*.

11 Sadik, 03/2006.

12 *Ibid*; O'Ballance, pp.73-74 & 102-103; Alfredo André, interview, September 2018.

13 Alfredo André, interview, September 2018 & Hoyt.

14 Alfredo André, interview, September 2018.

15 Sadik, 03/2006 (additional details published in Cooper *et al*, *La guerre Iran-Irak, No.23*).

16 Sadik, 10/2007; Murray *et al*, pp.70-71 & Hooton *et al*, *Iran-Iraq War Vol.1*, p.66. In exchange for KGB support, the Iraqis provided large sections of a downed Iranian F-4E Phantom to Moscow. Ultimately, it took the GMID and the Intelligence Directorate IrAF until 23 February 1986 to recognize the full capability of the IRIAF's Khoofashs. On that day, Unit 114 intercepted a message emitted by an Iranian aircraft underway at an

altitude of 8,000 metres over the town of Behbehan, about 100 kilometres east of Bandar-e Khomeini, and containing the text of an order for several IrAF air bases to launch a strike against Iranian ground units on the Faw Peninsula. It was only through the repeated analysis of this message that the startled Iraqis concluded that the Iranians were not only listening to and intercepting their military communications, but actually had broken their military code, too.

17 Hooton *et al*, *Iran-Iraq War Vol.1*, pp.66-68.

18 *Ibid*.

19 Namaki *et al*, pp.130-150.

20 There is a wide range of versions about what exactly happened during this engagement. According to some (unofficial) Iranian sources, both Mirages crashed while trying to avoid AIM-54s fired at them; according to another, just one crashed; and according to the third version, one 'touched' the ground before disappearing in the direction of Iraq while trailing smoke. Available Iraqi sources deny any such losses, but there is a confirmed report about one Mirage being written off following an in-flight engine fire, around the same time (pilot ejected safely).

21 Sadik, 03/2006 & Namaki *et al*, pp.142-150.

22 Namaki *et al*, pp.208-211 & Sadik, 03/2005.

23 *Ibid* & Shakibania *et al*, *Tomcat Fights*.

24 Sadik, 03/2005 & 10/2007 (as published in Cooper *et al*, *La guerre Iran-Irak, No.23*).

25 Sadik, 10/2005. The authors are fully aware of the fact that Lieutenant-General Mukhalad's family – and his son in particular – remain insistent on the total of 14 kills. There is also no doubt that Lieutenant-General Mukhalad was highly decorated and subsequently pursued a successful career with the IrAF. However, it would be intellectually dishonest not to cite related statements by Sadik and French sources. Repeated requests for the son to provide details, or at least copies of his father's pilot log-book for cross-examination with known IRIAF losses remained unanswered. The only conclusion possible on the basis of the currently available information is that Mukhalad achieved two confirmed victories.

26 Sadik, 03/2006 & Guillebon, 'Le Bazar de Bagdad, Troisième Partie'. According to the latter source, by September 1983, the number of claims issued by Iraqi Mirage-pilots increased to 'about 30'. Not only the Iraqis, but de Waubert too, were thus highly satisfied with the Super 530F, and the performance of IrAF's pilots. At least as much, the French were pleased with the performance of the Cyrano-IV radar – especially once they discovered that in at least six air combats, right after the Super 530F was fired, the radar that was designed to lock on one target at time, automatically locked on the second target, enabling a quick re-engagement. In comparison, the French and the Iraqis were less pleased with the R.550 Magic: while usually guiding very well, this tended to detonate prematurely. The probable reason was that the glass covering the seeker-head in the front of the missile tended to heat up the longer the flight lasted. By the time the missile entered the hot exhausts from engines of targeted enemy fighters, the overheating would prompt its proximity fuse to activate. This problem should have been solved on the R.550 Magic Mk.II, which was never delivered to Iraq. Another interesting observation by de Waubert was that – at least by 1982-1983 – not one Iraqi pilot ever attempted to engage any Iranian fighters with help of his cannons only.

27 Hooton *et al*, *Iran-Iraq War, Vol. 1*, pp.75-76.

28 *Ibid*.

29 Sadik, 03/2006.

30 Guillebon, 'Le Bazar de Bagdad, Deuxieme partie & '…Troisième partie'.

31 Sadik, 03/2006. Notably, while available Iraqi sources tend to declare every single Baz-AR (and/or Kh-28) ever fired as a 'hit', the IrAF *Analytical Study* (p.6), indicates that the IRIAF HAWK-sites were 'constantly moved', regularly employed 'in ambushes', deployed in the assault mode, and began using 'decoy transmitters'.

32 DIA, *EWFS-Iraq*, p.9.

33 J. H., interview, October 2002; Sadik, 03/2006 & Guillebon, 'Le Bazar de Bagdad, Troisième partie'. While unable to confirm or deny the total number of Baz-ARs delivered to Iraq, the latter source stressed that 31 were manufactured by Matra in 1982, at a price of FFR20 million apiece (US$3.6 million at contemporary rates), of which FFR1 million was for just the transport container, which was not reusable. In comparison, Sadik recalled the number of Baz-ARs delivered to Iraq as '80'.

34 CIA, *Iraq's Air Force* & Huertas, *Mirage: The Combat Log*, p.145. According to Timmerman, the Iraqis claimed no fewer than 12 Iranian F-14As as shot down during this period.

35 As usual, the only details available about both engagements are those released by Iranian sources (specifically by Shakibania *et al*, *Tomcat Fights*). Not one of the available Iraqi sources has proved able to find out or recall which IrAF pilots were involved. Notable is that in one of his numerous posts on the ACIG.info forum, Sadik fiercely criticised the IRIAF's F-4E crews for not deploying their ECM-pods to counter Cyrano-radars of IrAF's Mirages. Curiously, he seem not to have known that in this and several similar engagements, the Phantoms equipped with ALQ-101 and ALQ-119 pods of US origin were not targeted by the Iraqi interceptors and SAMs.

36 Namaki *et al*, p.220 & Sirous Ebrahimi (eyewitness of this clash), interview, September 2009.

37 IRIAF, *204 KIA & 58 POWs* & Manoucherians, 'RF-4E'.

38 *IrAF through British Eyes* & Sadik, 03/2005 & 10/2007 (according to Sadik, malfunctions in the fire-control system of Iraqi Mirages remained relatively frequent until 1986).

39 *IrAF through British Eyes*; Cooper *et al*, *La guerre Iran-Irak, No.22 & 23*; Hooton *et al*, *Iran-Iraq War, Volume 2*.

40 CIA, *Iraq's Air Force*.

41 *Ibid* & *IrAF through British Eyes*.

42 *Ibid*. It is notable that despite clear and indisputable evidence about losing dozens of aircraft and pilots to IRIAF F-14As, the majority of IrAF officers interviewed over time remain insistent that these shot down only eight Iraqi aircraft in all eight years of the war – which is also the figure cited in the IrAF *Analytical Study*. At the time of writing not one of the Iraqi sources interviewed proved able to explain why the eight aircraft they do admit to losing to the IRIAF F-14s were those both the best-equipped, and those flown by some of the best IrAF pilots.

43 CIA, *Iraq's Air Force*; Guillebon, 'Le Bazar de Bagdad, Troisième Partie'.

44 Sadik, 11/2007; DIA, *EWFS-Iraq*, pp.11 & 21.

45 DIA, *Air Force Intelligence Study – Iraq*, DDB-1300-IZ-87, October 1987 (acquired via Ted Hooton).

46 DIA, *EWFS-Iraq*, p.21, CIA/FOIA/ERR.

47 *Ibid*.

48 *Ibid*.

49 Sadik, 11/2007; *IrAF through British Eyes*; CIA, *Iraq: Major Weapons Deliveries and their Impact on Force Capabilities*, February 1987, CIA/FOIA/ERR & Guillebon, 'Le Bazar de Bagdad, Troisième Partie'. According to Guillebon, Captains Aimé Marion and Jean Andrieu returned to France in October 1984, when they were replaced by Jean-Michel Cantin and Jean-Marc Le Moel. Leroy remained in Iraq through this period. According to Sadik, one of the French pilots spent so much time in Iraq that he earned himself the nick-name 'Arab' at home.

50 Guillebon, 'Le Bazar de Bagdad, Troisième Partie'. The first Mirage F.1EQ-4s to reach Iraq were serial numbers 4503, 4506, 4507 and 4510. Serial numbers 4502 and 4511 followed during the second transfer, in July 1983.

51 Data provided by Hugues de Guillebon, 11/2017.

52 CIA, *Iraq's Air Force* & Dildy *et al*, pp.38-39.

53 Sadik, 03/2005; Cooper *et al*, *Arab MiGs, Volume 2*; *IAF through British Eyes*; 'The Agreement between the Governments of India and Iraq', *AirEnthusiast*, Vol.5/No.3 (September 1973). Indian Air Force instructors seconded to the IrAF dominated the Iraqi military flight training facilities at all levels since the early 1960s. According to another British report (FCO 8/5005, from 1983), no fewer than 68 of them served with the Air Force Academy, together with 9 instructors from Bangladesh, and 9 from Egypt (the presence of the latter, in turn,led to rumours in Iran that they would actually fly combat sorties for the IrAF). While a small number of Iraqi cadets underwent various advanced flight training courses in Pakistan, even more did so in France, Great Britain, Egypt, Czechoslovakia, and the USSR. Correspondingly, frequently published reports about a 'Pakistan-trained Iraqi Air Force' are within realms of science fiction.

54 CIA, *Iraq: Major Weapons Deliveries and their Impact on Force Capabilities*, February 1987 & *Iraq's Air Force*, CIA/FOIA/ERR; *SPEARTIP 014-90*; Dildy *et al*, pp.38-39.

55 *Ibid*.

Chapter 4

1 Nadimi, p.117 & CIA, *Khark Island: Iran's Principal Oil-Export Terminal*, June 1984, CIA/FOIA/ERR. Notable is that the 170 km-long trunkline connecting Agha Jari with Genaveh – consisting of two pipelines – had a throughput capacity of 2.7 million barrels a day, without pumping.

2 Nadimi, p.118. Notably, after four storage tanks were severely damaged by Iraqi air strikes early during the war, the remaining tanks still had a combined capacity of 19 million barrels as of early 1984 (or about two weeks of storage at contemporary export rates). Even then, the Iranian oil exports during the war never surpassed a maximum of about 2.5 million bpd, which means that claims in diverse French and Iraqi publications about the damage caused to the Khark during the war decreasing its daily output 'from 6 to less than 1 million bpd' belong within realms of science fiction.

3 Nadimi, p.21.

4 *Ibid*, pp.21-22 & 111-112 & Sadik, 10/2007.

5 Nadimi, p.22.

6 *Ibid*, p.73.

7 *Ibid*, pp.81 & 84.

8 *Ibid*, p.118.

9 *Ibid*, p.120.

10 Ebrahimi, 09/2009.

11 See also CIA, *Iraq/Iran Military Summary: Imagery analysis report*, October 1980, CIA/FOIA/ERR. The most prominent amongst these air defence ships were six Polish-built cargo vessels of the *Iran Kalaam* class (Ebrahimi, 09/2009). While the total amount of cargo ferried by the caravans to BIK remains unknown, the overall scope of this operation can be gauged by the details known about related pilotage operations. According to Ebrahimi, a total of 692 cargo ships made a total of 1,384 piloted trips to BIK between 24 September 1980 and June 1985. Considering that the average ship had a displacement of 15,000 tonnes, this means that the Operation *Caravan* delivered at least 10,380,000 tonnes of cargo to BIK in the first five years of the war alone.

12 Because Iraqi sources have only ever revealed the names of downed pilots, but never their target, there is still some uncertainty about the actual target of that air strike. According to Nadimi (pp.85-86), the four Sukhois were underway to attack oil rigs in the Dorud oilfield, west of Khark.

13 Navias *et al*, pp.46-48.

14 *Ibid* & Sadik, 10/2007.

15 Sadik, 03/2005 & 10/2007; Ebrahimi, 09/2009 & Nadimi, p.93. According to Sadik, *all* the decoys deployed by the Iranians had not only been designed and positioned by British advisors, but indeed: manufactured in the United Kingdom. The British team supposedly supporting this operation had been deployed on board the salvage ships named *Strance 11* and *Seaboard*. Both had a British skipper and crews consisting of up to a dozen, of which between five and six were Britons and Germans.

16 Unless stated otherwise, the content of this box is based on Interavia Data, 'AM 39 EXOCET'; Lennox, *Jane's Air-Launched Weapons*; Gunston, *Aircraft Armament* & Gunston, *Missiles*.

17 Details on the AM.39's seeker-head as provided by Sadik, 03/ 2005.

18 *Ibid.*

19 Nadimi, p.88.

20 *IAF through British Eyes*.

21 Sadik, 10/2007 & Nadimi, p.90.

22 Pierre Razoux, *Operation Sugar.*

23 *Ibid*. The five French pilots that delivered Super Etendards returned home on board of the Falcon 50 that guided them to Saddam AB. In turn, a team of French advisors brought in by the Falcon remained in the country to advise Iraqi pilots and ground crews.

24 Cooper *et al*, *Hawker Hunters at War*, pp.50-52 & CIA, *Iraq's Air Force* .

25 CIA, *Iraq's Air Force* & Woods, *Saddam's Generals*, pp.208-209. Notable in the case of the latter source is the bitter critique expressed by Major-General Abossi. According to him, Sha'ban was 'pretty weak' as a pilot, 'not effective' as C-in-C IrAF, and somebody who was 'not admired in the air force as much as al-Jabouri had been'. In comparison, Sadik considered Saddam's decision to return Hamid Sha'ban from retirement and appoint him the C-in-C IrAF for the 'crucial decision' of the war.

26 CIA, *Iraq's Air Force.*

27 Sadik, 07/2006; Nadimi, p.59 & CIA, *Iraq's Air Force.* Not a member of the Ba'ath Party, Basu is frequently 'forgotten' nowadays. After serving as Deputy Operations IrAF, he was promoted in rank in 1989, but then sent into retirement: as he was not a member of the Ba'ath, he could not be appointed the commander of the air force. Contrary to widespread rumours he did not become involved in the 1995 coup attempt against Saddam: Basu was arrested 'for political reasons' in July 1993, and executed on Saddam's order in November of the same year.

28 Sadik, 07/2006 & Nadimi, p.59.

29 'Bomber Harris' (also 'Butcher Harris') was the nickname of Sir Arthur Harris, 1st Baronet, Marshal of the Royal Air Force commanding the RAF Bomber Command during the Second World War. Harris initiated and ran the campaign of massive strategic bombing against Nazi Germany, with the aim of '...destroying German cities, the killing of German workers, and the disruption of civilised life throughout Germany… the creation of a refugee problem on an unprecedented scale, and the breakdown of morale both at home and at the battle fronts' – all of which were expected to shorten the war (Norman Longmate, *The Bombers: The RAF Offensive against Germany, 1939-1945*; London, Hutchinson; ISBN 0-09-151580-7). Arguably, while gulping at least one third of the contemporary British defence budget, overpowering the Luftwaffe, completely destroying all major urban centres and causing millions of civilian victims, the campaign failed to break the German morale, had only a minimal impact upon the German industrial output, and failed to shorten the war by a single day.

30 Shakibania *et al*, *Tomcat Fights*; Navias *et al*, pp.72-74; Iraqi Air Force Martyrs Website.

31 Murray *et al*, p.227 (citing orders of the President and Commander-in-Chief of the Armed Forces from 26 February 1984, and other dates in period February-December 1984) and p.237 (citing Saddam's own statements from discussion with diverse military officials, late 1988).

32 Sadik *et al*, 'Les "Mirage" de Bagdad' & Guillebon, 'Le Bazar de Bagdad, Troisième Partie'. Bakir eventually rose in rank to Major-General, and then commanded the IrAF in the mid-1990s. The test-deployment undertaken on his suggestion took place in July 1983, when the 1st Battalion of the 417th Infantry Brigade was cut off by the Iranians outside Zarbatya. Reluctantly, the GHQ then ordered four Mirages led by Major Salah Ismail Nasser into several air strikes. To the surprise of many in Baghdad, who expected the aircraft of No. 79 Squadron to be shot to pieces, not one was shot down, although Nasser and his wingmen identified about 20 Iranian anti-aircraft guns in the combat zone.

33 *Ibid.*

34 Ali Tobchi, interview, May 2014; Namaki *et al*, p.275.

35 DIA, *EWFS-Iraq*, p.10, CIA/FOIA/ERR.

36 CIA, *Iraq's Chemical Warfare Program: More Self-Reliant, More Deadly*, August 1990, CIA/FOIA/ERR & Woods *et al*, *Saddam's War*, pp.55-56.

37 Sadik, 03/ 2007 & 10/2007; Hooton *et al*, *Iran-Iraq War Vol.2*, pp.29-30. According to Sadik, the idea to buy Spanish-made versions of US-designed bombs was born during a visit by Lieutenant-Colonel Ali Raji to Mirage F.1-equipped units of the Royal Moroccan Air Force. These were deploying Mk.82 and Mk.84 bombs, initially equipped with so-called 'Daisy cutter' fuses that made them detonate above the ground, and later on with South African-made Jupiter fuses. De Guillebon, (in *Le Bazar de Bagdad, Troisième Partie*), cited a 'confidential' French report from August 1983, which noted that 'Commander Ryad, commanding officer of No. 89 Squadron, has just left for a two-weeks training course in Spain'. Furthermore, he cited the Iranians finding unexploded bombs of Spanish origin filled with CW agents, clearly marked as 'BR.250WP' on the warhead's body, and 'ESP MU-O9, Lot 83-01' on the fuse. The weapons in question may have been delivered to Iraq from Torrejon AB, in January 1984, aboard a transport operated by Iraqi Airways. Finally, he pointed out that the French advisors in Iraq were always kept away from 'such' operations, and never provided any kind of support for them.

38 Sadik, 03/2005, 03/2006 & 03/2007. Before long, the Iraqis were placing sufficient orders for EXPAL-made BR.250 and BR.500 general purpose bombs, for the Spaniards to establish a new company – International Technology SA – tasked with 'further development of designs based on the Mk.80 series, new domestic designs, and associated air-driven fuses' (Lennox, *Jane's Air-Launched Weapons*, pp.450-455). According to the leading Portuguese military aviation researcher, Jose Augusto Matos (interview, December 2018), related Portuguese documentation remains outside the public reach at present, but it seems that the Portuguese company COMETNA (a national metallurgical company supervised by the Ministry of Industry and Technology) was occasionally contracted by either Baghdad or EXPAL for the production of casings for aviation bombs: these would then be forwarded to the Trafaria Explosives Factory (in Portugal), which added their explosive content. The resulting production was undertaken only on sporadic requests, i.e. it was anything but 'continuous' (a fact important because at least officially, production of aviation bombs in Portugal ceased once the country withdrew from its overseas possessions in 1975, and was re-launched only once the EMPORDEF Group was established in 1997).

39 Sadik, 03/ 2005. On 9 December 1984, Cardoen CBUs may have caused the loss of two F.1EQ-2s from No. 89 Squadron. Both pilots – Captains Tariq Ibrahim Ramadan Bakr al-Azzawi and Captain Hamoud Abd al-Majid Ali an-Nuaimi – ejected successfully.

40 Navias *et al*, p.73 & Nadimi, p.117. Perhaps the best example for the Iraqi failure to influence the flow of the war through anti-ship attacks until this date was a large-scale attack against a caravan including 13 ships carrying troops and supplies to BIK, launched on 1 February 1984. According to information by Ebrahimi, Navias *et al* (p.73) and CIA, *Iraq-Iran: The War Moves into the Gulf*, 17 May 1984, CIA/FOIA/ERR, this included at least four, possibly six Super Frelons, and resulted in the firing of at least as many Exocets (each Super Frelon could carry two missiles, but they usually carried only one). While the Iraqi media subsequently claimed the 'destruction' of no fewer than eight ships, actually: one missile wrecked the bulk carrier *City of Rio* (subsequently written off), another severely damaged the freighter *Skaros* (later repaired), one failed to detonate after hitting the freighter *Neptune*, and the others either missed or hit decoys. The losses in men and material suffered by the Iranians in this way remain unknown. However, there is little doubt that this attack failed to prevent 12 out of 13 ships from reaching BIK, and thus from delivering troops and supplies used in Operation *Khyber*. Worse yet, only a week later, on 16 February 1984, another caravan including a dozen merchants reached BIK: while this time the Iraqis claimed the 'destruction' of seven ships, only one – the Liberian bulk carrier *al-Tariq* – was damaged by an Exocet while

entering the Khowr Mousa. Quickly repaired, the same ship was then hit by another Exocet while returning to Bushehr, a week later.

41 Interview with 'Major K' (former IrAF Mirage-pilot) to Brigadier-General Sadik, March 2007; Navias *et al*, pp.75-77. Claims according to which the Super Etendards flew their first combat sortie only on 24 March 1984, and that one of two Exocets fired on this opportunity hit the construction site of the nuclear reactor in Bushehr – lack support even from their supposed source, the Information Circular INFCIRC/319 of the International Atomic Energy Agency [IAEA], September 1984.

42 Navias *et al*, p.74 & Ebrahimi, 09/2009. The reason for the presence of *Heyang Ilho* was that in the light of exaggerated Iraqi claims, many service companies began deploying their salvage and supply ships in the shipping lines, hoping to become involved in operations related to the recovery of the cargo of damaged tankers, and thus earn handsome profits. For the Iranian seamen, they resembled 'vultures, waiting for one of them to get hit by the Iraqis'.

43 Sadik, 03/ 2005 & Navias *et al*, p.76.

44 *Ibid.*

45 Sadik, 10/2007; Shaw *et al*, p.89; Cooper *et al*, *La guerre Iran-Irak, No.23*.

46 Sadik, 10/2007; Ebrahimi, 09/2009; 'Saudi F-15 Fighters Down 2 Iranian Jets over Persian Gulf', *New York Times*, 6 June 1984. Ironically, the importance of the Fahd Line for the freedom of operations the Iraqis enjoyed over the western Persian Gulf during the next four years is entirely ignored in all of related Iraqi, Iranian, and Western accounts published since – although the existence of that 'no-fly-zone' meant that the IrAF was free to operate as far south as the United Arab Emirates and Oman, and then select the point from which to turn east or north and attack targets along more than 2,000 kilometres long Iranian coast.

47 Navias *et al*, p.74; Cooper *et al*, *Iran-Iraq War in the Air*, p.175; Sadik, 03/2006, 03/2007, 10/2007 & Nadimi. Notably, Baghdad claimed the downing of 'three F-14s into the sea off Bandar Khomeini', on 11 August 1984, and this claim was widely cited in the Western media too (see Spick, p.63 & Lake, p.197). The newest Iranian 'assessments' according to which All-e-Agha's Tomcat 'collided with an Iraqi SS-N-2 Styx anti-ship missile he was trying to intercept', or reports he was shot down by 'Iraqi Mirages', are within realms of science fiction. Provided independently from each other, recollections by All-e-Agha's RIO, 1st Lieutenant Mohammad Rostampour to All-e-Agha's son Babak (interview to co-author Cooper, September 2006), and a detailed description of the Giraffe operation run by two MiG-23MLs provided by Sadik (for details see Cooper, *MiG-23 Flogger in the Middle East*, pp.36-37) are mutually confirming.

48 CIA, *Iraq-Iran: The War Moves into the Gulf*, 17 May 1984 & CIA, *Iraq's Air Force*, CIA/FOIA/ERR.

49 Navias *et al*, pp.74-85; Sadik, 10/2007; Cooper *et al*, *Iran-Iraq War in the Air*, p.175; CIA, *Iraq-Iran: The War Moves into the Gulf*, 17 May 1984, CIA/FOIA/ERR; de Guillebon, 'L'affaire des "Super Étendard" irakiens, Troisième partie' & Nadimi, p.94. Diverse Iraqi sources have provided at least two versions about what happened to Kamal: according to one, he was shot down by an F-15C of the RSAF; according to the other, the pilot lost control of his low-flying aircraft that – after releasing the missile – became unstable. As in so many other cases, the Exocet fired by Kamal disappeared without a trace.

50 CIA, *Iraq-Iran: The War Moves into the Gulf*, 17 May 1984, CIA/FOIA/ERR & Murray *et al*, p.238. According to Sadik (03/ 2005), the primary means of obtaining intelligence about shipping along the Iranian coast were interceptions of related radio communications. For a drastic illustration of how blissfully unaware the IrAF was of its role in the Oil Campaign or what exactly was going on in the Persian Gulf – throughout the entire war – see the interview with Major-General Abossi in Woods *et al*, *Saddam's Generals*, pp.11 & 199- 214.

Chapter 5

1 Sadik, 03/2005 & 03/2006 & de Guillebon, 'Les "Mirage" traquent les pétroliers… Première partie'. Through this delivery the number of Mirages in Iraq grew to 65, for which there were 78 qualified pilots. According to Sadik, the original staff of No. 81 Squadron included three groups: 3 veteran Super Etendard-fliers, 11 Captains and 1st Lieutenants with good experience on earlier Mirage variants, and 8 pilots fresh from a conversion course at Orange AB. Based on the better-known Atlis II laser designator (originally developed for the Mirage 2000H sold to India), the LDP.1EQ Patrick was custom-tailored to fit the nav/attack system of the F.1EQ-5.

2 Sadik, 03/ 2005.

3 Navias *et al*, pp.101-102; Sadik, 03/2005 & 03/2006, and e-mail exchange with Farzin Nadimi, 07/2006.

4 Navias *et al*, pp.102-103; Nadimi, p.118; Ebrahimi, 12/2017. While proving at least reasonably effective, the Shuttle Tanker system remains a matter of quite a few controversies between Iranian experts until this very day. Furthermore, while many Iranian sources report that the caravans to BIK were abandoned in 1985, actually, they were run right until the end of the war, but were downsized to between 3 and 5 ships (Ebrahimi, 10/2018). Foremost, by 1986 the majority of military supplies were unloaded in Bandar Abbas, although the construction of that port was completed only after the war.

5 Navias *et al*, pp.102-103 & Nadimi, p.118.

6 Navias *et al*, pp.85-86.

7 K. M., USN's naval warfare expert, online interview, November 2013.

8 Sadik, 03/ 2007 & 10/2007; UN, *Note by the Secretary General S/1998/920*, 6 October 1998. According to the latter source, 1,550 parachute-retarded R-400s were produced over time (157 of these filled with biological warfare agents), of which about 1,000 should have been left over after the war with Iran.

9 CIA, *The Possibility that Iraq Will Finish the Job at Khark Island*, 26 August 1985, CIA/FOIA/ERR.

10 Sadik, 03/2007 & 10/2007.

11 DIA, *EWFS-Iraq*, p.21, CIA/FOIA/ERR. The Remora incorporated a superheterodyne receiver that carried out a frequency search function simultaneously from forward and aft facing antennas. The pilot could adjust the receiver to three or six pre-set frequencies: the digitally stored threat library enabled the pod to jam up to three frequencies at once by means of electronic switching and power management of the travelling wave tube (TWT) transmitter system.

12 DIA, *Air Force Intelligence Study – Iraq*, DDB-1300-IZ-87, October 1987; DIA, *EWFS-Iraq*, p.22. Earlier reports (see Timmerman) according to which the IrAF deployed Baz-ARs and AS.30Ls during this strike have proved to be unsubstantiated.

13 Sadik, 03/ 2007; Cooper *et al*, *La guerre Iran-Irak, No.23*; Navias *et al*, pp.104-105; Nadimi, pp-98-99.

14 Sadik, 03/2007 & 10/2007 & Navias *et al*, p.105.

15 CIA, *Iraq's Air Force*; Sadik, 03/2007 & 10/2007; Nadimi, pp.98-99.

16 Jackson, Mirage F.1, pp.48-50; Liébert *et al*, p.241; Jakowitsch, 09/2009 & DIA, *EWFS-Iraq*, p.18. By all available assessments, the Sherloc RWR was one of the most advanced in its class in the mid-1980s. It covered the frequency range between 1 and 18GHz, had a high-speed analogue and digital processor with a threat library of 100 modes, and was easy to re-program on the flight line.

Chapter 6

1 DIA, *EWFS-Iraq*, pp. iii & 12.

2 Sadik 03/2007 & 10/2007 (as published in Cooper *et al*, *La guerre Iran-Irak, No.23*).

3 *Ibid.*

4 Nadimi, p.119.

5 Sadik, 03/2007 & 10/2007; Navias *et al*, pp.114-116 & Nadimi, p.98.

6 Contemporary reports by INA & IRNA; Sadik, 03/2007 & 10/2007.

7 Sadik, 10/2007 & Ebrahimi, 09/2009. *Iran Sedaghat* met her ultimate fate while fulfilling her decoy-duty on 31 December 1987: she was hit and sunk by at least one Exocet while near Khark, with the loss of nine of the crew. Ironically, the Iraqi News Agency INA reported the first deployment of an AS.30L during the 15 August 1984 attack on Khark (see Timmerman).

8 'Air Marshal Hameed Sha'ban interviewed by al-Qaddessiya newspaper, ' *AFP*, 20 July 1986 & *MEES*, Vol. XXIX, No. 43, 4 August 1986, p.C2.

9 Sadik, e-mail exchange with Farzin Nadimi, 04/2006.

10 Nadimi, p.106.

11 Sadik, 03/2007 & 10/2007 (as published in Cooper *et al*, *La guerre Iran-Irak, No.23*).

12 *Ibid.*

13 *Ibid* & Navias *et al*, pp.115-118.

14 Sadik, 03/2007 & 10/2007; Yousef Samadarian (in an interview for an Iranian TV documentary). The Iranian formation actually consisted of two F-5Es sent to attack the oil refinery near Suleimaniyah: preoccupied with low-altitude navigation, neither of the Iranians ever saw the Mirage behind them.

15 Sadik, 03/2005 & Navias *et al*, p.119.

16 Sadik, 10/2007 & Nadimi, p.102.

17 Sadik, 03/2006, 03/2007 & 10/2007; According to Afshar and Afghan-Toloee (Shakibania *et al*, *Tomcat Fights*), their Sparrow downed one Mirage, while the following Sidewinder caused an Iraqi to crash into the sea while trying to evade. The crew was officially credited with a single Mirage kill.

18 Sadik, 03/2005, 03/2006, 03/2007 & 10/2007 & Sadik, interview to Nadimi, 01/2007.

19 Navias *et al*, pp.117-119 & Sadik, 03/2007.

20 Navias *et al*, p.117; Nadimi, p.107; 'If your enemy can squash you, strangle him first', *The Economist*, 23 August 1986.

21 Sadik, 03/2007 & 10/2007.

22 Nadimi, p.107 & Murray *et al*, p.257.

23 Sadik, 03/2007 & 10/2007; Hooton *et al*, *Iran-Iraq War, Vol.3*, pp.20-21; DIA, EWFS-Iraq, p.11. According to the latter document, the Iraqi electronic warfare operations during this period reached such complexity and intensity, and put such a massive strain upon involved aircraft and equipment that after each major air strike the entire system experienced 'significant downtimes'.

24 Sadik, 03/2005, 03/2006, 03/2007 & 10/2007.

25 *Ibid*; Shakibania *et al*, *Tomcat Fights*; Hooton *et al*, *Iran-Iraq War, Vol.3*, pp.20-21; Iraqi Air Force Martyrs Website & Ali Tobchi, interview, 09/2014.

26 ONI, *Request for Persian Gulf Related Info*, June 1987 & CIA, *Iraqi Air Operations in the Persian Gulf and the Attack on the USN Frigate Stark*, 18 May 1987 (CIA/FOIA/ERR). The latter report observed that, '...many of the Iraqi aircraft return to their base without attacking a ship, probably because they cannot locate a target'.

27 Nadimi, p.104.

28 Cooper *et al*, *Iran-Iraq War in the Air*, p.244 & Sadik, 03/2006.

29 Unless stated otherwise, this sub-chapter is based on Sadik, 10/2007 & Sadik *et al*, 'Un Falcon 50 lance-missiles'.

30 Information on deletion of the registration was provided by anonymous reader in France to the editor of the *Fana de l'Aviation* magazine in reaction to the publication of the article 'Un Falcon 50 lance-missiles', in 2007.

31 Navias *et al*, pp.147-148; CIA, *Iraqi Air Operations in the Persian Gulf and the Attack on the USN Frigate Stark*, 18 May 1987 (CIA/FOIA/ERR); Francona, p.5; Woods *et al*, p.201. The first citation of the deployment of a Falcon 50 in this attack was published in the French aviation magazine *International*, No. 942, on 1 July 1987.

32 *Ibid*.

33 Navias *et al*, p.149; Cooper *et al*, *Iran-Iraq War in the Air*, pp.250-251 (confirmed by Sadik, 10/2007); Nadimi, pp.104-106; Woods *et al*, p.201; *The Economist*, 17 October 1987. While neither Baghdad nor Tehran ever reported al-Hussein attacks on Lavan, it is on hand that this new missile was thus 'fine-tuned' on that island before being deployed against Tehran, in February 1988. What remains unclear is how the Iraqis knew – provided they ever found out – if their missiles came anywhere near their target.

34 Sadik, 10/2007.

35 Navias *et al*, p.149; Nadimi, p.106 & Ole Niklajsen (flight controller at Dubai International), interview, October 2006.

36 ONI, *SPEARTIP 009-88*, p.3.

37 Unless stated otherwise, the following sub-chapter is based on Sadik *et al*, 'Les "Mirage" de Bagdad'.

38 'Iran's Bomb: the making of a myth', *New Scientist*, Vol. 102, No. 1408, 3 May 1984; Anothny H Cordesman & Khalid R al-Rodhan, *Iran's Weapons of mass destruction: the real and potential threat*, CSIS, 2006.

39 Sadik (10/2007), added that in 1984 the 224th Missile Brigade fired three Scuds at the construction site, by night, from the southern Faw peninsula – but that all three missed.

40 Navias *et al*, pp.133,149; Cooper *et al*, *Iran-Iraq War in the Air*, p.251; Sadik, 03/2005 & 11/2007.

41 Navias *et al*, p.149.

42 'Iraq', *AirEnthusiast*, Vol.34/No.2 (February 1988) & Jakowitsch, 09/2009. As time was to show, none of these aircraft was to reach Iraq in time to take part in the war with Iran. Indeed, most of this order was never realised because of the UN-imposed arms embargo, prompted by the Iraqi invasion of Kuwait, in August 1990.

43 Jackson, 'Mirage F.1', pp.48-50; Liébert *et al*, p.241; Sadik, 10/2007. Raphael TH stood for *Radar de PHotographie Aérienne Electronique á transmission hertzienne* (airborne-photography radar with terrestrial electronic transmission).

Chapter 7

1 CIA, *Iraq: Major Weapons Deliveries and their Impact on Force Capabilities*, February 1987, CIA/FOIA/ERR.

2 ONI, *SPEARTIP 009-88*, p.3 & Cooper *et al*, *La guerre Iran-Irak, No.23*; Iraqi Air Force Martyrs Website.

3 Sadik *et al*, *'Les "Mirage" de Baghdad'* & Hooton *et al*, *Iran-Iraq War, Vol.4*, pp.50-58.

4 Hooton *et al*, *Iran-Iraq War, Vol.4*, pp.38-39 & Woods *et al*, *Saddam's War*, p.57. The Humans Rights Watch (in *The Anfal Campaign against the Kurds*, Yale University Press, 1995) precisely identified 3,200 victims, while other sources cited up to 6,800 killed. Saddam denied all knowledge of the decision to deploy CWs against Halabja and put the blame on Major-General Nizar al-Khazraji, who in turn claimed that no military leader was involved in the decision. Such and claims by IrAF veterans that the air force was not involved in the CW-attack on Halabja are countered not only by reports of dozens of eyewitnesses, or the fact that this town was only one of about 40 in Iran and Iraq attacked by chemical bombs in 1987 and 1988, and that one of the involved aircraft – the MiG-21bis flown by 1st Lieutenant Bassel Issa – was shot down by an IRIAF F-4E over the Darabandikahn Lake on the same day. On the contrary, claims that the, 'IrAF exterminated the 84th (Iranian) Division, frequently published in the Iraqi social media, belong within realms of science fiction: that unit did not participate in *Val Fajr-10*.

5 Navias *et al*, p.167; Sadik, 10/2007 & ONI, *SPEARTIP 009-88*, p.3. The ferocity of the attack on *Avaj* and *Sanandaj* was such that one of DIA's analysts concluded that the IrAF must have deployed Tu-22 bombers and their massive bombs in this strike (J. H., 10/2002). Notably, while the US intelligence confirmed the loss of one of the involved Mirages, the name of the downed pilot and that of the involved IRIAF crew currently remain unknown.

6 Nadimi, pp.95-96. Similar views were shared by foreign observers. For example, *The Economist* (17 October 1987) commented on the lack of success of the Iraqi Oil Campaign with the title 'Seven Years Mystery'.

7 Sadik, 10/2007 & Khademi, interview, July 2018; once again, the IRIAF claim was confirmed by the US intelligence (*SPEARTIP 009-88*, p.3), and – once again – the Iraqis remain insistent on the version according to which Abdullah's F.1EQ-5 was hit by an Iranian MANPAD, although his aircraft remained well outside the envelope of any such weapons throughout the mission.

8 Sadik, 10/2007 & 12/2007; Shakibania *et al*, *Tomcat Fights*.

9 Sadik, 03/2007, 10/2007 & 12/2007.

10 Sadik, 03/2007; Ebrahimi, 11/2018.

11 Table compiled by Sadik, 10/2007.

12 IrAF, *Analytical Study*, p.4.

13 *Ibid*. For comparison, while the same study cites 162 IrAF aircraft as lost during the war with Iran, in an interview run via Ali Tobchi in May 2014, Major-General Abossi stated that the IrAF lost '250 aircraft, 100 pilots killed and 50 missing in action'.

14 Navias *et al*, pp.86, 105. According to Timmerman, Iraqi Super Etendards fired 67 Exocets in 1984, 24 of which achieved a hit. Notably, at least 10 ships destroyed by Exocets between 1980 and 1988 have never been reported outside Iran – either because they were warships of the IRIN, or insured in Iran only – and thus remain unknown even to the Iraqis involved. This topic is to be discussed in one of the future volumes of the Middle East@War series.

15 Woods *et al*, Saddam's War, p.85.

16 According to Sadik (03/2007), an unknown number of F.1EQ-2s was upgraded to the F.1EQ-4 standard while undergoing repairs in France, 1983-1984.

17 The Mirage F.1EQ-5 serial number 4562 was retained in France for test purposes and never delivered, thus decreasing the actual number of single-seaters that reached Iraq by July 1988 to 85. By the time of the UN-imposed arms embargo in August 1990, the F.1EQ-2 serial number 4034 and the F.1EQ-5 serial number 4569, were still undergoing repairs in France, both related to combat damage from the war with Iran.

ABOUT THE AUTHORS

TOM COOPER

Tom Cooper is an Austrian aerial warfare analyst and historian. Following a career in worldwide transportation business – during which he established a network of contacts in the Middle East and Africa – he moved into narrow-focus analysis and writing on small, little-known air forces and conflicts, about which he has collected extensive archives. That resulted in specialisation in such Middle Eastern air forces as those of Egypt, Iran, Iraq and Syria, plus various African and Asian air forces. As well as authoring and co-authoring 30 other books and over 500 articles, he has co-authored an in-depth analysis of major Arab air forces at war with Israel in the period 1955–1973, resulting in the six-volume book series *Arab MiGs*.

MILOS SIPOS

Milos Sipos is a Slovakian military historian. During his career with a law firm, he has collected extensive documentation on inter-connected political, industrial, human resources and military-related affairs in Iran, Iraq and Syria. His core interest is a systematic approach to studies of their deep impacts upon combat efficiency and the general performance of local militaries. After more than 10 years of related work on the ACIG.info forum, this is his first instalment for Helion.